DISCOURSE ON THE ORIGIN OF INEQUALITY

DOVER THRIFT EDITIONS

Jean-Jacques Rousseau

DOVER PUBLICATIONS, INC.
MINEOLA, NEW YORK

DOVER THRIFT EDITIONS

GENERAL EDITOR: PAUL NEGRI
EDITOR OF THIS VOLUME: GREG BOROSON

Copyright

Bibliographical Note

This Dover edition, first published in 2004, is an unabridged republication of the text of the work originally published as "A Discourse Upon the Origin and the Foundation of the Inequality of Mankind" in *French and English Philosophers: Descartes, Rousseau, Voltaire, Hobbes*, Volume 34 of *The Harvard Classics*, published by P. F. Collier & Son, New York, in 1910. A new introductory note has been specially prepared for the present edition.

Library of Congress Cataloging-in-Publication Data

Rousseau, Jean-Jacques, 1712–1778.
    [Discours sur l'origine et les fondements de l'inégalité parmi les hommes. English]
    Discourse on the origin of inequality / Jean-Jacques Rousseau.
       p. cm. — (Dover thrift editions)
    Originally published in French and English philosophers. New York : P.F. Collier, 1910. (The Harvard classics ; v. 34)
    ISBN-13: 978-0-486-43414-8 (pbk.)
    ISBN-10: 0-486-43414-1 (pbk.)
     1. Equality. 2. Natural law. 3. Political science. I. Title. II. Series.

JC179.R814 2004
320'.01'1—dc22
                            2003067425

Manufactured in the United States by LSC Communications
43414110   2018
www.doverpublications.com

Note

JEAN-JACQUES ROUSSEAU (1712–1778), philosopher, novelist, composer—one of the foremost figures of the European Enlightenment—had an uncertain childhood. He was born in Geneva to French parents; his mother died a few days after his birth and he was abandoned by his father at the age of ten. After a few years of irregular schooling and apprenticeship to an engraver, he fled Switzerland in 1728. Rousseau traveled Europe and eventually settled in Paris, where he worked as a music copyist, teacher and secretary, occasionally writing on music theory and composing. He became involved with Thérèse Le Vasseur, a semi-literate servant girl. The couple did not marry until 1768, but they had five children, all of whom Rousseau consigned to the foundling hospital, later writing in his autobiographical (and thoroughly unreliable) *Confessions* that he deeply regretted doing so.

In 1749, Rousseau's career as a thinker and writer began suddenly when, one day on the road to Vincennes, he read that a contest was to be held by the Academy of Dijon for the best essay on the question: "Has the progress of the sciences and arts contributed to the corruption or to the improvement of human conduct?" He later wrote:

> All at once I found myself dazzled by a thousand sparkling lights; crowds of vivid ideas thronged into my head with a force and confusion that threw me into unspeakable agitation; I felt my head whirling in a giddiness like that of intoxication. Unable to walk for difficulty in breathing, I sank down under one of the trees by the road, and passed half an hour there in such a condition of excitement that when I rose I saw that the front of my waistcoat was all wet with tears. . . Ah, if ever I could have written a quarter of what I saw and felt under that tree, with what clarity I should have brought out all the contradictions of our social system! With what simplicity I should have demonstrated that man is by nature good, and that only our institutions have made him bad!

Rousseau's essay, *Discourse on the Arts and Sciences*, won first prize in the contest and was widely discussed. In 1752, Rousseau's career was truly launched after he rose to fame with the great success of his opera, *Le Devin du Village*, and he was able to begin devoting himself seriously to writing.

Discourse on the Origin of Inequality (Discours sur l'origine et les fondements de l'inégalité parmi les hommes) was written in 1754 in response to another contest held by the Academy. The resulting essay, though it did not fare as well with the judges as the so-called *First Discourse*, is one of Rousseau's most important works. The central belief that Rousseau had described as motivating his first essay—namely, "that man is by nature good, and that only our institutions have made him bad"—here receives its most powerful presentation, in an argument that addresses both the psychological and political implications of this belief.

Rousseau's bold conjectures about man's "natural state" were revolutionary and in many ways ran in opposition to the Enlightenment's reverence for civilized culture. Voltaire, Rousseau's intellectual rival, wrote to him about the *Discourse on the Origin of Inequality*: "I have received your new book against the human race, and thank you for it. Never was such cleverness used in the design of making us all stupid. One longs, in reading your book, to walk on all fours. But as I have lost that habit for more than sixty years, I feel unhappily the impossibility of resuming it."

The arguments Rousseau sets forth in the *Discourse on the Origin of Inequality* form the foundation for much of his future writing, in particular *Emile* (1762), which considers the problem of education, and *The Social Contract* (1762), which is undoubtedly the most influential of Rousseau's works, containing the politically potent notion of "the natural rights of man," a concept that would soon be incorporated into the rhetoric of both the French and American Revolutions.

Discourse on the Origin of Inequality

QUESTION

PROPOSED BY THE

ACADEMY OF DIJON

What is the Origin of the Inequality among Mankind;
and whether such Inequality is authorized by the Law of Nature?

A DISCOURSE

Upon the Origin and the Foundation
of the Inequality Among Mankind

'TIS OF MAN I am to speak; and the very question, in answer to which I am to speak of him, sufficiently informs me that I am going to speak to men; for to those alone, who are not afraid of honouring truth, it belongs to propose discussions of this kind. I shall therefore maintain with confidence the cause of mankind before the sages, who invite me to stand up in its defence; and I shall think myself happy, if I can but behave in a manner not unworthy of my subject and of my judges.

I conceive two species of inequality among men; one which I call natural, or physical inequality, because it is established by nature, and consists in the difference of age, health, bodily strength, and the qualities of the mind, or of the soul; the other which may be termed moral, or political inequality, because it depends on a kind of convention, and is established, or at least authorized, by the common consent of mankind. This species of inequality consists in the different privileges, which some men enjoy, to the prejudice of others, such as that of being richer, more honoured, more powerful, and even that of exacting obedience from them.

It were absurd to ask, what is the cause of natural inequality, seeing the bare definition of natural inequality answers the question: it would be more absurd still to enquire, if there might not be some essential connection between the two species of inequality, as it would be asking, in other words, if those who command are necessarily better men than those who obey; and if strength of body or of mind, wisdom or virtue are always to be found in individuals, in the same proportion with power, or riches: a question, fit perhaps to be discussed by slaves in the hearing of their masters, but unbecoming free and reasonable beings in quest of truth.

What therefore is precisely the subject of this discourse? It is to point out, in the progress of things, that moment, when, right taking place of

1

violence, nature became subject to law; to display that chain of surprising events, in consequence of which the strong submitted to serve the weak, and the people to purchase imaginary ease, at the expense of real happiness.

The philosophers, who have examined the foundations of society, have, every one of them, perceived the necessity of tracing it back to a state of nature, but not one of them has ever arrived there. Some of them have not scrupled to attribute to man in that state the ideas of justice and injustice, without troubling their heads to prove, that he really must have had such ideas, or even that such ideas were useful to him: others have spoken of the natural right of every man to keep what belongs to him, without letting us know what they meant by the word belong; others, without further ceremony ascribing to the strongest an authority over the weakest, have immediately struck out government, without thinking of the time requisite for men to form any notion of the things signified by the words authority and government. All of them, in fine, constantly harping on wants, avidity, oppression, desires and pride, have transferred to the state of nature ideas picked up in the bosom of society. In speaking of savages they described citizens. Nay, few of our own writers seem to have so much as doubted, that a state of nature did once actually exist; though it plainly appears by Sacred History, that even the first man, immediately furnished as he was by God himself with both instructions and precepts, never lived in that state, and that, if we give to the books of Moses that credit which every Christian philosopher ought to give to them, we must deny that, even before the deluge, such a state ever existed among men, unless they fell into it by some extraordinary event: a paradox very difficult to maintain, and altogether impossible to prove.

Let us begin therefore, by laying aside facts, for they do not affect the question. The researches, in which we may engage on this occasion, are not to be taken for historical truths, but merely as hypothetical and conditional reasonings, fitter to illustrate the nature of things, than to show their true origin, like those systems, which our naturalists daily make of the formation of the world. Religion commands us to believe, that men, having been drawn by God himself out of a state of nature, are unequal, because it is his pleasure they should be so; but religion does not forbid us to draw conjectures solely from the nature of man, considered in itself, and from that of the beings which surround him, concerning the fate of mankind, had they been left to themselves. This is then the question I am to answer, the question I propose to examine in the present discourse. As mankind in general have an interest in my subject, I shall endeavour to use a language suitable to all nations; or rather, forgetting the circumstances of time and place in order to think of nothing but the men I speak to, I shall suppose myself in the Lyceum of Athens, repeating the lessons of my masters before the Platos and the Xenocrates of that famous seat of philosophy as my judges, and in presence of the whole human species as my audience.

O man, whatever country you may belong to, whatever your opinions may be, attend to my words; you shall hear your history such as I think I have read it, not in books composed by those like you, for they are liars, but in the book of nature which never lies. All that I shall repeat after her, must be true, without any intermixture of falsehood, but where I may happen, without intending it, to introduce my own conceits. The times I am going to speak of are very remote. How much you are changed from what you once were! 'Tis in a manner the life of your species that I am going to write, from the qualities which you have received, and which your education and your habits could deprave, but could not destroy. There is, I am sensible, an age at which every individual of you would choose to stop; and you will look out for the age at which, had you your wish, your species had stopped. Uneasy at your present condition for reasons which threaten your unhappy posterity with still greater uneasiness, you will perhaps wish it were in your power to go back; and this sentiment ought to be considered, as the panegyric of your first parents, the condemnation of your contemporaries, and a source of terror to all those who may have the misfortune of succeeding you.

DISCOURSE

FIRST PART

However important it may be, in order to form a proper judgment of the natural state of man, to consider him from his origin, and to examine him, as it were, in the first embryo of the species; I shall not attempt to trace his organization through its successive approaches to perfection: I shall not stop to examine in the animal system what he might have been in the beginning, to become at last what he actually is; I shall not inquire whether, as Aristotle thinks, his neglected nails were no better at first than crooked talons; whether his whole body was not, bear-like, thick covered with rough hair; and whether, walking upon all-fours, his eyes, directed to the earth, and confined to a horizon of a few paces extent, did not at once point out the nature and limits of his ideas. I could only form vague, and almost imaginary, conjectures on this subject. Comparative anatomy has not as yet been sufficiently improved; neither have the observations of natural philosophy been sufficiently ascertained, to establish upon such foundations the basis of a solid system. For this reason, without having recourse to the supernatural informations with which we have been favoured on this head, or paying any attention to the changes, that must have happened in the conformation of the interior and exterior parts of man's body, in proportion as he applied his members to new purposes, and took to new aliments, I shall suppose his conformation to have always been, what we now behold it; that he always walked on two feet, made the same use of his hands that we do of ours, extended his looks over the whole face of nature, and measured with his eyes the vast extent of the heavens.

If I strip this being, thus constituted, of all the supernatural gifts which he may have received, and of all the artificial faculties, which we could not have acquired but by slow degrees; if I consider him, in a word, such as he must have issued from the hands of nature; I see an animal less strong than some, and less active than others, but, upon the whole, the most advantageously organized of any; I see him satisfying the calls of hunger under the first oak, and those of thirst at the first rivulet; I see him laying himself down to sleep at the foot of the same tree that afforded him his meal; and behold, this done, all his wants are completely supplied.

The earth left to its own natural fertility and covered with immense woods, that no hatchet ever disfigured, offers at every step food and shelter to every species of animals. Men, dispersed among them, observe and imitate their industry, and thus rise to the instinct of beasts; with this advantage, that, whereas every species of beasts is confined to one peculiar instinct, man, who perhaps has not any that particularly belongs to him, appropriates to himself those of all other animals, and lives equally upon most of the different aliments, which they only divide among themselves; a circumstance which qualifies him to find his subsistence, with more ease than any of them.

Men, accustomed from their infancy to the inclemency of the weather, and to the rigour of the different seasons; inured to fatigue, and obliged to defend, naked and without arms, their life and their prey against the other wild inhabitants of the forest, or at least to avoid their fury by flight, acquire a robust and almost unalterable habit of body; the children, bringing with them into the world the excellent constitution of their parents, and strengthening it by the same exercises that first produced it, attain by this means all the vigour that the human frame is capable of. Nature treats them exactly in the same manner that Sparta treated the children of her citizens; those who come well formed into the world she renders strong and robust, and destroys all the rest; differing in this respect from our societies, in which the state, by permitting children to become burdensome to their parents, murders them all without distinction, even in the wombs of their mothers.

The body being the only instrument that savage man is acquainted with, he employs it to different uses, of which ours, for want of practice, are incapable; and we may thank our industry for the loss of that strength and agility, which necessity obliges him to acquire. Had he a hatchet, would his hand so easily snap off from an oak so stout a branch? Had he a sling, would it dart a stone to so great a distance? Had he a ladder, would he run so nimbly up a tree? Had he a horse, would he with such swiftness shoot along the plain? Give civilized man but time to gather about him all his machines, and no doubt he will be an overmatch for the savage: but if you have a mind to see a contest still more unequal, place them naked and unarmed one opposite to the other; and you will soon discover the advantage there is in perpetually having all our forces at our disposal, in being constantly prepared against all events, and in always carrying ourselves, as it were, whole and entire about us.

Hobbes would have it that man is naturally void of fear, and always intent upon attacking and fighting. An illustrious philosopher thinks on the contrary, and Cumberland and Puffendorff likewise affirm it, that nothing is more fearful than man in a state of nature, that he is always in a tremble, and ready to fly at the first motion he perceives, at the first noise that strikes his ears. This, indeed, may be very true in regard to objects with which he is not acquainted; and I make no doubt of his being terrified at every new sight that presents itself, as often as he cannot distinguish the physical good and evil which he may expect from it, nor compare his forces with the dangers he has to encounter; circumstances that seldom occur in a state of nature, where all things proceed in so uniform a manner, and the face of the earth is not liable to those sudden and continual changes occasioned in it by the passions and inconstancies of collected bodies. But savage man living among other animals without any society or fixed habitation, and finding himself early under a necessity of measuring his strength with theirs, soon makes a comparison between both, and finding that he surpasses them more in address, than they surpass him in strength, he learns not to be any longer in dread of them. Turn out a bear or a wolf against a sturdy, active, resolute savage, (and this they all are,) provided with stones and a good stick; and you will soon find that the danger is at least equal on both sides, and that after several trials of this kind, wild beasts, who are not fond of attacking each other, will not be very fond of attacking man, whom they have found every whit as wild as themselves. As to animals who have really more strength than man has address, he is, in regard to them, what other weaker species are, who find means to subsist notwithstanding; he has even this great advantage over such weaker species, that being equally fleet with them, and finding on every tree an almost inviolable asylum, he is always at liberty to take it or leave it, as he likes best, and of course to fight or to fly, whichever is most agreeable to him. To this we may add that no animal naturally makes war upon man, except in the case of self-defence or extreme hunger; nor ever expresses against him any of these violent antipathies, which seem to indicate that some particular species are intended by nature for the food of others.

But there are other more formidable enemies, and against which man is not provided with the same means of defence; I mean natural infirmities, infancy, old age, and sickness of every kind, melancholy proofs of our weakness, whereof the two first are common to all animals, and the last chiefly attends man living in a state of society. It is even observable in regard to infancy, that the mother being able to carry her child about with her, wherever she goes, can perform the duty of a nurse with a great deal less trouble, than the females of many other animals, who are obliged to be constantly going and coming with no small labour and fatigue, one way to look out for their own subsistence, and another to suckle and feed their young ones. True it is that, if the woman happens to perish, her child is exposed to the greatest danger of perishing with her; but this danger is common to a hundred other species, whose young ones require a great deal of time to be able to provide for themselves; and if our infancy is longer than theirs, our life is longer likewise; so that, in this respect too, all things are in a manner equal; not but that there are other rules concerning the duration of the first age of life, and the number of the young of man and other animals, but they do not belong to my subject. With old men, who stir and perspire but little, the demand for food diminishes with their abilities to provide it; and as a savage life would exempt them from the gout and the rheumatism, and old age is of all ills that which human assistance is least capable of alleviating, they would at last go off, without its being perceived by others that they ceased to exist, and almost without perceiving it themselves.

In regard to sickness, I shall not repeat the vain and false declamations made use of to discredit medicine by most men, while they enjoy their health; I shall only ask if there are any solid observations from which we may conclude that in those countries where the healing art is most neglected, the mean duration of man's life is shorter than in those where it is most cultivated? And how is it possible this should be the case, if we inflict more diseases upon ourselves than medicine can supply us with remedies! The extreme inequalities in the manner of living of the several classes of mankind, the excess of idleness in some, and of labour in others, the facility of irritating and satisfying our sensuality and our appetites, the too exquisite and out of the way aliments of the rich, which fill them with fiery juices, and bring on indigestions, the unwholesome food of the poor, of which even, bad as it is, they very often fall short, and the want of which tempts them, every opportunity that offers, to eat greedily and overload their stomachs; watchings, excesses of every kind, immoderate transports of all the passions, fatigues, waste of spirits, in a word, the numberless pains and anxieties annexed to every condition, and which the mind of man is constantly a prey to; these are the fatal proofs that most of our ills are of our own making, and that we might have avoided them all by adhering to the simple, uniform and solitary way of life prescribed to us by nature. Allowing that nature intended we should always enjoy good health, I dare almost affirm that a state of reflection is a state against nature, and that the man who meditates is a depraved animal. We need only call to mind the good constitution of savages, of those at least whom we have not destroyed by our strong liquors; we need only reflect, that they are strangers to almost every disease, except those occasioned by wounds and old age, to be in a manner convinced that the history of human diseases might be easily composed by pursuing that of civil societies. Such at least was the opinion of Plato, who concluded from certain remedies made use of or approved by Podalyrus and Macaon at the Siege of Troy, that several disorders, which these remedies were found to bring on in his days, were not known among men at that remote period.

Man therefore, in a state of nature where there are so few sources of sickness, can have no great occasion for physic, and still less for physicians; neither is the human species more to be pitied in this respect, than any other species of animals. Ask those who make hunting their recreation or business, if in their excursions they meet with many sick or feeble animals. They meet with many carrying the marks of considerable wounds, that have been perfectly well healed and closed up; with many, whose bones formerly broken, and whose limbs almost torn off, have completely knit and united, without any other surgeon but time, any other regimen but their usual way of living, and whose cures were not the less perfect for their not having been tortured with incisions, poisoned with drugs, or worn out by diet and abstinence. In a word, however useful medicine well administered may be to us who live in a state of society, it is still past doubt, that if, on the one hand, the sick savage, destitute of help, has nothing to hope from nature, on the other, he has nothing to fear but from his disease; a circumstance, which often renders his situation preferable to ours.

Let us therefore beware of confounding savage man with the men, whom we daily see and converse with. Nature behaves towards all

animals left to her care with a predilection, that seems to prove how
jealous she is of that prerogative. The horse, the cat, the bull, nay the
ass itself, have generally a higher stature, and always a more robust constitution, more vigour, more strength and courage in their forests than
in our houses; they lose half these advantages by becoming domestic
animals; it looks as if all our attention to treat them kindly, and to feed
them well, served only to bastardize them. It is thus with man himself.
In proportion as he becomes sociable and a slave to others, he becomes
weak, fearful, mean-spirited, and his soft and effeminate way of living
at once completes the enervation of his strength and of his courage. We
may add, that there must be still a wider difference between man and
man in a savage and domestic condition, than between beast and beast;
for as men and beasts have been treated alike by nature, all the conveniences with which men indulge themselves more than they do the
beasts tamed by them, are so many particular causes which make them
degenerate more sensibly.

Nakedness therefore, the want of houses, and of all these unneces-
saries, which we consider as so very necessary, are not such mighty evils
in respect to these primitive men, and much less still any obstacle to
their preservation. Their skins, it is true, are destitute of hair; but then
they have no occasion for any such covering in warm climates; and in
cold climates they soon learn to apply to that use those of the animals
they have conquered; they have but two feet to run with, but they have
two hands to defend themselves with, and provide for all their wants; it
costs them perhaps a great deal of time and trouble to make their children walk; but the mothers carry them with ease; an advantage not
granted to other species of animals, with whom the mother, when pursued, is obliged to abandon her young ones, or regulate her steps by
theirs. In short, unless we admit those singular and fortuitous concur-
rences of circumstances, which I shall speak of hereafter, and which, it
is very possible, may never have existed, it is evident, in every state of
the question, that the man, who first made himself clothes and built
himself a cabin, supplied himself with things which he did not much
want, since he had lived without them till then; and why should he not
have been able to support in his riper years, the same kind of life,
which he had supported from his infancy?

Alone, idle, and always surrounded with danger, savage man must be
fond of sleep, and sleep lightly like other animals, who think but little,
and may, in a manner, be said to sleep all the time they do not think:
self-preservation being almost his only concern, he must exercise those
faculties most, which are most serviceable in attacking and in defending, whether to subdue his prey, or to prevent his becoming that of
other animals: those organs, on the contrary, which softness and sensu-

ality can alone improve, must remain in a state of rudeness, utterly incompatible with all manner of delicacy; and as his senses are divided on this point, his touch and his taste must be extremely coarse and blunt; his sight, his hearing, and his smelling equally subtle: such is the animal state in general, and accordingly if we may believe travellers, it is that of most savage nations. We must not therefore be surprised, that the Hottentots of the Cape of Good Hope, distinguish with their naked eyes ships on the ocean, at as great a distance as the Dutch can discern them with their glasses; nor that the savages of America should have tracked the Spaniards with their noses, to as great a degree of exactness, as the best dogs could have done; nor that all these barbarous nations support nakedness without pain, use such large quantities of Pimento to give their food a relish, and drink like water the strongest liquors of Europe.

As yet I have considered man merely in his physical capacity; let us now endeavour to examine him in a metaphysical and moral light.

I can discover nothing in any mere animal but an ingenious machine, to which nature has given senses to wind itself up, and guard, to a certain degree, against everything that might destroy or disorder it. I perceive the very same things in the human machine, with this difference, that nature alone operates in all the operations of the beast, whereas man, as a free agent, has a share in his. One chooses by instinct; the other by an act of liberty; for which reason the beast cannot deviate from the rules that have been prescribed to it, even in cases where such deviation might be useful, and man often deviates from the rules laid down for him to his prejudice. Thus a pigeon would starve near a dish of the best flesh-meat, and a cat on a heap of fruit or corn, though both might very well support life with the food which they disdain, did they but bethink themselves to make a trial of it: it is in this manner dissolute men run into excesses, which bring on fevers and death itself; because the mind depraves the senses, and when nature ceases to speak, the will still continues to dictate.

All animals must be allowed to have ideas, since all animals have senses; they even combine their ideas to a certain degree, and, in this respect, it is only the difference of such degree, that constitutes the difference between man and beast: some philosophers have even advanced, that there is a greater difference between some men and some others, than between some men and some beasts; it is not therefore so much the understanding that constitutes, among animals, the specifical distinction of man, as his quality of a free agent. Nature speaks to all animals, and beasts obey her voice. Man feels the same impression, but he at the same time perceives that he is free to resist or to acquiesce; and it is in the consciousness of this liberty, that the spirituality of

.his soul chiefly appears: for natural philosophy explains, in some measure, the mechanism of the senses and the formation of ideas; but in
the power of willing, or rather of choosing, and in the consciousness of
this power, nothing can be discovered but acts, that are purely spiritual,
and cannot be accounted for by the laws of mechanics.

But though the difficulties, in which all these questions are involved,
should leave some room to dispute on this difference between man and
beast, there is another very specific quality that distinguishes them, and
a quality which will admit of no dispute; this is the faculty of improvement; a faculty which, as circumstances offer, successively unfolds all
the other faculties, and resides among us not only in the species, but in
the individuals that compose it; whereas a beast is, at the end of some
months, all he ever will be during the rest of his life; and his species, at
the end of a thousand years, precisely what it was the first year of that
long period. Why is man alone subject to dotage? Is it not, because he
thus returns to his primitive condition? And because, while the beast,
which has acquired nothing and has likewise nothing to lose, continues always in possession of his instinct, man, losing by old age, or by accident, all the acquisitions he had made in consequence of his perfectibility, thus falls back even lower than beast themselves? It would be
a melancholy necessity for us to be obliged to allow, that this distinctive
and almost unlimited faculty is the source of all man's misfortunes; that
it is this faculty, which, though by slow degrees, draws them out of their
original condition, in which his days would slide away insensibly in
peace and innocence; that it is this faculty, which, in a succession of
ages, produces his discoveries and mistakes, his virtues and his vices,
and, at long run, renders him both his own and nature's tyrant. It would
be shocking to be obliged to commend, as a beneficent being, whoever
he was that first suggested to the *Oronoco* Indians the use of those
boards which they bind on the temples of their children, and which secure to them the enjoyment of some part at least of their natural im-
becility and happiness.

Savage man, abandoned by nature to pure instinct, or rather indem-
nified for that which has perhaps been denied to him by faculties capable of immediately supplying the place of it, and of raising him afterwards a great deal higher, would therefore begin with functions that
were merely animal: to see and to feel would be his first condition,
which he would enjoy in common with other animals. To will and not
to will, to wish and to fear, would be the first, and in a manner, the only
operations of his soul, till new circumstances occasioned new developments.

Let moralists say what they will, the human understanding is greatly
indebted to the passions, which, on their side, are likewise universally

allowed to be greatly indebted to the human understanding. It is by the activity of our passions, that our reason improves: we covet knowledge merely because we covet enjoyment, and it is impossible to conceive why a man exempt from fears and desires should take the trouble to reason. The passions, in their turn, owe their origin to our wants, and their increase to our progress in science; for we cannot desire or fear anything, but in consequence of the ideas we have of it, or of the simple impulses of nature; and savage man, destitute of every species of knowledge, experiences no passions but those of this last kind; his desires never extend beyond his physical wants; he knows no goods but food, a female, and rest; he fears no evil but pain, and hunger; I say pain, and not death; for no animal, merely as such, will ever know what it is to die, and the knowledge of death, and of its terrors, is one of the first acquisitions made by man, in consequence of his deviating from the animal state.

I could easily, were it requisite, cite facts in support of this opinion, and show, that the progress of the mind has everywhere kept pace exactly with the wants, to which nature had left the inhabitants exposed, or to which circumstances had subjected them, and consequently to the passions, which inclined them to provide for these wants. I could exhibit in Egypt the arts starting up, and extending themselves with the inundations of the Nile; I could pursue them in their progress among the Greeks, where they were seen to bud forth, grow, and rise to the heavens, in the midst of the sands and rocks of Attica, without being able to take root on the fertile banks of the Eurotas; I would observe that, in general, the inhabitants of the north are more industrious than those of the south, because they can less do without industry; as if nature thus meant to make all things equal, by giving to the mind that fertility she has denied to the soil.

But exclusive of the uncertain testimonies of history, who does not perceive that everything seems to remove from savage man the temptation and the means of altering his condition? His imagination paints nothing to him; his heart asks nothing from him. His moderate wants are so easily supplied with what he everywhere finds ready to his hand, and he stands at such a distance from the degree of knowledge requisite to covet more, that he can neither have foresight nor curiosity. The spectacle of nature, by growing quite familiar to him, becomes at last equally indifferent. It is constantly the same order, constantly the same revolutions; he has not sense enough to feel surprise at the sight of the greatest wonders; and it is not in his mind we must look for that philosophy, which man must have to know how to observe once, what he has every day seen. His soul, which nothing disturbs, gives itself up entirely to the consciousness of its actual existence, without any thought of even the nearest futurity; and his projects, equally confined with his views, scarce extend to the end of the day. Such is, even at present, the degree of foresight in the Caribbean: he sells his cotton bed in the morning, and comes in the evening, with tears in his eyes, to buy it back, not having foreseen that he should want it again the next night.

The more we meditate on this subject, the wider does the distance between mere sensation and the most simple knowledge become in our eyes; and it is impossible to conceive how man, by his own powers alone, without the assistance of communication, and the spur of necessity, could have got over so great an interval. How many ages perhaps revolved, before men beheld any other fire but that of the heavens? How many different accidents must have concurred to make them acquainted with the most common uses of this element? How often have they let it go out, before they knew the art of reproducing it? And how often perhaps has not every one of these secrets perished with the discoverer? What shall we say of agriculture, an art which requires so much labour and foresight; which depends upon other arts; which, it is very evident, cannot be practised but in a society, if not a formed one, at least one of some standing, and which does not so much serve to draw aliments from the earth, for the earth would yield them without all that trouble, as to oblige her to produce those things, which we like best, preferably to others? But let us suppose that men had multiplied to such a degree, that the natural products of the earth no longer sufficed for their support; a supposition which, by the bye, would prove that this kind of life would be very advantageous to the human species; let us suppose that, without forge or anvil, the instruments of husbandry had dropped from the heavens into the hands of savages, that these men had got the better of that mortal aversion they all have for constant labour; that they had learned to foretell their wants at so great a distance of time; that they had guessed exactly how they were to break the earth, commit their seed to it, and plant trees; that they had found out the art of grinding their corn, and improving by fermentation the juice of their grapes; all operations which we must allow them to have learned from the gods, since we cannot conceive how they should make such discoveries of themselves; after all these fine presents, what man would be mad enough to cultivate a field, that may be robbed by the first comer, man or beast, who takes a fancy to the produce of it. And would any man consent to spend his day in labour and fatigue, when the rewards of his labour and fatigue became more and more precarious in proportion to his want of them? In a word, how could this situation engage men to cultivate the earth, as long as it was not parcelled out among them, that is, as long as a state of nature subsisted.

Though we should suppose savage man as well versed in the art of thinking, as philosophers make him; though we were, after them, to make him a philosopher himself, discovering of himself the sublimest truths, forming to himself, by the most abstract arguments, maxims of justice and reason drawn from the love of order in general, or from the known will of his Creator: in a word, though we were to suppose his mind as intelligent and enlightened, as it must, and is, in fact, found to be dull and stupid; what benefit would the species receive from all these metaphysical discoveries, which could not be communicated, but must perish with the individual who had made them? What progress could mankind make in the forests, scattered up and down among the other animals? And to what degree could men mutually improve and enlighten each other, when they had no fixed habitation, nor any need of each other's assistance; when the same persons scarcely met twice in their whole lives, and on meeting neither spoke to, or so much as knew each other?

Let us consider how many ideas we owe to the use of speech; how much grammar exercises, and facilitates the operations of the mind; let us, besides, reflect on the immense pains and time that the first invention of languages must have required: Let us add these reflections to the preceding; and then we may judge how many thousand ages must have been requisite to develop successively the operations, which the human mind is capable of producing.

I must now beg leave to stop one moment to consider the perplexities attending the origin of languages. I might here barely cite or repeat the researches made, in relation to this question, by the Abbé de Condillac, which all fully confirm my system, and perhaps even suggested to me the first idea of it. But, as the manner, in which the philosopher resolves the difficulties of his own starting, concerning the origin of arbitrary signs, shows that he supposes, what I doubt, namely a kind of society already established among the inventors of languages; I think it my duty, at the same time that I refer to his reflections, to give my own, in order to expose the same difficulties in a light suitable to my subject. The first that offers is how languages could become necessary; for as there was no correspondence between men, nor the least necessity for any, there is no conceiving the necessity of this invention, nor the possibility of it, if it was not indispensable. I might say, with many others, that languages are the fruit of the domestic intercourse between fathers, mothers, and children: but this, besides its not answering any difficulties, would be committing the same fault with those, who reasoning on the state of nature, transfer to it ideas collected in society, always consider families as living together under one roof, and their members as observing among themselves an union, equally intimate and permanent with that which we see exist in a civil state, where so many common interests conspire to unite them; whereas in this primitive state, as there were neither houses nor cabins, nor any kind of property, every one took up his lodging at random, and seldom continued above one night in the same place; males and females united without any premeditated design, as chance, occasion, or desire brought them together, nor had they any great occasion for language to make known their thoughts to each other. They parted with the same ease. The mother suckled her children, when just born, for her own sake; but afterwards out of love and affection to them, when habit and custom had made them dear to her; but they no sooner gained strength enough to run about is quest of food than they separated even from her of their own accord; and as they scarce had any other method of not losing each other, than that of remaining constantly in each other's sight, they soon came to such a pass of forgetfulness, as not even to know each other, when they happened to meet again. I must further observe that the child having all his wants to explain, and consequently more things to say to his mother, than the mother can have to say to him, it is he that must be at the chief expense of invention, and the language he makes use of must be in a great measure his own work; this makes the number of languages equal to that of the individuals who are to speak them; and this multiplicity of languages is further increased by their roving and vagabond kind of life, which allows no idiom time enough to acquire any consistency; for to say that the mother would have dictated to the child the words he must employ to ask her this thing and that, may well enough explain in what manner languages, already formed, are taught, but it does not show us in what manner they are first formed.

Let us suppose this first difficulty conquered: Let us for a moment consider ourselves at this side of the immense space, which must have separated the pure state of nature from that in which languages became necessary, and let us, after allowing such necessity, examine how languages could begin to be established. A new difficulty this, still more stubborn than the preceding; for if men stood in need of speech to learn to think, they must have stood in still greater need of the art of thinking to invent that of speaking; and though we could conceive how the sounds of the voice came to be taken for the conventional interpreters of our ideas we should not be the nearer knowing who could have been the interpreters of this convention for such ideas, as, in consequence of their not having any sensible objects, could not be made manifest by gesture or voice; so that we can scarce form any tolerable conjectures concerning the birth of this art of communicating our thoughts, and establishing a correspondence between minds: a sublime art which, though so remote from its origin, philosophers still behold at such a prodigious distance from its perfection, that I never met with one of them bold enough to affirm it would ever arrive there, though the revolutions necessarily produced by time were suspended in its favour; though prejudice could be banished from, or would be at least content to sit silent in the presence of our academies, and though these societies should consecrate themselves, entirely and during whole ages, to the study of this intricate object.

The first language of man, the most universal and most energetic of all languages, in short, the only language he had occasion for, before there was a necessity of persuading assembled multitudes, was the cry of nature. As this cry was never extorted but by a kind of instinct in the most urgent cases, to implore assistance in great danger, or relief in great sufferings, it was of little use in the common occurrences of life, where more moderate sentiments generally prevail. When the ideas of men began to extend and multiply, and a closer communication began to take place among them, they laboured to devise more numerous signs, and a more extensive language: they multiplied the inflections of the voice, and added to them gestures, which are, in their own nature, more expressive, and whose meaning depends less on any prior determination. They therefore expressed visible and movable objects by gestures and those which strike the ear, by imitative sounds: but as gestures scarcely indicate anything except objects that are actually present or can be easily described, and visible actions; as they are not of general use, since darkness or the interposition of an opaque medium renders them useless; and as besides they require attention rather than excite it: men at length bethought themselves of substituting for them the articulations of voice, which, without having the same relation to any determinate object, are, in quality of instituted signs, fitter to represent all our ideas; a substitution, which could only have been made by common consent, and in a manner pretty difficult to practise by men, whose rude organs were unimproved by exercise; a substitution, which is in itself more difficult to be conceived, since the motives to this unanimous agreement must have been somehow or another expressed, and speech therefore appears to have been exceedingly requisite to establish the use of speech.

We must allow that the words, first made use of by men, had in their minds a much more extensive signification, than those employed in languages of some standing, and that, considering how ignorant they were of the division of speech into its constituent parts; they at first gave every word the meaning of an entire proposition. When afterwards they began to perceive the difference between the subject and attribute, and between verb and noun, a distinction which required no mean effort of genius, the substantives for a time were only so many proper names, the infinitive was the only tense, and as to adjectives, great difficulties must have attended the development of the idea that represents them, since every adjective is an abstract word, and abstraction is an unnatural and very painful operation.

At first they gave every object a peculiar name, without any regard to its genus or species, things which these first institutors of language were in no condition to distinguish; and every individual presented itself solitary to their minds, as it stands in the table of nature. If they called one oak A, they called another oak B: so that their dictionary must have been more extensive in proportion as their knowledge of things was more confined. It could not but be a very difficult task to get rid of so diffuse and embarrassing a nomenclature; as in order to marshal the several beings under common and generic denominations, it was necessary to be first acquainted with their properties, and their differences; to be stocked with observations and definitions, that is to say, to understand natural history and metaphysics, advantages which the men of these times could not have enjoyed.

Besides, general ideas cannot be conveyed to the mind without the assistance of words, nor can the understanding seize them without the assistance of propositions. This is one of the reasons, why mere animals cannot form such ideas, nor ever acquire the perfectibility which depends on such an operation. When a monkey leaves without the least hesitation one nut for another, are we to think he has any general idea of that kind of fruit, and that he compares these two individual bodies with his archetype notion of them? No, certainly; but the sight of one of these nuts calls back to his memory the sensations which he has received from the other; and his eyes, modified after some certain manner, give notice to his palate of the modification it is in its turn going to receive. Every general idea is purely intellectual; let the imagination tamper ever so little with it, it immediately becomes a particular idea. Endeavour to represent to yourself the image of a tree in general, you never will be able to do it; in spite of all your efforts it will appear big or little, thin or tufted, or a bright or a deep colour; and were you master to see nothing in it, but what can be seen in every tree, such a picture would no longer resemble any tree. Beings perfectly abstract are perceivable in the same manner, or are only conceivable by the assistance of speech. The definition of a triangle can alone give you a just idea of that figure: the moment you form a triangle in your mind, it is this or that particular triangle and no other, and you cannot avoid giving breadth to its lines and colour to its area. We must therefore make use of propositions; we must therefore speak to have general ideas; for the moment the imagination stops, the mind must stop too, if not assisted by speech. If therefore the first inventors could give no names to any ideas but those they had already, it follows that the first substantives could never have been anything more than proper names.

But when by means, which I cannot conceive, our new grammarians began to extend their ideas, and generalize their words, the ignorance of the inventors must have confined this method to very narrow bounds; and as they had at first too much multiplied the names of individuals for want of being acquainted with the distinctions called genus and species, they afterwards made too few genera and species for want of having considered beings in all their differences; to push the divisions far enough, they must have had more knowledge and experience than we can allow them, and have made more researches and taken more pains, than we can suppose them willing to submit to. Now if, even at this present time, we every day discover new species, which had before escaped all our observations, how many species must have escaped the notice of men, who judged of things merely from their first appearances! As to the primitive classes and the most general notions, it were superfluous to add that these they must have likewise overlooked: how, for example, could they have thought of or understood the words, matter, spirit, substance, mode, figure, motion, since even our philosophers, who for so long a time have been constantly employing these terms, can themselves scarcely understand them, and since the ideas annexed to these words being purely metaphysical, no models of them could be found in nature?

I stop at these first advances, and beseech my judges to suspend their lecture a little, in order to consider, what a great way language has still to go, in regard to the invention of physical substantives alone, (though the easiest part of language to invent,) to be able to express all the sentiments of man, to assume an invariable form, to bear being spoken in public and to influence society: I earnestly entreat them to consider how much time and knowledge must have been requisite to find out numbers, abstract words, the aorists, and all the other tenses of verbs, the particles, and syntax, the method of connecting propositions and arguments, of forming all the logic of discourse. For my own part, I am so scared at the difficulties that multiply at every step, and so convinced of the almost demonstrated impossibility of languages owing their birth and establishment to means that were merely human, that I must leave to whoever may please to take it up, the task of discussing this difficult problem. "Which was the most necessary, society already formed to invent languages, or languages already invented to form society?"

But be the case of these origins ever so mysterious, we may at least infer from the little care which nature has taken to bring men together by mutual wants, and make the use of speech easy to them, how little she has done towards making them sociable, and how little she has contributed to anything which they themselves have done to become so. In fact, it is impossible to conceive, why, in this primitive state, one man should have more occasion for the assistance of another, than one monkey, or one wolf for that of another animal of the same species; or supposing that he had, what motive could induce another to assist him; or even, in this last case, how he, who wanted assistance, and he from whom it was wanted, could agree among themselves upon the conditions. Authors, I know, are continually telling us, that in this state man would have been a most miserable creature; and if it is true, as I fancy I have proved it, that he must have continued many ages without either the desire or the opportunity of emerging from such a state, this their assertion could only serve to justify a charge against nature, and not any against the being which nature had thus constituted; but, if I thoroughly understand this term miserable, it is a word, that either has no meaning, or signifies nothing, but a privation attended with pain, and a suffering state of body or soul; now I would fain know what kind of misery can be that of a free being, whose heart enjoys perfect peace, and body perfect health? And which is aptest to become insupportable to those who enjoy it, a civil or a natural life? In civil life we can scarcely meet a single person who does not complain of his existence; many even throw away as much of it as they can, and the united force of divine and human laws can hardly put bounds to this disorder. Was ever any free savage known to have been so much as tempted to complain of life, and lay violent hands on himself? Let us therefore judge with less pride on which side real misery is to be placed. Nothing, on the contrary, must have been so unhappy as savage man, dazzled by flashes of knowledge, racked by passions, and reasoning on a state different from that in which he saw himself placed. It was in consequence of a very wise Providence, that the faculties, which he potentially enjoyed, were not to develop themselves but in proportion as there offered occasions to exercise them, lest they should be superfluous or troublesome to him when he did not want them, or tardy and useless when he did. He had in his instinct alone everything requisite to live in a state of nature; in his cultivated reason he has barely what is necessary to live in a state of society.

It appears at first sight that, as there was no kind of moral relations between men in this state, nor any known duties, they could not be either good or bad, and had neither vices nor virtues, unless we take these words in a physical sense, and call vices, in the individual, the qualities which may prove detrimental to his own preservation, and virtues those which may contribute to it; in which case we should be obliged to consider him as most virtuous, who made least resistance against the simple impulses of nature. But without deviating from the usual meaning of these terms, it is proper to suspend the judgment we might form of such a situation, and be upon our guard against prejudice, till, the balance in hand, we have examined whether there are more virtues or vices among civilized men; or whether the improvement of their understanding is sufficient to compensate the damage which they mutually do to each other, in proportion as they become better informed of the services which they ought to do; or whether, upon the whole, they would not be much happier in a condition, where they had nothing to fear or to hope from each other, than in that where they had submitted to an universal subserviency, and have obliged themselves to depend for everything upon the good will of those, who do not think themselves obliged to give anything in return.

But above all things let us beware concluding with Hobbes, that man, as having no idea of goodness, must be naturally bad; that he is vicious because he does not know what virtue is; that he always refuses to do any service to those of his own species, because he believes that none is due to them; that, in virtue of that right which he justly claims to everything he wants, he foolishly looks upon himself as proprietor of the whole universe. Hobbes very plainly saw the flaws in all the modern definitions of natural right: but the consequences, which he draws from his own definition, show that it is, in the sense he understands it, equally exceptionable. This author, to argue from his own principles, should say that the state of nature, being that where the care of our own preservation interferes least with the preservation of others, was of course the most favourable to peace, and most suitable to mankind; whereas he advances the very reverse in consequence of his having injudiciously admitted, as objects of that care which savage man should take of his preservation, the satisfaction of numberless passions which are the work of society, and have rendered laws necessary. A bad man, says he, is a robust child. But this is not proving that savage man is a robust child; and though we were to grant that he was, what could this philosopher infer from such a concession? That if this man, when robust, depended on others as much as when feeble, there is no excess that he would not be guilty of. He would make nothing of striking his mother when she delayed ever so little to give him the breast; he would claw, and bite, and strangle without remorse the first of his younger brothers, that ever so accidentally jostled or otherwise disturbed him. But these are two contradictory suppositions in the state of nature, to be robust and dependent. Man is weak when dependent, and his own master before he grows robust. Hobbes did not consider that the same cause, which hinders savages from making use of their reason, as our jurisconsults pretend, hinders them at the same time from making an ill use of their faculties, as he himself pretends; so that we may say that savages are not bad, precisely because they don't know what it is to be good; for it is neither the development of the understanding, nor the curb of the law, but the calmness of their passions and their ignorance of vice that hinders them from doing ill: *tantus plus in illis proficit vitiorum ignorantia, quam in his cognito virtutis.* There is besides another principle that has escaped Hobbes, and which, having been given to man to moderate, on certain occasions, the blind and impetuous sallies of self-love, or the desire of self-preservation previous to the appearance of that passion, allays the ardour, with which he naturally pursues his private welfare, by an innate abhorrence to see beings suffer that resemble him. I shall not surely be contradicted, in granting to man the only natural virtue, which the most passionate detractor of human virtues could not deny him, I mean that of pity, a disposition suitable to creatures weak as we are, and liable to so many evils; a virtue so much the more universal, and withal useful to man, as it takes place in him of all manner of reflection; and so natural, that the beasts themselves sometimes give evident signs of it. Not to speak of the tenderness of mothers for their young; and of the dangers they face to screen them from danger; with what reluctance are horses known to trample upon living bodies; one animal never passes unmoved by the dead carcass of another animal of the same species: there are even some who bestow a kind of sepulture upon their dead fellows; and the mournful lowings of cattle, on their entering the slaughter-house, publish the impression made upon them by the horrible spectacle they are there struck with. It is with pleasure we see the author of the fable of the bees, forced to acknowledge man a compassionate and sensible being; and lay aside, in the example he offers to confirm it, his cold and subtle style, to place before us the pathetic picture of a man, who, with his hands tied up, is obliged to behold a beast of prey tear a child from the arms of his mother, and then with his teeth grind the tender limbs, and with his claws rend the throbbing entrails of the innocent victim. What horrible emotions must not such a spectator experience at the sight of an event which does not personally concern him? What anguish must he not suffer at his not being able to assist the fainting mother or the expiring infant?

Such is the pure motion of nature, anterior to all manner of reflection; such is the force of natural pity, which the most dissolute manners have as yet found it so difficult to extinguish, since we every day see, in our theatrical representation, those men sympathize with the unfortunate and weep at their sufferings, who, if in the tyrant's place, would aggravate the torments of their enemies. Mandeville was very sensible that men, in spite of all their morality, would never have been better than monsters, if nature had not given them pity to assist reason: but he did not perceive that from this quality alone flow all the social virtues, which he would dispute mankind the possession of. In fact, what is generosity, what clemency, what humanity, but pity applied to the weak, to the guilty, or to the human species in general? Even benevolence and friendship, if we judge right, will appear the effects of a constant pity, fixed upon a particular object: for to wish that a person may not suffer, what is it but to wish that he may be happy? Though it were true that commiseration is no more than a sentiment, which puts us in the place of him who suffers, a sentiment obscure but active in the savage, developed but dormant in civilized man, how could this notion affect the truth of what I advance, but to make it more evident. In fact, commiseration must be so much the more energetic, the more intimately the animal, that beholds any kind of distress, identifies himself with the animal that labours under it. Now it is evident that this identification must have been infinitely more perfect in the state of nature than in the state of reason. It is reason that engenders self-love, and reflection that strengthens it; it is reason that makes man shrink into himself; it is reason that makes him keep aloof from everything that can trouble or afflict him: it is philosophy that destroys his connections with other men; it is in consequence of her dictates that he mutters to himself at the sight of another in distress, You may perish for aught I care, nothing can hurt me. Nothing less than those evils, which theaten the whole species, can disturb the calm sleep of the philosopher, and force him from his bed. One man may with impunity murder another under his windows; he has nothing to do but clap his hands to his ears, argue a little with himself to hinder nature, that startles within him, from identifying him with the unhappy sufferer. Savage man wants this admirable talent; and for want of wisdom and reason, is always ready foolishly to obey the first whispers of humanity. In riots and street-brawls the populace flock together, the prudent man sneaks off. They are the dregs of the people, the poor basket and barrow-women, that part the combatants, and hinder gentle folks from cutting one another's throats.

It is therefore certain that pity is a natural sentiment, which, by moderating in every individual the activity of self-love, contributes to the mutual preservation of the whole species. It is this pity which hurries us without reflection to the assistance of those we see in distress; it is this pity which, in a state of nature, stands for laws, for manners, for virtue, with this advantage, that no one is tempted to disobey her sweet and gentle voice: it is this pity which will always hinder a robust savage from plundering a feeble child, or infirm old man, of the subsistence they have acquired with pain and difficulty, if he has but the least prospect of providing for himself by any other means: it is this pity which, instead of that sublime maxim of argumentative justice, Do to others as you would have others do to you, inspires all men with that other maxim of natural goodness a great deal less perfect, but perhaps more useful, Consult your own happiness with as little prejudice as you can to that of others. It is in a word, in this natural sentiment, rather than in fine-spun arguments, that we must look for the cause of that reluctance which every man would experience to do evil, even independently of the maxims of education. Though it may be the peculiar happiness of Socrates and other geniuses of his stamp, to reason themselves into virtue, the human species would long ago have ceased to exist, had it depended entirely for its preservation on the reasonings of the individuals that compose it.

With passions so tame, and so salutary a curb, men, rather wild than wicked, and more attentive to guard against mischief than to do any to other animals, were not exposed to any dangerous dissensions: As they kept up no manner of correspondence with each other, and were of course strangers to vanity, to respect, to esteem, to contempt; as they had no notion of what we call Meum and Tuum, nor any true idea of justice; as they considered any violence they were liable to, as an evil that could be easily repaired, and not as an injury that deserved punishment; and as they never so much as dreamed of revenge, unless perhaps mechanically and unpremeditatedly, as a dog who bites the stone that has been thrown at him; their disputes could seldom be attended with bloodshed, were they never occasioned by a more considerable stake than that of subsistence: but there is a more dangerous subject of contention, which I must not leave unnoticed.

Among the passions which ruffle the heart of man, there is one of a hot and impetuous nature, which renders the sexes necessary to each other; a terrible passion which despises all dangers, bears down all obstacles, and to which in its transports it seems proper to destroy the human species which it is destined to preserve. What must become of men abandoned to this lawless and brutal rage, without modesty, without shame, and every day disputing the objects of their passion at the expense of their blood?

We must in the first place allow that the more violent the passions, the more necessary are laws to restrain them: but besides that the disorders and the crimes, to which these passions daily give rise among us, sufficiently prove the insufficiency of laws for that purpose, we would do well to look back a little further and examine, if these evils did not spring up with the laws themselves; for at this rate, though the laws were capable of repressing these evils, it is the least that might be expected from them, seeing it is no more than stopping the progress of a mischief which they themselves have produced.

Let us begin by distinguishing between what is moral and what is physical in the passion called love. The physical part of it is that general desire which prompts the sexes to unite with each other; the moral part is that which determines that desire, and fixes it upon a particular object to the exclusion of all others, or at least gives it a greater degree of energy for this preferred object. Now it is easy to perceive that the moral part of love is a factitious sentiment, engendered by society, and cried up by the women with great care and address in order to establish their empire, and secure command to that sex which ought to obey. This sentiment, being founded on certain notions of beauty and merit which a savage is not capable of having, and upon comparisons which he is not capable of making, can scarcely exist in him: for as his mind was never in a condition to form abstract ideas of regularity and proportion, neither is his heart susceptible of sentiments of admiration and love, which, even without our perceiving it, are produced by our application of these ideas; he listens solely to the dispositions implanted in him by nature, and not to taste which he never was in a way of acquiring; and every woman answers his purpose.

Confined entirely to what is physical in love, and happy enough not to know these preferences which sharpen the appetite for it, at the same time that they increase the difficulty of satisfying such appetite, men, in a state of nature, must be subject to fewer and less violent fits of that passion, and of course there must be fewer and less violent disputes among them in consequence of it. The imagination which causes so many ravages among us, never speaks to the heart of savages, who peaceably wait for the impulses of nature, yield to these impulses without choice and with more pleasure than fury; and whose desires never outlive their necessity for the thing desired.

Nothing therefore can be more evident, than that it is society alone, which has added even to love itself as well as to all the other passions, that impetuous ardour, which so often renders it fatal to mankind; and it is so much the more ridiculous to represent savages constantly murdering each other to glut their brutality, as this opinion is diametrically opposite to experience, and the Caribbeans, the people in the world who have as yet deviated least from the state of nature, are to all intents and purposes the most peaceable in their amours, and the least subject to jealousy, though they live in a burning climate which seems always to add considerably to the activity of these passions.

As to the inductions which may be drawn, in respect to several species of animals, from the battles of the males, who in all seasons cover our poultry yards with blood, and in spring particularly cause our forests to ring again with the noise they make in disputing their females, we must begin by excluding all those species, where nature has evidently established, in the relative power of the sexes, relations different from those which exist among us: thus from the battle of cocks we can form no induction that will affect the human species. In the species, where the proportion is better observed, these battles must be owing entirely to the fewness of the females compared with the males, or, which is all one, to the exclusive intervals, during which the females constantly refuse the addresses of the males; for if the female admits the male but two months in the year, it is all the same as if the number of females were five-sixths less than what it is: now neither of these cases is applicable to the human species, where the number of females generally surpasses that of males, and where it has never been observed that, even among savages, the females had, like those of other animals, stated times of passion and indifference. Besides, among several of these animals the whole species takes fire all at once, and for some days nothing is to be seen among them but confusion, tumult, disorder and bloodshed; a state unknown to the human species where love is never periodical. We can not therefore conclude from the battles of certain animals for the possession of their females, that the same would be the case of man in a state of nature; and though we might, as these contests do not destroy the other species, there is at least equal room to think they would not be fatal to ours; nay it is very probable that they would cause fewer ravages than they do in society, especially in those countries where, morality being as yet held in some esteem, the jealousy of lovers, and the vengeance of husbands every day produce duels, murders and even worse crimes; where the duty of an eternal fidelity serves only to propagate adultery; and the very laws of continence and honour necessarily contribute to increase dissoluteness, and multiply abortions.

Let us conclude that savage man, wandering about in the forests, without industry, without speech, without any fixed residence, an equal stranger to war and every social connection, without standing in any shape in need of his fellows, as well as without any desire of hurting them, and perhaps even without ever distinguishing them individually one from the other, subject to few passions, and finding in himself all he wants, let us, I say, conclude that savage man thus circumstanced had no knowledge or sentiment but such as are proper to that condition, that he was alone sensible of his real necessities, took notice of nothing but what it was his interest to see, and that his understanding made as little progress as his vanity. If he happened to make any discovery, he could the less communicate it as he did not even know his children. The art perished with the inventor; there was neither education nor improvement; generations succeeded generations to no purpose; and as all constantly set out from the same point, whole centuries rolled on in the rudeness and barbarity of the first age; the species was grown old, while the individual still remained in a state of childhood.

If I have enlarged so much upon the supposition of this primitive condition, it is because I thought it my duty, considering what ancient errors and inveterate prejudices I have to extirpate, to dig to the very roots, and show in a true picture of the state of nature, how much even natural inequality falls short in this state of that reality and influence which our writers ascribe to it.

In fact, we may easily perceive that among the differences, which distinguish men, several pass for natural, which are merely the work of habit and the different kinds of life adopted by men living in a social way. Thus a robust or delicate constitution, and the strength and weakness which depend on it, are oftener produced by the hardy or effeminate manner in which a man has been brought up, than by the primitive constitution of his body. It is the same thus in regard to the forces of the mind; and education not only produces a difference between those minds which are cultivated and those which are not, but even increases that which is found among the first in proportion to their culture; for let a giant and a dwarf set out in the same path, the giant at every step will acquire a new advantage over the dwarf. Now, if we compare the prodigious variety in the education and manner of living of the different orders of men in a civil state, with the simplicity and uniformity that prevails in the animal and savage life, where all the individuals make use of the same aliments, live in the same manner, and do exactly the same things, we shall easily conceive how much the difference between man and man in the state of nature must be less than in the state of society, and how much every inequality of institution must increase the natural inequalities of the human species.

But though nature in the distribution of her gifts should really affect all the preferences that are ascribed to her, what advantage could the most favoured derive from her partiality, to the prejudice of others, in a state of things, which scarce admitted any kind of relation between her pupils? Of what service can beauty be, where there is no love? What will wit avail people who don't speak, or craft those who have no affairs to transact? Authors are constantly crying out, that the strongest would oppress the weakest; but let them explain what they mean by the word oppression. One man will rule with violence, another will groan under a constant subjection to all his caprices: this is indeed precisely what I observe among us, but I don't see how it can be said of savage men, into whose heads it would be a harder matter to drive even the meaning of the words domination and servitude. One man might, indeed, seize on the fruits which another had gathered, on the game which another had killed, on the cavern which another had occupied for shelter; but how is it possible he should ever exact obedience from him, and what chains of dependence can there be among men who possess nothing? If I am driven from one tree, I have nothing to do but look out for another; if one place is made uneasy to me, what can hinder me from taking up my quarters elsewhere? But suppose I should meet a man so much superior to me in strength, and withal so wicked, so lazy and so barbarous as to oblige me to provide for his subsistence while he remains idle; he must resolve not to take his eyes from me a single moment, to bind me fast before he can take the least nap, lest I should kill him or give him the slip during his sleep: that is to say, he must expose himself voluntarily to much greater troubles than what he seeks to avoid, than any he gives me. And after all, let him abate ever so little of his vigilance; let him at some sudden noise but turn his head another way; I am already buried in the forest, my fetters are broke, and he never sees me again.

But without insisting any longer upon these details, every one must see that, as the bonds of servitude are formed merely by the mutual dependence of men one upon another and the reciprocal necessities which unite them, it is impossible for one man to enslave another, without having first reduced him to a condition in which he can not live without the enslaver's assistance; a condition which, as it does not exist in a state of nature, must leave every man his own master, and render the law of the strongest altogether vain and useless.

Having proved that the inequality, which may subsist between man and man in a state of nature, is almost imperceivable, and that it has very little influence, I must now proceed to show its origin, and trace its progress, in the successive developments of the human mind. After having showed, that perfectibility, the social virtues, and the other faculties, which natural man had received *in potentia*, could never be developed of themselves, that for that purpose there was a necessity for the fortuitous concurrence of several foreign causes, which might never happen, and without which he must have eternally remained in his primitive condition; I must proceed to consider and bring together the different accidents which may have perfected the human understanding by debasing the species, render a being wicked by rendering him sociable, and from so remote a term bring man at last and the world to the point in which we now see them.

I must own that, as the events I am about to describe might have happened many different ways, my choice of these I shall assign can be grounded on nothing but mere conjecture; but besides these conjectures becoming reasons, when they are not only the most probable that can be drawn from the nature of things, but the only means we can have of discovering truth, the consequences I mean to deduce from mine will not be merely conjectural, since, on the principles I have just established, it is impossible to form any other system, that would not supply me with the same results, and from which I might not draw the same conclusions.

This will authorize me to be the more concise in my reflections on the manner, in which the lapse of time makes amends for the little verisimilitude of events; on the surprising power of very trivial causes, when they act without intermission; on the impossibility there is on the one hand of destroying certain Hypotheses, if on the other we can not give them the degree of certainty which facts must be allowed to possess; on its being the business of history, when two facts are proposed, as real, to be connected by a chain of intermediate facts which are either unknown or considered as such, to furnish such facts as many actually connect them; and the business of philosophy, when history is silent, to point out similar facts which may answer the same purpose; in fine on the privilege of similitude, in regard to events, to reduce facts to a much smaller number of different classes than is generally imagined. It suffices me to offer these objects to the consideration of my judges; it suffices me to have conducted my inquiry in such a manner as to save common readers the trouble of considering them.

SECOND PART

The first man, who, after enclosing a piece of ground, took it into his head to say, "This is mine," and found people simple enough to believe him, was the true founder of civil society. How many crimes, how many wars, how many murders, how many misfortunes and horrors, would that man have saved the human species, who pulling up the stakes or filling up the ditches should have cried to his fellows: Be sure not to listen to this imposter; you are lost, if you forget that the fruits of the earth belong equally to us all, and the earth itself to nobody! But it is highly probable that things were now come to such a pass, that they could not continue much longer in the same way; for as this idea of property depends on several prior ideas which could only spring up gradually one after another, it was not formed all at once in the human mind: men must have great progress; they must have acquired a great stock of industry and knowledge, and transmitted and increased it from age to age before they could arrive at this last term of the state of nature. Let us therefore take up things a little higher, and collect into one point of view, and in their most natural order, this slow succession of events and mental improvements.

The first sentiment of man was that of his existence, his first care that of preserving it. The productions of the earth yielded him all the assistance he required; instinct prompted him to make use of them. Among

the various appetites, which made him at different times experience
different modes of existence, there was one that excited him to perpetuate his species; and this blind propensity, quite void of anything like
pure love or affection, produced nothing but an act that was merely animal. The present heat once allayed, the sexes took no further notice of
each other, and even the child ceased to have any tie in his mother, the
moment he ceased to want her assistance.

Such was the condition of infant man; such was the life of an animal
confined at first to pure sensations, and so far from harbouring any
thought of forcing her gifts from nature, that he scarcely availed himself of those which she offered to him of her own accord. But difficulties soon arose, and there was a necessity for learning how to surmount
them: the height of some trees, which prevented his reaching their
fruits; the competition of other animals equally fond of the same fruits;
the fierceness of many that even aimed at his life; these were so many
circumstances, which obliged him to apply to bodily exercise. There
was a necessity for becoming active, swift-footed, and sturdy in battle.
The natural arms, which are stones and the branches of trees, soon offered themselves to his assistance. He learned to surmount the obstacles of nature, to contend in case of necessity with other animals, to dispute his subsistence even with other men, or indemnify himself for the
loss of whatever he found himself obliged to part with to the strongest.

In proportion as the human species grew more numerous, and extended itself, its pains likewise multiplied and increased. The difference of soils, climates and seasons, might have forced men to observe
some difference in their way of living. Bad harvests, long and severe
winters, and scorching summers which parched up all the fruits of the
earth, required extraordinary exertions of industry. On the sea shore,
and the banks of rivers, they invented the line and the hook, and became fishermen and ichthyophagous. In the forests they made themselves bows and arrows, and became huntsmen and warriors. In the
cold countries they covered themselves with the skins of the beasts they
had killed; thunder, a volcano, or some happy accident made them acquainted with fire, a new resource against the rigours of winter: they
discovered the method of preserving this element, then that of reproducing it, and lastly the way of preparing with it the flesh of animals,
which heretofore they devoured raw from the carcass.

This reiterated application of various beings to himself, and to one
another, must have naturally engendered in the mind of man the idea
of certain relations. These relations, which we express by the words,
great, little, strong, weak, swift, slow, fearful, bold, and the like, compared occasionally, and almost without thinking of it, produced in him
some kind of reflection, or rather a mechanical prudence, which

pointed out to him the precautions most essential to his preservation and safety.

The new lights resulting from this development increased his superiority over other animals, by making him sensible of it. He laid himself out to ensnare them; he played them a thousand tricks; and though several surpassed him in strength or in swiftness, he in time became the master of those that could be of any service to him, and a sore enemy to those that could do him any mischief. 'Tis thus, that the first look he gave into himself produced the first emotion of pride in him; 'tis thus that, at a time he scarce knew how to distinguish between the different ranks of existence, by attributing to his species the first rank among animals in general, he prepared himself at a distance to pretend to it as an individual among those of his own species in particular.

Though other men were not to him what they are to us, and he had scarce more intercourse with them than with other animals, they were not overlooked in his observations. The conformities, which in time he might discover between them, and between himself and his female, made him judge of those he did not perceive; and seeing that they all behaved as himself would have done in similar circumstances, he concluded that their manner of thinking and willing was quite conformable to his own; and this important truth, when once engraved deeply on his mind, made him follow, by a presentiment as sure as any logic, and withal much quicker, the best rules of conduct, which for the sake of his own safety and advantage it was proper he should observe towards them.

Instructed by experience that the love of happiness is the sole principle of all human actions, he found himself in a condition to distinguish the few cases, in which common interest might authorize him to build upon the assistance of his fellows, and those still fewer, in which a competition of interests might justly render it suspected. In the first case he united with them in the same flock, or at most by some kind of free association which obliged none of its members, and lasted no longer than the transitory necessity that had given birth to it. In the second case every one aimed at his own private advantage, either by open force if he found himself strong enough, or by cunning and address if he thought himself too weak to use violence.

Such was the manner in which men might have insensibly acquired some gross idea of their mutual engagements and the advantage of fulfilling them, but this only as far as their present and sensible interest required; for as to foresight they were utter strangers to it, and far from troubling their heads about a distant futurity, they scarce thought of the day following. Was a deer to be taken? Every one saw that to succeed he must faithfully stand to his post; but suppose a hare to have slipped by within reach of any one of them, it is not to be doubted but he pursued it without scruple, and when he had seized his prey never reproached himself with having made his companions miss theirs.

We may easily conceive that such an intercourse scarce required a more refined language than that of crows and monkeys, which flock together almost in the same manner. Inarticulate exclamations, a great many gestures, and some imitative sounds, must have been for a long time the universal language of mankind, and by joining to these in every country some articulate and conventional sounds, of which, as I have already hinted, it is not very easy to explain the institution, there arose particular languages, but rude, imperfect, and such nearly as are to be found at this day among several savage nations. My pen straightened by the rapidity of time, the abundance of things I have to say, and the almost insensible progress of the first improvements, flies like an arrow over numberless ages, for the slower the succession of events, the quicker I may allow myself to be in relating them.

At length, these first improvements enabled man to improve at a greater rate. Industry grew perfect in proportion as the mind became more enlightened. Men soon ceasing to fall asleep under the first tree, or take shelter in the first cavern, lit upon some hard and sharp kinds of stone resembling spades or hatchets, and employed them to dig the ground, cut down trees, and with the branches build huts, which they afterwards bethought themselves of plastering over with clay or dirt. This was the epoch of a first revolution, which produced the establishment and distinction of families, and which introduced a species of property, and along with it perhaps a thousand quarrels and battles. As the strongest however were probably the first to make themselves cabins, which they knew they were able to defend, we may conclude that the weak found it much shorter and safer to imitate than to attempt to dislodge them: and as to those, who were already provided with cabins, no one could have any great temptation to seize upon that of his neighbour, not so much because it did not belong to him, as because it could be of no service to him; and as besides to make himself master of it, he must expose himself to a very sharp conflict with the present occupiers.

The first developments of the heart were the effects of a new situation, which united husbands and wives, parents and children, under one roof; the habit of living together gave birth to the sweetest sentiments the human species is acquainted with, conjugal and paternal love. Every family became a little society, so much the more firmly united, as a mutual attachment and liberty were the only bonds of it; and it was now that the sexes, whose way of life had been hitherto the same, began to adopt different manners and customs. The women became more sedentary, and accustomed themselves to stay at home and look after the children, while the men rambled abroad in quest of subsistence for the whole family. The two sexes likewise by living a little more at their ease began to lose somewhat of their usual ferocity and sturdiness; but if on the one hand individuals became less able to engage separately with wild beasts, they on the other were more easily got together to make a common resistance against them.

In this new state of things, the simplicity and solitariness of man's life, the limitedness of his wants, and the instruments which he had invented to satisfy them, leaving him a great deal of leisure, he employed it to supply himself with several conveniences unknown to his ancestors; and this was the first yoke he inadvertently imposed upon himself, and the first source of mischief which he prepared for his children; for besides continuing in this manner to soften both body and mind, these conveniences having through use lost almost all their aptness to please, and even degenerated into real wants, the privation of them became far more intolerable than the possession of them had been agreeable; to lose them was a misfortune, to possess them no happiness.

Here we may a little better discover how the use of speech insensibly commences or improves in the bosom of every family, and may likewise from conjectures concerning the manner in which divers particular causes might have propagated language, and accelerated its progress by rendering it every day more and more necessary. Great inundations or earthquakes surrounded inhabited districts with water or precipices, portions of the continent were by revolutions of the globe torn off and split into islands. It is obvious that among men thus collected, and forced to live together, a common idiom must have started up much sooner, than among those who freely wandered through the forests of the main land. Thus it is very possible that the inhabitants of the islands formed in this manner, after their first essays in navigation, brought among us the use of speech; and it is very probable at least that society and languages commenced in islands and even acquired perfection there, before the inhabitants of the continent knew anything of either.

Everything now begins to wear a new aspect. Those who heretofore wandered through the woods, by taking to a more settled way of life, gradually flock together, coalesce into several separate bodies, and at length form in every country distinct nations, united in character and manners, not by any laws or regulations, but by an uniform manner of life, a sameness of provisions, and the common influence of the climate. A permanent neighborhood must at last infallibly create some connection between different families. The transitory commerce required by nature soon produced, among the youth of both sexes living

in contiguous cabins, another kind of commerce, which besides being
equally agreeable is rendered more durable by mutual intercourse.
Men begin to consider different objects, and to make comparisons;
they insensibly acquire ideas of merit and beauty, and these soon produce sentiments of preference. By seeing each other often they contract a habit, which makes it painful not to see each other always.
Tender and agreeable sentiments steal into the soul, and are by the
smallest opposition wound up into the most impetuous fury: Jealousy
kindles with love; discord triumphs; and the gentlest of passions requires sacrifices of human blood to appease it.

In proportion as ideas and sentiments succeed each other, and the
head and the heart exercise themselves, men continue to shake off their
original wildness, and their connections become more intimate and extensive. They now begin to assemble round a great tree: singing and
dancing, the genuine offspring of love and leisure, become the amusement or rather the occupation of the men and women, free from care,
thus gathered together. Every one begins to survey the rest, and wishes
to be surveyed himself; and public esteem acquires a value. He who
sings or dances best; the handsomest, the strongest, the most dexterous,
the most eloquent, comes to be the most respected: this was the first
step towards inequality, and at the same time towards vice. From these
first preferences there proceeded on one side vanity and contempt,
on the other envy and shame; and the fermentation raised by these
new leavens at length produced combinations fatal to happiness and
innocence.

Men no sooner began to set a value upon each other, and know what
esteem was, than each laid claim to it, and it was no longer safe for any
man to refuse it to another. Hence the first duties of civility and politeness, even among savages; and hence every voluntary injury became an
affront, as besides the mischief, which resulted from it as an injury, the
party offended was sure to find in it a contempt for his person more intolerable than the mischief itself. It was thus that every man, punishing
the contempt expressed for him by others in proportion to the value he
set upon himself, the effects of revenge became terrible, and men
learned to be sanguinary and cruel. Such precisely was the degree at-
tained by most of the savage nations with whom we are acquainted.
And it is for want of sufficiently distinguishing ideas, and observing at
how great a distance these people were from the first state of nature,
that so many authors have hastily concluded that man is naturally
cruel, and requires a regular system of police to be reclaimed; whereas
nothing can be more gentle than he in his primitive state, when placed
by nature at an equal distance from the stupidity of brutes, and the pernicious good sense of civilized man; and equally confined by instinct

and reason to the care of providing against the mischief which threatens him, he is withheld by natural compassion from doing any injury to others, so far from being ever so little prone even to return that which he has received. For according to the axiom of the wise Locke, Where there is no property, there can be no injury.

But we must take notice, that the society now formed and the relations now established among men required in them qualities different from those, which they derived from their primitive constitution; that as a sense of morality began to insinuate itself into human actions, and every man, before the enacting of laws, was the only judge and avenger of the injuries he had received, that goodness of heart suitable to the pure state of nature by no means suited infant society; that it was necessary punishments should become severer in the same proportion that the opportunities of offending became more frequent, and the dread of vengeance add strength to the too weak curb of the law. Thus, though men were become less patient, and natural compassion had already suffered some alteration, this period of the development of the human faculties, holding a just mean between the indolence of the primitive state, and the petulant activity of self-love, must have been the happiest and most durable epoch. The more we reflect on this state, the more convinced we shall be, that it was the least subject of any to revolutions, the best for man, and that nothing could have drawn him out of it but some fatal accident, which, for the public good, should never have happened. The example of the savages, most of whom have been found in this condition, seems to confirm that mankind was formed ever to remain in it, that this condition is the real youth of the world, and that all ulterior improvements have been so many steps, in appearance towards the perfection of individuals, but in fact towards the decrepitness of the species.

As long as men remained satisfied with their rustic cabins; as long as they confined themselves to the use of clothes made of the skins of other animals, and the use of thorns and fish-bones, in putting these skins together; as long as they continued to consider feathers and shells as sufficient ornaments, and to paint their bodies of different colours, to improve or ornament their bows and arrows, to form and scoop out with sharp-edged stones some little fishing boats, or clumsy instruments of music; in a word, as long as they undertook such works only as a single person could finish, and stuck to such arts as did not require the joint endeavours of several hands, they lived free, healthy, honest and happy, as much as their nature would admit, and continued to enjoy with each other all the pleasures of an independent intercourse; but from the moment one man began to stand in need of another's assistance; from the moment it appeared an advantage for one man to possess the quantity of provisions requisite for two, all equality vanished; property started up; labour became necessary; and boundless forests became smiling fields, which it was found necessary to water with human sweat, and in which slavery and misery were soon seen to sprout out and grow with the fruits of the earth.

Metallurgy and agriculture were the two arts whose invention produced this great revolution. With the poet, it is gold and silver, but with the philosopher it is iron and corn, which have civilized men, and ruined mankind. Accordingly both one and the other were unknown to the savages of America, who for that very reason have always continued savages; nay other nations seem to have continued in a state of barbarism, as long as they continued to exercise one only of these arts without the other; and perhaps one of the best reasons that can be assigned, why Europe has been, if not earlier, at least more constantly and better civilized than the other quarters of the world, is that she both abounds most in iron and is best qualified to produce corn.

It is a very difficult matter to tell how men came to know anything of iron, and the art of employing it: for we are not to suppose that they should of themselves think of digging it out of the mines, and preparing it for fusion, before they knew what could be the result of such a process. On the other hand, there is the less reason to attribute this discovery to any accidental fire, as mines are formed nowhere but in dry and barren places, and such as are bare of trees and plants, so that it looks as if nature had taken pains to keep from us so mischievous a secret. Nothing therefore remains but the extraordinary circumstance of some volcano, which, belching forth metallic substances ready fused, might have given the spectators a notion of imitating that operation of nature; and after all we must suppose them endued with an extraordinary stock of courage and foresight to undertake so painful a work, and have, at so great a distance, an eye to the advantages they might derive from it; qualities scarcely suitable but to heads more exercised, than those of such discoverers can be supposed to have been.

As to agriculture, the principles of it were known a long time before the practice of it took place, and it is hardly possible that men, constantly employed in drawing their subsistence from trees and plants, should not have early hit on the means employed by nature for the generation of vegetables; but in all probability it was very late before their industry took a turn that way, either because trees, which with their land and water game supplied them with sufficient food, did not require their attention; or because they did not know the use of corn; or because they had no instruments to cultivate it; or because they were destitute of foresight in regard to future necessities; or in fine, because they wanted means to hinder others from running away with the fruit

of their labours. We may believe that on their becoming more industrious they began their agriculture by cultivating with sharp stones and
pointed sticks a few pulse or roots about their cabins; and that it was a
long time before they knew the method of preparing corn, and were
provided with instruments necessary to raise it in large quantities; not
to mention the necessity there is, in order to follow this occupation and
sow lands, to consent to lose something at present to gain a great deal
hereafter; a precaution very foreign to the turn of man's mind in a savage state, in which, as I have already taken notice, he can hardly foresee his wants from morning to night.

For this reason the invention of other arts must have been necessary
to oblige mankind to apply to that of agriculture. As soon as men were
wanted to fuse and forge iron, others were wanted to maintain them.
The more hands were employed in manufactures, the fewer hands
were left to provide subsistence for all, though the number of mouths
to be supplied with food continued the same; and as some required
commodities in exchange for their iron, the rest at last found out the
method of making iron subservient to the multiplication of commodities. Hence on the one hand husbandry and agriculture, and on the
other the art of working metals and of multiplying the uses of them.

To the tilling of the earth the distribution of it necessarily succeeded,
and to property one acknowledged, the first rules of justice: for to secure every man his own, every man must have something. Moreover,
as men began to extend their views to futurity, and all found themselves
in possession of more or less goods capable of being lost, every one in
particular had reason to fear, lest reprisals should be made on him for
any injury he might do to others. This origin is so much the more natural, as it is impossible to conceive how property can flow from any
other source but industry; for what can a man add but his labour to
things which he has not made, in order to acquire a property in them?
'Tis the labour of the hands alone, which giving the husbandman a title
to the produce of the land he has tilled gives him a title to the land itself, at least till he has gathered in the fruits of it, and so on from year
to year; and this enjoyment forming a continued possession is easily
transformed into a property. The ancients, says Grotius, by giving to
Ceres the epithet of Legislatrix, and to a festival celebrated in her honour the name of Thesmorphoria, insinuated that the distribution of
lands produced a new kind of right; that is, the right of property different from that which results from the law of nature.

Things thus circumstanced might have remained equal, if men's talents had been equal, and if, for instance, the use of iron, and the con-
sumption of commodities had always held an exact proportion to each
other; but as this proportion had no support, it was soon broken. The

man that had most strength performed most labour; the most dexterous
turned his labour to best account; the most ingenious found out meth-
ods of lessening his labour; the husbandman required more iron, or the
smith more corn, and while both worked equally, one earned a great
deal by his labour, while the other could scarce live by his. It is thus
that natural inequality insensibly unfolds itself with that arising from a
variety of combinations, and that the difference among men, developed by the difference of their circumstances, becomes more sensible,
more permanent in its effects, and begins to influence in the same proportion the condition of private persons.

Things once arrived at this period, it is an easy matter to imagine the
rest. I shall not stop to describe the successive inventions of other arts,
the progress of language, the trial and employments of talents, the inequality of fortunes, the use or abuse of riches, nor all the details which
follow these, and which every one may easily supply. I shall just give a
glance at mankind placed in this new order of things.

Behold then all our faculties developed; our memory and imagination at work, self-love interested; reason rendered active; and the mind
almost arrived at the utmost bounds of that perfection it is capable of.
Behold all our natural qualities put in motion; the rank and condition
of every man established, not only as to the quantum of property and
the power of serving or hurting others, but likewise as to genius, beauty,
strength or address, merit or talents; and as these were the only qualities which could command respect, it was found necessary to have or
at least to affect them. It was requisite for men to be thought what they
really were not. To be and to appear became two very different things,
and from this distinction sprang pomp and knavery, and all the vices
which form their train. On the other hand, man, heretofore free and independent, was now in consequence of a multitude of new wants
brought under subjection, as it were, to all nature, and especially to his
fellows, whose slave in some sense he became even by becoming their
master; if rich, he stood in need of their services, if poor, of their assistance; even mediocrity itself could not enable him to do without them.
He must therefore have been continually at work to interest them in his
happiness, and make them, if not really, at least apparently find their
advantage in labouring for his: this rendered him sly and artful in his
dealings with some, imperious and cruel in his dealings with others,
and laid him under the necessity of using ill all those whom he stood
in need of, as often as he could not awe them into a compliance with
his will, and did not find it his interest to purchase it at the expense of
real services. In fine, an insatiable ambition, the rage of raising their
relative fortunes, not so much through real necessity, as to over-top others, inspire all men with a wicked inclination to injure each other, and

with a secret jealousy so much the more dangerous, as to carry its point with the greater security, it often puts on the face of benevolence. In a word, sometimes nothing was to be seen but a contention of endeavours on the one hand, and an opposition of interests on the other, while a secret desire of thriving at the expense of others constantly prevailed. Such were the first effects of property, and the inseparable attendants of infant inequality.

Riches, before the invention of signs to represent them, could scarce consist in anything but lands and cattle, the only real goods which men can possess. But when estates increased so much in number and in extent as to take in whole countries and touch each other, it became impossible for one man to aggrandise himself but at the expense of some other; and the supernumerary inhabitants, who were too weak or too indolent to make such acquisitions in their turn, impoverished without losing anything, because while everything about them changed they alone remained the same, were obliged to receive or force their subsistence from the hands of the rich. And hence began to flow, according to the different characters of each, domination and slavery, or violence and rapine. The rich on their side scarce began to taste the pleasure of commanding, when they preferred it to every other; and making use of their old slaves to acquire new ones, they no longer thought of anything but subduing and enslaving their neighbours; like those ravenous wolves, who having once tasted human flesh, despise every other food, and devour nothing but men for the future.

It is thus that the most powerful or the most wretched, respectively considering their power and wretchedness as a kind of title to the substance of others, even equivalent to that of property, the equality once broken was followed by the most shocking disorders. It is thus that the usurpations of the rich, the pillagings of the poor, and the unbridled passions of all, by stifling the cries of natural compassion, and the as yet feeble voice of justice, rendered man avaricious, wicked and ambitious. There arose between the title of the strongest, and that of the first occupier a perpetual conflict, which always ended in battery and bloodshed. Infant society became a scene of the most horrible warfare: Mankind thus debased and harassed, and no longer able to retreat, or renounce the unhappy acquisitions it had made; labouring, in short merely to its confusion by the abuse of those faculties, which in themselves do it so much honour, brought itself to the very brink of ruin and destruction.

> *Attonitus novitate mali, divesque miserque,*
> *Effugere optat opes; et quae modò voverat, odit.*

But it is impossible that men should not sooner or later have made reflections on so wretched a situation, and upon the calamities with which they were overwhelmed. The rich in particular must have soon perceived how much they suffered by a perpetual war, of which they alone supported all the expense, and in which, though all risked life, they alone risked any substance. Besides, whatever colour they might pretend to give their usurpations, they sufficiently saw that these usurpations were in the main founded upon false and precarious titles, and that what they had acquired by mere force, others could again by mere force wrest out of their hands, without leaving them the least room to complain of such a proceeding. Even those, who owed all their riches to their own industry, could scarce ground their acquisitions upon a better title. It availed them nothing to say, 'Twas I built this wall; I acquired this spot by my labour. Who traced it out for you, another might object, and what right have you to expect payment at our expense for doing that we did not oblige you to do? Don't you know that numbers of your brethren perish, or suffer grievously for want of what you possess more than suffices nature, and that you should have had the express and unanimous consent of mankind to appropriate to yourself of their common, more than was requisite for your private subsistence? Destitute of solid reasons to justify, and sufficient force to defend himself; crushing individuals with ease, but with equal ease crushed by numbers; one against all, and unable, on account of mutual jealousies, to unite with his equals against banditti united by the common hopes of pillage; the rich man, thus pressed by necessity, at last conceived the deepest project that ever entered the human mind: this was to employ in his favour the very forces that attacked him, to make allies of his enemies, to inspire them with other maxims, and make them adopt other institutions as favourable to his pretensions, as the law of nature was unfavourable to them.

With this view, after laying before his neighbours all the horrors of a situation, which armed them all one against another, which rendered their possessions as burdensome as their wants were intolerable, and in which no one could expect any safety either in poverty or riches, he easily invented specious arguments to bring them over to his purpose. "Let us unite," said he, "to secure the weak from oppression, restrain the ambitious, and secure to every man the possession of what belongs to him: Let us form rules of justice and peace, to which all may be obliged to conform, which shall not except persons, but may in some sort make amends for the caprice of fortune, by submitting alike the powerful and the weak to the observance of mutual duties. In a word, instead of turning our forces against ourselves, let us collect them into a sovereign power, which may govern us by wise laws, may protect and defend all the members of the association, repel common enemies, and maintain a perpetual concord and harmony among us."

Much fewer words of this kind were sufficient to draw in a parcel of rustics, whom it was an easy matter to impose upon, who had besides too many quarrels among themselves to live without arbiters, and too much avarice and ambition to live long without masters. All offered their necks to the yoke in hopes of securing their liberty; for though they had sense enough to perceive the advantages of a political constitution, they had not experience enough to see beforehand the dangers of it; those among them, who were best qualified to foresee abuses, were precisely those who expected to benefit by them; even the soberest judged it requisite to sacrifice one part of their liberty to ensure the other, as a man, dangerously wounded in any of his limbs, readily parts with it to save the rest of his body.

Such was, or must have been, had man been left to himself, the origin of society and of the laws, which increased the fetters of the weak, and the strength of the rich; irretrievably destroyed natural liberty, fixed for ever the laws of property and inequality; changed an artful usurpation into an irrevocable title; and for the benefit of a few ambitious individuals subjected the rest of mankind to perpetual labour, servitude, and misery. We may easily conceive how the establishment of a single society rendered that of all the rest absolutely necessary, and how, to make head against united forces, it became necessary for the rest of mankind to unite in their turn. Societies once formed in this manner, soon multiplied or spread to such a degree, as to cover the face of the earth; and not to leave a corner in the whole universe, where a man could throw off the yoke, and withdraw his head from under the often ill-conducted sword which he saw perpetually hanging over it. The civil law being thus become the common rule of citizens, the law of nature no longer obtained but among the different societies, in which, under the name of the law of nations, it was qualified by some tacit conventions to render commerce possible, and supply the place of natural compassion, which, losing by degrees all that influence over societies which it originally had over individuals, no longer exists but in some great souls, who consider themselves as citizens of the world, and forcing the imaginary barriers that separate people from people, after the example of the Sovereign Being from whom we all derive our existence, make the whole human race the object of their benevolence.

Political bodies, thus remaining in a state of nature among themselves, soon experienced the inconveniences which had obliged individuals to quit it; and this state became much more fatal to these great bodies, than it had been before to the individuals which now composed them. Hence those national wars, those battles, those murders, those reprisals, which make nature shudder and shock reason; hence all those horrible prejudices, which make it a virtue and an honour to shed human blood. The worthiest men learned to consider the cutting of the throats of their fellows as a duty; at length men began to butcher each other by thousands without knowing for what; and more murders were committed in a single action, and more horrible disorders at the taking of a single town, than had been committed in the state of nature during ages together upon the whole face of the earth. Such are the first effects we may conceive to have arisen from the division of mankind into different societies. Let us return to their institution.

I know that several writers have assigned other origins of political society; as for instance, the conquests of the powerful, or the union of the weak; and it is no matter which of these causes we adopt in regard to what I am going to establish; that, however, which I have just laid down, seems to me the most natural, for the following reasons: First, because, in the first case, the right of conquest being in fact no right at all, it could not serve as a foundation for any other right, the conqueror and the conquered ever remaining with respect to each other in a state of war, unless the conquered, restored to the full possession of their liberty, should freely choose their conqueror for their chief. Till then, whatever capitulations might have been made between them, as these capitulations were founded upon violence, and of course *de facto* null and void, there could not have existed in this hypothesis either a true society, or a political body, or any other law but that of the strongest. Second, because these words strong and weak, are ambiguous in the second case; for during the interval between the establishment of the right of property or prior occupation and that of political government, the meaning of these terms is better expressed by the words poor and rich, as before the establishment of laws men in reality had no other means of reducing their equals, but by invading the property of these equals, or by parting with some of their own property to them. Third, because the poor having nothing but their liberty to lose, it would have been the height of madness in them to give up willingly the only blessing they had left without obtaining some consideration for it: whereas the rich being sensible, if I may say so, in every part of their possessions, it was much easier to do them mischief, and therefore more incumbent upon them to guard against it; and because, in fine, it is but reasonable to suppose, that a thing has been invented by him to whom it could be of service rather than by him to whom it must prove detrimental.

Government in its infancy had no regular and permanent form. For want of a sufficient fund of philosophy and experience, men could see no further than the present inconveniences, and never thought of providing remedies for future ones, but in proportion as they arose. In spite of all the labours of the wisest legislators, the political state still continued imperfect, because it was in a manner the work of chance; and, as the foundations of it were ill laid, time, though sufficient to discover its defects and suggest the remedies for them, could never mend its original vices. Men were continually repairing; whereas, to erect a good edifice, they should have begun as Lycurgus did at Sparta, by clearing the area, and removing the old materials. Society at first consisted merely of some general conventions which all the members bound themselves to observe, and for the performance of which the whole body became security to every individual. Experience was necessary to show the great weakness of such a constitution, and how easy it was for those, who infringed it, to escape the conviction or chastisement of faults, of which the public alone was to be both the witness and the judge; the laws could not fail of being eluded a thousand ways; inconveniences and disorders could not but multiply continually, till it was at last found necessary to think of committing to private persons the dangerous trust of public authority, and to magistrates the care of enforcing obedience to the people: for to say that chiefs were elected before confederacies were formed, and that the ministers of the laws existed before the laws themselves, is a supposition too ridiculous to deserve I should seriously refute it.

It would be equally unreasonable to imagine that men at first threw themselves into the arms of an absolute master, without any conditions or consideration on his side; and that the first means contrived by jealous and unconquered men for their common safety was to run hand over head into slavery. In fact, why did they give themselves superiors, if it was not to be defended by them against oppression, and protected in their lives, liberties, and properties, which are in a manner the constitutional elements of their being? Now in the relations between man and man, the worst that can happen to one man being to see himself at the discretion of another, would it not have been contrary to the dictates of good sense to begin by making over to a chief the only things for the preservation of which they stood in need of his assistance? What equivalent could he have offered them for so fine a privilege? And had he presumed to exact it on pretense of defending them, would he not have immediately received the answer in the apologue? What worse treatment can we expect from an enemy? It is therefore past dispute, and indeed a fundamental maxim of political law, that people gave themselves chiefs to defend their liberty and not be enslaved by them. If we have a prince, said Pliny to Trajan, it is in order that he may keep us from having a master.

Political writers argue in regard to the love of liberty with the same philosophy that philosophers do in regard to the state of nature; by the things they see they judge of things very different which they have never seen, and they attribute to men a natural inclination to slavery, on account of the patience with which the slaves within their notice carry the yoke; not reflecting that it is with liberty as with innocence and virtue, the value of which is not known but by those who possess them, though the relish for them is lost with the things themselves. I know the charms of your country, said Brasidas to a satrap who was comparing the life of the Spartans with that of the Persepolites; but you can not know the pleasures of mine.

As an unbroken courser erects his mane, paws the ground, and rages at the bare sight of the bit, while a trained horse patiently suffers both whip and spur, just so the barbarian will never reach his neck to the yoke which civilized man carries without murmuring but prefers the most stormy liberty to a calm subjection. It is not therefore by the servile disposition of enslaved nations that we must judge of the natural dispositions of man for or against slavery, but by the prodigies done by every free people to secure themselves from oppression. I know that the first are constantly crying up that peace and tranquillity they enjoy in their irons, and that *miserrimam servitutem pacem appellant:* but when I see the others sacrifice pleasures, peace, riches, power, and even life itself to the preservation of that single jewel so much slighted by those who have lost it; when I see free-born animals through a natural abhorrence of captivity dash their brains out against the bars of their prison; when I see multitudes of naked savages despise European pleasures, and brave hunger, fire and sword, and death itself to preserve their independency; I feel that it belongs not to slaves to argue concerning liberty.

As to paternal authority, from which several have derived absolute government and every other mode of society, it is sufficient, without having recourse to Locke and Sidney, to observe that nothing in the world differs more from the cruel spirit of despotism that the gentleness of that authority, which looks more to the advantage of him who obeys than to the utility of him who commands; that by the law of nature the father continues master of his child no longer than the child stands in need of his assistance; that after that term they become equal, and that then the son, entirely independent of the father, owes him no obedience, but only respect. Gratitude is indeed a duty which we are bound to pay, but which benefactors can not exact. Instead of saying that civil society is derived from paternal authority, we should rather say that it is to the former that the latter owes its principal force: No one individual was acknowledged as the father of several other individuals, till they settled about him. The father's goods, which he can indeed dispose of as he pleases, are the ties which hold his children to their dependence upon him, and he may divide his substance among them in proportion as they shall have deserved his attention by a continual deference to his commands. Now the subjects of a despotic chief, far from having any such favour to expect from him, as both themselves and all they have are his property, or at least are considered by him as such, are obliged to receive as a favour what he relinquishes to them of their own property. He does them justice when he strips them; he treats them with mercy when he suffers them to live. By continuing in this manner to compare facts with right, we should discover as little solidity as truth in the voluntary establishment of tyranny; and it would be a hard matter to prove the validity of a contract which was binding only on one side, in which one of the parties should stake everything and the other nothing, and which could turn out to the prejudice of him alone who had bound himself.

This odious system is even, at this day, far from being that of wise and good monarchs, and especially of the kings of France, as may be seen by divers passages in their edicts, and particularly by that of a celebrated piece published in 1667 in the name and by the orders of Louis XIV. "Let it therefore not be said that the sovereign is not subject to the laws of his realm, since, that he is, is a maxim of the law of nations which flattery has sometimes attacked, but which good princes have always defended as the tutelary divinity of their realms. How much more reasonable is it to say with the sage Plato, that the perfect happiness of a state consists in the subjects obeying their prince, the prince obeying the laws, and the laws being equitable and always directed to the good of the public? I shall not stop to consider, if, liberty being the most noble faculty of man, it is not degrading one's nature, reducing one's self to the level of brutes, who are the slaves of instinct, and even offending the author of one's being, to renounce without reserve the most precious of his gifts, and submit to the commission of all the crimes he has forbid us, merely to gratify a mad or a cruel master; and if this sublime artist ought to be more irritated at seeing his work destroyed than at seeing it dishonoured. I shall only ask what right those, who were not afraid thus to degrade themselves, could have to subject their dependants to the same ignominy, and renounce, in the name of their posterity, blessings for which it is not indebted to their liberality, and without which life itself must appear a burthen to all those who are worthy to live.

Puffendorf says that, as we can transfer our property from one to another by contracts and conventions, we may likewise divest ourselves of our liberty in favour of other men. This, in my opinion, is a very poor way of arguing; for, in the first place, the property I cede to another becomes by such cession a thing quite foreign to me, and the abuse of which can no way affect me; but it concerns me greatly that my liberty is not abused, and I can not, without incurring the guilt of the crimes I may be forced to commit, expose myself to become the instrument of any. Besides, the right of property being of mere human convention and institution, every man may dispose as he pleases of what he possesses: But the case is otherwise with regard to the essential gifts of nature, such as life and liberty, which every man is permitted to enjoy, and of which it is doubtful at least whether any man has a right to divest himself: By giving up the one, we degrade our being; by giving up the other we annihilate it as much as it is our power to do so; and as no temporal enjoyments can indemnify us for the loss of either, it would be at once offending both nature and reason to renounce them for any consideration. But though we could transfer our liberty as we do our substance, the difference would be very great with regard to our children, who enjoy our substance but by a cession of our right; whereas liberty being a blessing, which as men they hold from nature, their parents have no right to strip them of it; so that as to establish slavery it was necessary to do violence to nature, so it was necessary to alter nature to perpetuate such a right; and the jurisconsults, who have gravely pronounced that the child of a slave comes a slave into the world, have in other words decided, that a man does not come a man into the world.

It therefore appears to me incontestably true, that not only governments did not begin by arbitrary power, which is but the corruption and extreme term of government, and at length brings it back to the law of the strongest, against which governments were at first the remedy, but even that, allowing they had commenced in this manner, such power being illegal in itself could never have served as a foundation to the rights of society, nor of course to the inequality of institution.

I shall not now enter upon the inquiries which still remain to be made into the nature of the fundamental pacts of every kind of government, but, following the common opinion, confine myself in this place to the establishment of the political body as a real contract between the multitude and the chiefs elected by it. A contract by which both parties oblige themselves to the observance of the laws that are therein stipulated, and form the bands of their union. The multitude having, on occasion of the social relations between them, concentered all their wills in one person, all the articles, in regard to which this will explains itself, become so many fundamental laws, which oblige without exception all the members of the state, and one of which laws regulates the choice and the power of the magistrates appointed to look to the execution of the rest. This power extends to everything that can maintain the constitution, but extends to nothing that can alter it. To this power are added honours, that may render the laws and the ministers of them respectable; and the persons of the ministers are distinguished by certain prerogatives, which may make them amends for the great fatigues inseparable from a good administration. The magistrate, on his side, obliges himself not to use the power with which he is intrusted but conformably to the intention of his constituents, to maintain every one of them in the peaceable possession of his property, and upon all occasions prefer the good of the public to his own private interest.

Before experience had demonstrated, or a thorough knowledge of the human heart had pointed out, the abuses inseparable from such a constitution, it must have appeared so much the more perfect, as those appointed to look to its preservation were themselves most concerned therein; for magistracy and its rights being built solely on the fundamental laws, as soon as these ceased to exist, the magistrates would cease to be lawful, the people would no longer be bound to obey them, and, as the essence of the state did not consist in the magistrates but in the laws, the members of it would immediately become entitled to their primitive and natural liberty.

A little reflection would afford us new arguments in confirmation of this truth, and the nature of the contract might alone convince us that it can not be irrevocable: for if there was no superior power capable of guaranteeing the fidelity of the contracting parties and of obliging them to fulfil their mutual engagements, they would remain sole judges in their own cause, and each of them would always have a right to renounce the contract, as soon as he discovered that the other had broke the conditions of it, or that these conditions ceased to suit his private convenience. Upon this principle, the right of abdication may probably be founded. Now, to consider as we do nothing but what is human in this institution, if the magistrate, who has all the power in his own hands, and who appropriates to himself all the advantages of the contract, has notwithstanding a right to divest himself of his authority; how much a better right must the people, who pay for all the faults of its chief, have to renounce their dependence upon him. But the shocking dissensions and disorders without number, which would be the necessary consequence of so dangerous a privilege, show more than anything else how much human governments stood in need of a more solid basis than that of mere reason, and how necessary it was for the public tranquillity, that the will of the Almighty should interpose to give to sovereign authority, a sacred and inviolable character, which should deprive subjects of the mischievous right to dispose of it to whom they pleased. If mankind had received no other advantages from religion, this alone would be sufficient to make them adopt and cherish it, since it is the means of saving more blood than fanaticism has been the cause of spilling. But to resume the thread of our hypothesis.

The various forms of government owe their origin to the various degrees of inequality between the members, at the time they first coalesced into a political body. Where a man happened to be eminent for power, for virtue, for riches, or for credit, he became sole magistrate, and the state assumed a monarchical form; if many of pretty equal eminence out-topped all the rest, they were jointly elected, and this election produced an aristocracy; those, between whose fortune or talents there happened to be no such disproportion, and who had deviated less from the state of nature, retained in common the supreme administration, and formed a democracy. Time demonstrated which of these forms suited mankind best. Some remained altogether subject to the laws; others soon bowed their necks to masters. The former laboured to preserve their liberty; the latter thought of nothing but invading that of their neighbours, jealous at seeing others enjoy a blessing which themselves had lost. In a word, riches and conquest fell to the share of the one, and virtue and happiness to that of the other.

In these various modes of government the offices at first were all elective; and when riches did not preponderate, the preference was given to merit, which gives a natural ascendant, and to age, which is the parent of deliberateness in council, and experience in execution. The ancients among the Hebrews, the Geronts of Sparta, the Senate of Rome, nay, the very etymology of our word seigneur, show how much gray hairs were formerly respected. The oftener the choice fell upon old men, the oftener it became necessary to repeat it, and the more the trouble of such repetitions became sensible; electioneering took place; factions arose; the parties contracted ill blood; civil wars blazed forth; the lives of the citizens were sacrificed to the pretended happiness of the state; and things at last came to such a pass, as to be ready to relapse into their primitive confusion. The ambition of the principal men induced them to take advantage of these circumstances to perpetuate the hitherto temporary charges in their families; the people already inured to dependence, accustomed to ease and the conveniences of life, and too much enervated to break their fetters, consented to the increase of their slavery for the sake of securing their tranquillity; and it is thus that chiefs, become hereditary, contracted the habit of considering magistracies as a family estate, and themselves as proprietors of those communities, of which at first they were but mere officers; to call their fellow-citizens their slaves; to look upon them, like so many cows or sheep, as a part of their substance; and to style themselves the peers of Gods, and Kings of Kings.

By pursuing the progress of inequality in these different revolutions, we shall discover that the establishment of laws and of the right of property was the first term of it; the institution of magistrates the second; and the third and last the changing of legal into arbitrary power; so that the different states of rich and poor were authorized by the first epoch; those of powerful and weak by the second; and by the third those of master and slave, which formed the last degree of inequality, and the term in which all the rest at last end, till new revolutions entirely dissolve the government, or bring it back nearer to its legal constitution.

To conceive the necessity of this progress, we are not so much to consider the motives for the establishment of political bodies, as the forms these bodies assume in their administration; and the inconveniences with which they are essentially attended; for those vices, which render social institutions necessary, are the same which render the abuse of such institutions unavoidable; and as (Sparta alone expected, whose laws chiefly regarded the education of children, and where Lycurgus established such manners and customs, as in a great measure made laws needless,) the laws, in general less strong than the passions, restrain men without changing them; it would be no hard matter to prove that every government, which carefully guarding against all alteration and corruption should scrupulously comply with the ends of its institution, was unnecessarily instituted; and that a country, where no one either eluded the laws, or made an ill use of magistracy, required neither laws nor magistrates.

Political distinctions are necessarily attended with civil distinctions. The inequality between the people and the chiefs increase so fast as to be soon felt by the private members, and appears among them in a thousand shapes according to their passions, their talents, and the circumstances of affairs. The magistrate can not usurp any illegal power without making himself creatures, with whom he must divide it. Besides, the citizens of a free state suffer themselves to be oppressed merely in proportion as, hurried on by a blind ambition, and looking rather below than above them, they come to love authority more than independence. When they submit to fetters, 'tis only to be the better able to fetter others in their turn. It is no easy matter to make him obey, who does not wish to command; and the most refined policy would find it impossible to subdue those men, who only desire to be independent; but inequality easily gains ground among base and ambitious souls, ever ready to run the risks of fortune, and almost indifferent whether they command or obey, as she proves either favourable or adverse to them. Thus then there must have been a time, when the eyes of the people were bewitched to such a degree, that their rulers needed only to have said to the most pitiful wretch, "Be great you and all your posterity," to make him immediately appear great in the eyes of every one as well as in his own; and his descendants took still more upon them, in proportion to their removes from him: the more distant and uncertain the cause, the greater the effect; the longer the line of drones a family produced, the more illustrious it was reckoned.

Were this a proper place to enter into details, I could easily explain in what manner inequalities in point of credit and authority become unavoidable among private persons the moment that, united into one body, they are obliged to compare themselves one with another, and to note the differences which they find in the continual use every man must make of his neighbour. These differences are of several kinds; but riches, nobility or rank, power and personal merit, being in general the principal distinctions, by which men in society measure each other, I could prove that the harmony or conflict between these different forces is the surest indication of the good or bad original constitution of any state: I could make it appear that, as among these four kinds of inequality, personal qualities are the source of all the rest, riches is that in which they ultimately terminate, because, being the most immediately useful to the prosperity of individuals, and the most easy to communicate, they are made use of to purchase every other distinction. By this observation we are enabled to judge with tolerable exactness, how much any people has deviated from its primitive institution, and what steps it has still to make to the extreme term of corruption. I could show how much this universal desire of reputation, of honours, of preference, with which we are all devoured, exercises and compares our talents and our forces: how much it excites and multiplies our passions; and, by creating an universal competition, rivalship, or rather enmity among men, how many disappoinments, successes, and catastrophes of every kind it daily causes among the innumerable pretenders whom it engages in the same career. I could show that it is to this itch of being spoken of, to this fury of distinguishing ourselves which seldom or never gives us a moment's respite, that we owe both the best and the worst things among us, our virtues and our vices, our sciences and our errors, our conquerors and our philosophers; that is to say, a great many bad things to a very few good ones. I could prove, in short, that if we behold a handful of rich and powerful men seated on the pinnacle of fortune and greatness, while the crowd grovel in obscurity and want, it is merely because the first prize what they enjoy but in the same degree that others want it, and that, without changing their condition, they would cease to be happy the minute the people ceased to be miserable.

But these details would alone furnish sufficient matter for a more considerable work, in which might be weighed the advantages and disadvantages of every species of government, relatively to the rights of man in a state of nature, and might likewise be unveiled all the different faces under which inequality has appeared to this day, and may hereafter appear to the end of time, according to the nature of these several governments, and the revolutions time must unavoidably occasion in them. We should then see the multitude oppressed by domestic tyrants in consequence of those very precautions taken by them to guard against foreign masters. We should see oppression increase continually without its being ever possible for the oppressed to know where it would stop, nor what lawful means they had left to check its progress. We should see the rights of citizens, and the liberties of nations extinguished by slow degrees, and the groans, and protestations and appeals of the weak treated as seditious murmurings. We should see policy confine to a mercenary portion of the people the honour of defending the common sense. We should see imposts made necessary by such measures, the disheartened husbandman desert his field even in time of peace, and quit the plough to take up the sword. We should see fatal and whimsical rules laid down concerning the point of honour. We should see the champions of their country sooner or later become her enemies, and perpetually holding their poniards to the breasts of their fellow citizens. Nay, the time would come when they might be heard to say to the oppressor of their country:

> Pectore si fratris gladium juguloque parentis
> Condere me jubeas, gravidæque in viscera partu
> Conjugis, in vitâ peragam tamen omnia dextrâ.

From the vast inequality of conditions and fortunes, from the great variety of passions and of talents, of useless arts, of pernicious arts, of frivolous sciences, would issue clouds of prejudices equally contrary to reason, to happiness, to virtue. We should see the chiefs foment everything that tends to weaken men formed into societies by dividing them; everything that, while it gives society an air of apparent harmony, sows in it the seeds of real division; everything that can inspire the different orders with mutual distrust and hatred by an opposition of their rights and interest, and of course strengthen that power which contains them all.

'Tis from the bosom of this disorder and these revolutions, that despotism gradually rearing up her hideous crest, and devouring in every part of the state all that still remained sound and untainted, would at last issue to trample upon the laws and the people, and establish herself upon the ruins of the republic. The times immediately preceding this last alteration would be times of calamity and trouble: but at last everything would be swallowed up by the monster; and the people would no longer have chiefs or laws, but only tyrants. At this fatal period all regard to virtue and manners would likewise disappear; for despotism, *cui ex honesto nulla est spes*, tolerates no other master, wherever it reigns; the moment it speaks, probity and duty lose all their influence, and the blindest obedience is the only virtue the miserable slaves have left them to practise.

This is the last term of inequality, the extreme point which closes the circle and meets that from which we set out. 'Tis here that all private men return to their primitive equality, because they are no longer of any account; and that, the subjects having no longer any law but that of their master, nor the master any other law but his passions, all notions of good and principles of justice again disappear. 'Tis here that everything returns to the sole law of the strongest, and of course to a new state of nature different from that with which we began, in as much as the first was the state of nature in its purity, and the last the consequence of excessive corruption. There is, in other respects, so little difference between these two states, and the contract of government is so much dissolved by despotism, that the despot is no longer master than he continues the strongest, and that, as soon as his slaves can expel him, they may do it without his having the least right to complain of their using him ill. The insurrection, which ends in the death or despotism of a sultan, is as juridical an act as any by which the day before he disposed of the lives and fortunes of his subjects. Force alone upheld him, force alone overturns him. Thus all things take place and succeed in their natural order; and whatever may be the upshot of these hasty and frequent revolutions, no one man has reason to complain of another's injustice, but only of his own indiscretion or bad fortune.

By thus discovering and following the lost and forgotten tracks, by which man from the natural must have arrived at the civil state; by restoring, with the intermediate positions which I have been just indicating, those which want of leisure obliges me to suppress, or which my imagination has not suggested, every attentive reader must unavoidably be struck at the immense space which separates these two states. 'Tis in this slow succession of things he may meet with the solution of an infinite number of problems in morality and politics, which philosophers are puzzled to solve. He will perceive that, the mankind of one age not being the mankind of another, the reason why Diogenes could not find a man was, that he sought among his contemporaries the man of an earlier period: Cato, he will then see, fell with Rome and with liberty, because he did not suit the age in which he lived; and the greatest of men served only to astonish that world, which would have cheerfully obeyed him, had he come into it five hundred years earlier. In a word, he will find himself in a condition to understand how the soul and the passions of men by insensible alterations change as it were their nature;

how it comes to pass, that at the long run our wants and our pleasures change objects; that, original man vanishing by degrees, society no longer offers to our inspection but an assemblage of artificial men and factitious passions, which are the work of all these new relations, and have no foundation in nature. Reflection teaches us nothing on that head, but what experience perfectly confirms. Savage man and civilised man differ so much at bottom in point of inclinations and passions, that what constitutes the supreme happiness of the one would reduce the other to despair. The first sighs for nothing but repose and liberty; he desires only to live, and to be exempt from labour; nay, the ataraxy of the most confirmed Stoic falls short of his consummate indifference for every other object. On the contrary, the citizen always in motion, is perpetually sweating and toiling, and racking his brains to find out occupations still more laborious: He continues a drudge to his last minute; nay, he courts death to be able to live, or renounces life to acquire immortality. He cringes to men in power whom he hates, and to rich men whom he despises; he sticks at nothing to have the honour of serving them; he is not ashamed to value himself on his own weakness and the protection they afford him; and proud of his chains, he speaks with disdain of those who have not the honour of being the partner of his bondage. What a spectacle must the painful and envied labours of an European minister of state form in the eyes of a Caribbean! How many cruel deaths would not this indolent savage prefer to such a horrid life, which very often is not even sweetened by the pleasure of doing good? But to see the drift of so many cares, his mind should first have affixed some meaning to these words power and reputation; he should be apprised that there are men who consider as something the looks of the rest of mankind, who know how to be happy and satisfied with themselves on the testimony of others sooner than upon their own. In fact, the real source of all those differences, is that the savage lives within himself, whereas the citizen, constantly beside himself, knows only how to live in the opinion of others; insomuch that it is, if I may say so, merely from their judgment that he derives the consciousness of his own existence. It is foreign to my subject to show how this disposition engenders so much indifference for good and evil, notwithstanding so many and such fine discourses of morality; how everything, being reduced to appearances, becomes mere art and mummery; honour, friendship, virtue, and often vice itself, which we at last learn the secret to boast of; how, in short, ever inquiring of others what we are, and never daring to question ourselves on so delicate a point, in the midst of so much philosophy, humanity, and politeness, and so many sublime maxims, we have nothing to show for ourselves but a deceitful and frivolous exterior, honour without virtue, reason without wisdom, and pleasure without happiness. It is sufficient that I have proved that this is not the original condition of man, and that it is merely the spirit of society, and the inequality which society engenders, that thus change and transform all our natural inclinations.

I have endeavoured to exhibit the origin and progress of inequality, the institution and abuse of political societies, as far as these things are capable of being deduced from the nature of man by the mere light of reason, and independently of those sacred maxims which give to the sovereign authority the sanction of divine right. It follows from this picture, that as there is scarce any inequality among men in a state of nature, all that which we now behold owes its force and its growth to the development of our faculties and the improvement of our understanding, and at last becomes permanent and lawful by the establishment of property and of laws. It likewise follows that moral inequality, authorised by any right that is merely positive, clashes with natural right, as often as it does not combine in the same proportion with physical inequality: a distinction which sufficiently determines, what we are able to think in that respect of that kind of inequality which obtains in all civilised nations, since it is evidently against the law of nature that infancy should command old age, folly conduct wisdom, and a handful of men should be ready to choke with superfluities, while the famished multitude want the commonest necessaries of life.

FICTION

FLATLAND: A ROMANCE OF MANY DIMENSIONS, Edwin A. Abbott.
(0-486-27263-X)

PRIDE AND PREJUDICE, Jane Austen. (0-486-28473-5)

CIVIL WAR SHORT STORIES AND POEMS, Edited by Bob Blaisdell.
(0-486-48226-X)

THE DECAMERON: Selected Tales, Giovanni Boccaccio. Edited by Bob
Blaisdell. (0-486-41113-3)

JANE EYRE, Charlotte Brontë. (0-486-42449-9)

WUTHERING HEIGHTS, Emily Brontë. (0-486-29256-8)

THE THIRTY-NINE STEPS, John Buchan. (0-486-28201-5)

ALICE'S ADVENTURES IN WONDERLAND, Lewis Carroll. (0-486-27543-4)

MY ÁNTONIA, Willa Cather. (0-486-28240-6)

THE AWAKENING, Kate Chopin. (0-486-27786-0)

HEART OF DARKNESS, Joseph Conrad. (0-486-26464-5)

LORD JIM, Joseph Conrad. (0-486-40650-4)

THE RED BADGE OF COURAGE, Stephen Crane. (0-486-26465-3)

THE WORLD'S GREATEST SHORT STORIES, Edited by James Daley.
(0-486-44716-2)

A CHRISTMAS CAROL, Charles Dickens. (0-486-26865-9)

GREAT EXPECTATIONS, Charles Dickens. (0-486-41586-4)

A TALE OF TWO CITIES, Charles Dickens. (0-486-40651-2)

CRIME AND PUNISHMENT, Fyodor Dostoyevsky. Translated by Constance
Garnett. (0-486-41587-2)

THE ADVENTURES OF SHERLOCK HOLMES, Sir Arthur Conan Doyle.
(0-486-47491-7)

THE HOUND OF THE BASKERVILLES, Sir Arthur Conan Doyle. (0-486-28214-7)

BLAKE: PROPHET AGAINST EMPIRE, David V. Erdman. (0-486-26719-9)

WHERE ANGELS FEAR TO TREAD, E. M. Forster. (0-486-27791-7)

BEOWULF, Translated by R. K. Gordon. (0-486-27264-8)

THE RETURN OF THE NATIVE, Thomas Hardy. (0-486-43165-7)

THE SCARLET LETTER, Nathaniel Hawthorne. (0-486-28048-9)

SIDDHARTHA, Hermann Hesse. (0-486-40653-9)

THE ODYSSEY, Homer. (0-486-40654-7)

THE TURN OF THE SCREW, Henry James. (0-486-26684-2)

DUBLINERS, James Joyce. (0-486-26870-5)

FICTION

THE METAMORPHOSIS AND OTHER STORIES, Franz Kafka. (0-486-29030-1)

SONS AND LOVERS, D. H. Lawrence. (0-486-42121-X)

THE CALL OF THE WILD, Jack London. (0-486-26472-6)

GREAT AMERICAN SHORT STORIES, Edited by Paul Negri. (0-486-42119-8)

THE GOLD-BUG AND OTHER TALES, Edgar Allan Poe. (0-486-26875-6)

ANTHEM, Ayn Rand. (0-486-49277-X)

FRANKENSTEIN, Mary Shelley. (0-486-28211-2)

THE JUNGLE, Upton Sinclair. (0-486-41923-1)

THREE LIVES, Gertrude Stein. (0-486-28059-4)

THE STRANGE CASE OF DR. JEKYLL AND MR. HYDE, Robert Louis Stevenson. (0-486-26688-5)

DRACULA, Bram Stoker. (0-486-41109-5)

UNCLE TOM'S CABIN, Harriet Beecher Stowe. (0-486-44028-1)

ADVENTURES OF HUCKLEBERRY FINN, Mark Twain. (0-486-28061-6)

THE ADVENTURES OF TOM SAWYER, Mark Twain. (0-486-40077-8)

CANDIDE, Voltaire. Edited by Francois-Marie Arouet. (0-486-26689-3)

THE COUNTRY OF THE BLIND: and Other Science-Fiction Stories, H. G. Wells. Edited by Martin Gardner. (0-486-48289-8)

THE WAR OF THE WORLDS, H. G. Wells. (0-486-29506-0)

ETHAN FROME, Edith Wharton. (0-486-26690-7)

THE PICTURE OF DORIAN GRAY, Oscar Wilde. (0-486-27807-7)

MONDAY OR TUESDAY: Eight Stories, Virginia Woolf. (0-486-29453-6)

NONFICTION

THE DECLARATION OF INDEPENDENCE AND OTHER GREAT DOCUMENTS OF AMERICAN HISTORY: 1775-1865, Edited by John Grafton. (0-486-41124-9)

INCIDENTS IN THE LIFE OF A SLAVE GIRL, Harriet Jacobs. (0-486-41931-2)

GREAT SPEECHES, Abraham Lincoln. (0-486-26872-1)

THE WIT AND WISDOM OF ABRAHAM LINCOLN: A Book of Quotations, Abraham Lincoln. Edited by Bob Blaisdell. (0-486-44097-4)

THE SECOND TREATISE OF GOVERNMENT AND A LETTER CONCERNING TOLERATION, John Locke. (0-486-42464-2)

THE PRINCE, Niccolò Machiavelli. (0-486-27274-5)

MICHEL DE MONTAIGNE: Selected Essays, Michel de Montaigne. Translated by Charles Cotton. Edited by William Carew Hazlitt. (0-486-48603-6)

UTOPIA, Sir Thomas More. (0-486-29583-4)

THE RUNAWAY WIFE

ALSO BY ELIZABETH BIRKELUND

The Dressmaker
(*under the name* Elizabeth Birkelund Oberbeck)

THE RUNAWAY WIFE

A NOVEL

Elizabeth Birkelund

HARPER

NEW YORK • LONDON • TORONTO • SYDNEY

HARPER

HarperCollins books may be purchased for educational, business, or sales promotional use. For information please e-mail the Special Markets Department at SPsales@harpercollins.com.

FIRST EDITION

Designed by Jamie Lynn Kerner

Library of Congress Cataloging-in-Publication Data has been applied for.

ISBN 978-0-06-243175-2

16 17 18 19 20   OV/RRD   10 9 8 7 6 5 4 3 2 1

To the French muses in my life:
M.T., Pascale, Valerie, Sophie, Nathalie,
Alexandra, Isabelle, Moumoune, and Zou Zou

THE RUNAWAY WIFE

PART ONE

CALLIOPE, THE MUSE

ONE

LA CABANE DES AUDANNES

JIM OLSEN, YOU ARE HERE. IN SWITZERLAND, WALK-ing on the rock ledges of the Swiss Alps. If this was not the end of the world, at least it felt like it. In this moonscape ten thousand feet high, in this land of rock and rock and more rock, and sky and sky and more sky, one misguided step and Jim could plunge from one of thousands of vertiginous, crusted cliffs. The only thing that reassured Jim that he was not on a planet in a far-flung galaxy was his ability, on this clear day, to pinpoint several small patches of green that re-sembled colored pieces in a stained-glass window—these he knew to be farmland in the Swiss valley far, far below.

Jim had expected a movie-set Alpine cabin flush with red and orange impatiens cascading from window boxes. Instead, La Cabane des Audannes was a squat tin box that

resembled an abandoned trailer home in the Arctic. Six small square windows punctured the front of the shiny bubble. It was hard to believe that just a few days earlier, he and his college friend Ambrose had been enjoying chilled beer on a sunny veranda overlooking the lush lower Alpine meadows, with clanking bells on lolling cows as their background music.

Back in New York City, when he had searched the cabin's website, the tag line for the Cabane that had caught his eye was "*la grande aventure du sauvetage dans les Alpes*," roughly translated as "the great adventure of rescue in the Alps." It had seemed a strange description at the time.

Ambrose, half-French, half-American, had been trying for years to convince Jim to join him on a late-summer hike from *hutte* to *hutte* in the Bernese Alps, but Jim had always been too busy at work. Had he ever taken a vacation while he was at KKT? He'd sacrificed the bulk of his twenties, even the summers when he was in business school, to the small investment boutique that had promised him a future. Well, no time like the present.

"This hutte," Ambrose was saying—he pronounced it *hoote* with a silent *h,* "was carried up the Geltenhorn in one piece, suspended from a military helicopter."

Approaching the shining shelter, now unobstructed by the mountain shadow that had covered it from a distance, Jim didn't care how it had been transported. He would have stopped anywhere to escape the incessant, chafing wind and to rest his sore feet. The blisters on his left heel were bleed-

ing; he cursed himself again for not heeding the advice of the saleswoman back in New York who'd suggested he break in his new boots two weeks before the trip. Jim guessed that by the time he returned to New York the following week, his boots would feel . . . well, just perfect.

Firewood burning. A pale wisp of smoke rose from the side of the metal bubble into the achingly blue late-afternoon sky. A deep breath. They were finally there. A gust of cold wind set the sign, LA CABANE DES AUDANNES, jangling on its chain. Jim paused on the rocky terrace outside the threshold to gaze back at the thread-thin serpentine path along the tip of the range they'd hiked for most of the day. The expanse of gray and black craggy peaks extended out of sight into the distance.

"I smell Wiener schnitzel," said Ambrose, dashing into the hutte. Jim followed, the KKT door slamming behind him.

Inside was a world of charm and warmth. The room was alive with voices and laughter. Clusters of hikers sprawled across chairs; small round tables crowded with mugs of beer were lit with lamps with red shades, as if each table hosted a small campfire. The bleached wooden walls and floors were scrubbed clean, and the peephole windows, which from the exterior resembled insect eyes, were dressed with red-and-white-checked curtains. Even the straight-backed wooden chairs were softened by plump gingham cushions tied with bows. At the far end of the room, a fire crackled and sparked under an arched metal mantel.

Jim overheard Germans, with their hard *k*'s; Aussies, with their loosened vowels; French, with their rolling *r*'s. A few Italians entered the cabin behind them, with laughter and words that rippled into arias. They settled at one of the long refectory tables in the middle of the room. Despite the human commotion, the cozy scene was crisply clean, a testament to Swiss perfection.

With a smile that pumped up his already ample cheeks, Michel Acolas introduced himself as *"le capitain du chalet."* He signed the new guests in and, pointing to the ladder at the center of the compact interior of the hutte, told them to claim their beds. As Ambrose engaged in French chatter with the *capitain*, Jim climbed the ladder. Perched on the top step, he counted thirty sheeted mattresses in a circular room that resembled the inside of a lighthouse. Three movable walls had been placed to form sections—for families, perhaps, or lovers—but otherwise, thirty hikers slept in one room. His fiancée—that is, his ex-fiancée—would have bristled at the sight.

"Une bière?" Ambrose asked Jim as he dropped down from the ladder.

"Sure," said Jim.

"Don't look so excited."

"Thinking of Sally."

"One minute on your own, and you're back to your old, destructive ruminations! Nothing a cold beer can't handle."

Ambrose addressed a young waiter whose bulbous nose resembled that of Monsieur Acolas. It had to be his son.

They followed him to one of the few open tables near the fire.

"What beautiful women," Ambrose said, nodding at the next table as they took their seats. The three, the only women in the room, were an unlikely trio in the midst of the mostly bearded male hikers; Jim was surprised he hadn't noticed them earlier. They leaned in toward one another with the intensity of people telling secrets.

When the frosted mugs of beers arrived at their small table, so, surprisingly, did one of the young women. She was smiling, tall and slender, with dark, wavy hair that fell below her shoulders, and she carried a half-full glass of red wine. She introduced herself to them in English; Jim forgot her name as soon as they'd shaken hands.

"Please join us," Ambrose said, standing and offering her his chair. "Ambrose Vincelles. *Enchanté.*"

In their college days, Ambrose had merely to open his mouth—Jim was convinced it was his French-American accent—for women to appear at his side. Eight years out of college seemed not to have diminished his appeal.

"Thalia Castellane," she said to Jim as if she had guessed that her name needed repeating. He pulled up another chair.

She placed her glass on their table and sat in the chair Ambrose had offered, crossing her long legs. She had deep-set blue eyes, the lightness of which he had never seen before, a long, slim nose; curvaceous lips; and an angular jaw. Her face looked sculpted.

"Forgive me," began Ambrose, "I know this sounds

sexist, but before you glided over to our table I was asking myself how three beautiful women ended up in this remote tin-can cabin at the very end of the world at the very end of the hiking season."

Thalia laughed, throwing back her head of thick hair. "In your world, I suppose beauty must be preserved in a jar," she said.

Jim detected a British accent on top of the French one.

"Yes, as a matter of fact, with beauty like yours——"

"What should be preserved in a jar," interrupted Jim, "is Ambrose. The label would read: THE LAST LIVING ROMAN-TIC."

"Those are my sisters," the woman said, pointing at the two women at the nearby table, who were deep in conversation. Their new friend seemed to desire her sisters' company.

"No, really," said Ambrose, "what brings you here?"

"I'm sure the same thing that brought all of us to this funny little metal cigarette lighter! The vigor of the mountains, the way they compel you"—she raised her arms above her head—"upward and upward until you see them kiss the sky like a lover." She dropped her hands and winked at Jim. "As a child, I would sit all day long and watch the shadows of clouds on this graphite mountain canvas. The mountains are art in constant motion."

"You know them well," said Ambrose.

"Our mother is half-Swiss, half-French; our father, French," said Thalia, leaning forward. "*Maman* grew up in these Alps during the summers, as did we when we visited

our grandparents, our mother's parents, who had a chalet in the valley of the Elghorn, just above Gstaad. Sadly for us, they sold the chalet two years ago. We hike up here every few years, but—oh, did you just hear that howling wind? My sisters and I prefer the lower Alps."

"Your English, it's so fluent," Jim said.

"*Merci*," she said, nodding and smiling broadly at Jim. The red wine had stained her lips, which made her smile seem brighter. "Educated in England. You're American, aren't you?" She squinted at him as if she were a buyer surveying a parcel of land.

"I suppose my accent gave me away."

"Excuse Jim," interrupted Ambrose. "He's never been out of the States. Jim, in case you haven't noticed, you stand leagues taller than most of the men in the room—your football days aren't that far behind you. In addition to your very American accent, you have a look in your eyes that the world is yours, or *could* be yours at any moment—and that, my friend, among Europeans, is American."

A certain "American" look? Since when had Ambrose fallen prey to stereotyping? Thalia leaned back and placed her arms behind her head, a gesture that seemed unnatural, as if she were posing.

"Don't tell me you speak no French?" she asked, directing her large eyes at Jim.

"Only a little. In the suburban town outside Chicago where I grew up," Jim said, "French people are considered an exotic species. I took French in high school and for a year

in college, but not until this trip have I understood the merits of a fluent second language."

As Ambrose chronicled their trek up the Wildhorn in French, Jim watched the restless Thalia shift in her seat. Would she ever stop moving? There. She finally settled, as would a butterfly, perched on the edge of her chair.

It was amazing how Ambrose could ramble—especially in French, with a beautiful woman. As he watched them converse, Jim concluded that his college pal had been right: this mountain trek up the Wildhorn had been a welcome distraction for him after months of brooding about his lost love and job. He would start his new job on September 8, in ten days.

"Voilà," said Monsieur Acolas, his face rosy from tending the fire. He placed onto their table two wineglasses and a bottle of red wine that Jim and Ambrose had not ordered. He uncorked the bottle, poured two glasses, and refilled Thalia's glass. The monsieur tilted his chin in the direction of Thalia's sisters' table.

"A gift," he said in English with his thick accent.

"From your sisters?" Ambrose asked the young woman, who nodded.

"How unusual," said Jim.

"I think my sisters wish to get you two drunk," said Thalia, raising her glass with a smile and a wink, again at Jim.

"I like the way your sisters are thinking," Jim said, lift-

ing his glass to match hers in the air. "But *we* should have sent a bottle to *their* table."

A frigid wind tunneled into the room along with a long string of men—Jim counted fifteen—dressed in folkloric Alpine gear, some bearded, some mustached, most wearing green feathered caps, green jackets or vests, and black pants. They lined up in front of the fireplace and, with no introduction, began to yodel. The small room resembled an accordion, the bellows swelling and compressing in rhythm; the music had a mournful, nostalgic tone. To complete the picture, tears appeared on the stubbled, wrinkled cheek of the elderly vocalist at the end of the line. As the band of men segued into the Swiss national anthem, hikers began to clap along.

Ambrose leaned over the table to tell Jim that the troupe traveled across the Alps.

"They stop at each hutte only once a year," yelled Ambrose above the singing. "After this, they'll probably sing at the Geltenhütte. How lucky we are that they're here this late in the season!"

After the yodelers finished and they scattered, Ambrose suggested that Thalia invite her sisters to join them. Thalia jumped up quickly, as if she'd been waiting for the invitation. Within moments Thalia's two sisters were tableside, wineglasses in hand. As Jim rose to fetch their chairs, he noticed that the women's strong family resemblance resided in their sharp chins and the lush curve of their lips.

Jim refilled the wineglasses. He guessed that the oldest was the sister who now introduced herself as Clio. She was tall, around five feet eleven, and had wide cheekbones and startlingly white teeth, gleaming perhaps because of her suntan. Her dark-brown hair was pulled back into a ponytail, emphasizing her high forehead. She appeared to be the opposite of the impetuous Thalia; her movements and bearing were measured and self-contained, as if she rationed them.

The last sister to arrive at the table extended her hand awkwardly, as if it were an unnatural gesture. In a light voice, she introduced herself as Hélène.

She was clearly the youngest of the sisters, blonde to their brunette; her hair looked as if she'd cut it herself. Jim had the impression that she'd worked hard to underplay her prettiness. The measure hadn't worked: the haircut accentuated her very long neck and narrow shoulders.

She was a shy yet stirring beauty, but as she greeted them, her face grew animated. Was she staring at Jim? Her hazel eyes asked questions.

"*Three Sisters*!" said Ambrose playfully. "I feel like I'm in the Chekhov play! Olga, Masha, and Irina stuck in the provinces, yearning for Moscow. But perhaps in this case you're yearning for Paris?"

"We *are* yearning," said Helene quickly, "but not for a city." Her voice seemed to erupt from her, and she looked surprised at the sound.

Clio shot Helene a look. A yodeler launched into an encore in the corner of the room.

Ambrose stood and raised his glass. "To yearning and yodeling through life."

"To yodeling," the sisters repeated with uplifted chins: those delicate yet sharp chins! Clio was expressionless, Thalia's smile looked forced, and Helene looked gloomy.

"And here's to toasting, a tradition that originated in France," continued Ambrose, glass still raised.

"Is that true?" asked Thalia.

"It was a French wedding tradition," said Ambrose, addressing Jim, "to drop a piece of toast into a couple's Champagne to ensure a healthy life. The couple would lift their glasses to raise the toast! I raise a toast to you three graces."

"However generous it might seem for us to have treated you to this bottle of wine—not a bad year, actually," Thalia noted, looking skeptically at the label—"it *does* have a price tag."

Was that another wink from Thalia? Sitting so close to her at the small table, Jim could smell her perfume, some flower that he'd known in another time but couldn't identify.

"*Aha!*" laughed Ambrose. "Never a free lunch, nor bottle of wine, not even in this remote region of the Alps."

"You have to forgive my sister, she is always playing a game," said Clio. "The challenge is to know when the game ends and reality begins, eh, Thalia?"

"That's what actors are *supposed* to do." Thalia pushed out her chair, stood, and curtsied to Jim and Ambrose. "Make you think and feel that you're watching *life*, so that you forget you're in a theater."

"If you couldn't already tell," said Clio, "Thalia is the actress of the family."

"Actor," Thalia said.

Clio rolled her eyes.

"While Thalia is the ac*tor* of the family," Clio continued, then looked at Helene, "Helene is—"

"I can speak for myself," Helene interrupted. "Really, Clio, it's not as if you're an anchor on the morning news. I'm an editor at Gallimard."

"Gallimard?" Jim looked at Ambrose for a translation.

"Major publishing house in Paris," said Ambrose.

"Don't look so self-important," Thalia said, facing Helene. "It's not as if Papa didn't help you get the job."

"Thalia!" said Clio.

"Excuse me," said Helene, "did he not help you get your last role by introducing you to Gérard Depardieu's producer?"

Eyes flashing, the two sisters began speaking in rapid French.

"Enough! Let's not forget why—" Clio tilted her head in Jim's direction. "Just before we sat down, I overheard someone say that there's one death in the Alps every single day of the year!"

"That's not possible!" said Helene.

"I don't know if it's true," said Clio. "The Aussies over there were talking about it."

"What a horrid thought," said Thalia. She stood and lifted the knapsack that was slung over her chair, and threw it over her shoulder.

"I'm feeling claustrophobic in here," she said, and left the table.

"Nice excuse," Helene said when she was gone. "She's sneaking a cigarette."

"She's smoking too much," said Clio.

"Clio, say something to her. You're the only one she'll listen to."

Jim watched Thalia walk to the door, her hips swaying smoothly and loosely, as if to a song that she was singing to herself. He leaned back in his chair and sipped his wine.

Full of soft yellow light from the battery-run lamps on the tables and the glow from the crackling fire, the hushed voices of Helene, Ambrose, and Clio now engaged in conversation in French, and the occasional bursts of laughter at the tables nearby, every corner of the place brimmed with what Jim, in his limited experience, considered a comforting and warm humanity.

TWO

THE REQUEST

THEY WERE SILENT WITHOUT THE RESTLESS
Thalia in the room. Jim gazed at the fire and thought of
Sally and wished she were next to him, her warm, freck-
led arm resting on his. Clio reminded him of Sally in her
neat, organized body, the way her jawbone lined up with
her collarbone. Sally was safety for him. And he for Sally.
They had both been dumped by their previous "others," as
Sally called them. What she and Jim had created together
was close to a pact between two nation-states that agree not
to disappoint each other. Their romantic little NATO. Sally
would joke with Jim that she was attracted to him because
he was handsome, tall, and strong, but what she loved him
for most was his earnestness and integrity. He'd heard from
mutual friends that his replacement was charismatic, the life

of the party. Maybe Jim was too earnest? Whatever the case, how weak their little NATO had proved.

"I met someone else," she'd told him over the phone during the half hour he took for lunch at his desk. He heard a loud grinding sound in the background; he pictured her standing by the paper shredder.

"You *what?*" he'd asked.

"I'm so sorry, Jim. I found someone else," she'd said.

It was as casual an admission as if she'd located an article of clothing or an umbrella that had gone missing. They'd been a couple for five years. Sally worked in client relations at an asset-management firm where the hours were as predictable as her daily maintenance routine: her shower, her "Whaat?" through the noise of the blow-dryer when she thought Jim was talking to her but he wasn't, her application of moisturizing cream, her makeup session, the donning of her final accoutrement: her red-framed eyeglasses.

Three days before she delivered her news ("This is a breakup. Drop your weapons and place your hands behind your head. You will now be entirely vulnerable, and I will crush you"), Jim had turned thirty years old.

Jim caught Helene looking at him, her head tilted toward him, her neck long and swanlike.

"Did you enjoy your hike today?" Clio asked, interrupting his brief eye contact with her sister.

"Despite my poor, sore feet, it was magnificent. The Alps are awe inspiring. Thanks to Ambrose's persistence,

this is my first vacation—sandwiched between years of accumulated and future slavery."

"Slavery?" asked Helene.

"Jim is an investment banker," explained Ambrose.

A few years ago, Jim would have characterized himself as the master of his universe, not a slave. After Princeton, he had attended Harvard Business School and then nailed a job at KKT; he'd even bought an apartment in Tribeca. But truth be told, he still felt like a kid from out of town.

"He's a slave to his blind ambition," said Ambrose. "Some of us are quick to exchange our freedom for money and power. I can't wait until Jim makes his first hundred million so that he can do what he was meant to do on this earth."

"And you know what that is?" Jim asked.

"You'll change the world for the better, of course," said Ambrose.

Helene asked Ambrose about his work.

"Art dealer, married to a lawyer. We have two children, a son who is six and a daughter who is four."

"He's also a loyal friend who continues to rescue me from myself," Jim added, laughing.

Thalia returned with the fresh air and the smell of cigarette smoke on her breath, and Jim rose to welcome her back to her chair. When she leaned toward him, Jim identified her scent: Underneath her cigarette breath she smelled like summertime roses, like the ones on Mrs. Day's fence. The

peach-colored ones that Mrs. Day, whose lawn he mowed, had asked him to cut. How sweet they had smelled. Like sugar. He hadn't thought of them in years.

"It's chilly out there!" Thalia said, hugging herself as she sat down.

"Oh, maman . . ." said Helene.

A worried glance passed from one sister to the next.

The yodelers had formed a line for the buffet and were heaping their plates high with stew, gravy, and potatoes.

"They will clear away the buffet if we don't go now," Clio interrupted.

JIM ASKED ABOUT CLIO'S WORK AS THE FIVE OF THEM moved along in the line. She was a commercial artist and the mother of two young sons. Thalia told them about her role in a film coming out in the next few weeks.

"Have you heard of *Le dernier rendez-vous* or *Savage*?" she asked, turning to them.

The men shook their heads.

She pouted. "You've missed out!"

"Stop boasting, Thalia," said Helene.

"I also work in theater groups, some commercials . . ."

"Does one act in a commercial?" asked Helene. "I always think of one 'appearing'—"

"What accomplishment in a family," interrupted Ambrose.

"Maman is the most accomplished of us all," said Helene of the brown-blue-green eyes.

They returned to the table, plates full.

"She is everything we are and more," Helene continued, taking her seat. "She embodies us—is that the right word?—and surpasses us. Sometimes I have to shake her out of me—that's how close she is to us, isn't that right?" She looked at Clio and Thalia. "To Maman." She lifted her glass. "To Maman, wherever you are right now."

Jim noticed that the sisters, even the fitful Thalia, had frozen. Helene placed her wineglass carefully onto the table and lifted her red-and-white gingham napkin to her eye. Clio and Thalia raised their glasses in silence. The moment passed.

"Have you been in these Alps before?" Helene asked, gazing at Jim, then Ambrose.

"Are you experienced hikers?" Clio added before they could respond. From flirtation to interview.

"I've been hiking the Alps since I was a child," said Ambrose, "but this is my first time on the Wildhorn. During the summers when I was a teenager, my father woke me daily to hike to the summit of Chamechaude in the Chartreuse Alps before breakfast."

"And you?" Clio's eyes attacked Jim. Helene gazed down at her plate. Everything was hanging on his answer, it seemed.

"This is Jim's first visit to Europe," Thalia said. "I discovered that over our first glass of wine."

His intuition was correct: the mood at the table deflated instantly.

Clio furrowed her brow and began scanning the center of the room, where a few Italians were leaning back in their chairs, laughing loudly.

Thalia ran her fingers through her hair. "Helene stop kicking me! Helene wants me to tell you— Have they had enough wine?" Thalia interrupted herself to ask her sisters.

"It's growing colder outside by the minute," said Helene.

"Jim, Ambrose," Thalia began. "We've decided in the short time since we met you—actually, before we met you, to be honest: when we first saw you. It was your height, Jim, I suppose, and your sturdy build, and maybe it was because you are both handsome, too—"

"Thalia!" interrupted Clio. "She can't help herself—"

"That you would be . . ." Thalia hesitated and looked at Clio. " . . . suitable for a job we cannot do by ourselves. This is Helene's idea. Why aren't *you* doing the asking? I still think we should contact the Swiss Air Ambulance . . . They are experienced with life-threatening mountain emergencies . . ."

Jim noticed color appear in Helene's cheeks, a red bloom that looked soft enough to blow away.

Ambrose, about to bring his wineglass to his lips, paused with his glass in midair.

A small group of yodelers gathered not far from their table.

"Before they start their yodeling again, hurry, Thalia," prodded Helene.

"We'd like you to help us find our mother," Thalia said.

The man in the corner picked up an accordion and another man began to yodel softly, as if accompanying the sisters' request.

Thalia continued, "According to the guest records of this cabin, our mother stayed here for one night on June 21, and we think—"

"*You* think," interrupted Helene.

Thalia glared at her sister. "Some of us think she departed the next morning toward the Col du Brochet, one of the highest mountain passes in this region, and Monsieur Acolas' guest records confirm this. The trail starts above this hutte and is the only route we know of that leads up to the Col du Brochet and back down. Helene thinks she's in the Lower Alps, that she wrote the Col du Brochet as her destination in the guest ledger to dodge father. But for the last two weeks, we've hiked to all her favorite Lower Alpine haunts and still have no clue where she is."

Thalia's lips moved the way she walked, smoothly but self-consciously. He imagined her watching herself speak in front of the mirror.

"We thought we'd have found her by now, that we'd be on our way home." Clio jumped in, her pointed elbows on the table. "The only places we haven't checked are the mountain trails above here. Thalia and I think she must be camping out near the Col du Brochet, a two-day hike from here. She *has* to be there."

Helene inhaled deeply. Jim didn't hear her exhale.

Thalia's eyes filled with tears, and for a moment Jim wondered whether the tears were part of the act.

"So we thought—" continued Thalia, "that there'd be some hikers heading in that direction who could keep an eye out for her—"

"And if, on their *descent*," interrupted Helene, "those hikers found her, they could accompany her down the mountain and let us know that she was safe."

"We three would hike this last part," added Clio, "but we've been up here for two weeks and we have to get back to our lives. My kids are about to start school; Helene has a thousand books to edit at Gallimard and rehearsals start on Tuesday for a play that Thalia has the lead in. Within the week the entrance to the Col du Brochet will be blocked off or if it's not blocked, it could be impassable by the early snow that is forecast. And this hutte . . . Who knows when Monsieur Acolas will decide to shut it down for the season."

She was already scanning the room for her next target. Her eyes settled on a bearded man whose belly hung over his belt. He would be on Jim's list, too. He was even wearing suspenders.

"According to Monsieur Acolas," Clio continued, "only one person stays up this high during the winter, and it's a female hermit. Monsieur calls her the hermitess. He says she's gone mad up in the mountains. I've been asking everyone I meet about this hermitess, because it would be just like Maman to take care of this woman and bring her food."

"They say that before she became a hermitess," volunteered Helene, puckering her lips as she spoke, "she was a shepherdess in the low Alps who talked to her sheep—you know, to comfort them. When wolves ate her sheep, the story goes, she came up here to live in a cave as a young woman and vowed never to speak to another living being again. And she didn't, unless Maman has found her and inspired her to sing, which is highly likely. Apparently, she was sighted a year ago. "

"There she goes with her stories," said Thalia. "While I like to act, Helene likes to make things up."

"Can you imagine?" said Helene, settling her large hazel eyes on Jim. "Being alone for years—let alone one year? Do you think you'd unlearn how to speak, actually forget how to form words with your lips?"

Jim thought Helene seemed to have a pretty difficult time already forming English words with her French accent.

"But this hermitess, if there is one," said Ambrose, "could be living in any one of the thousands of caves in the Bernese mountain range."

"True," said Thalia, sinking into her chair. "But the point is—"

"The point is," interrupted Clio, clearly impatient, "it's freezing up there, and getting colder."

"I agree with Clio. This hermitess could be a clue to Maman's whereabouts," added Helene, perched at the edge of her chair. "Maman *would* feel an affinity to someone who

wished to be so true to herself that she couldn't live in the world."

"Enough of the hermitess," pronounced Thalia, tossing her head dramatically. "Wasn't Clio just telling us that someone dies every day up here in these Alps? I would have thought that Monsieur Acolas or *someone* up here would have tried to dissuade Maman from climbing to the Col all by herself."

"How would they have stopped her? She's not *that* old, Thalia," said Helene. "She's forty-nine, but she's really fit, and it was early summer when she left, so the days were longer. And about the daily death in the Alps—I don't believe it either. I won't."

"I'll look it up," said Thalia. She dipped her hand into her jacket pocket to retrieve her phone. "*Merde.* Forgot, no service up here."

Ambrose reached for the wine bottle. "I've heard the same statistic," he said softly. "We *are* talking about the Wildhorn in the Bernese, the most glaciated region of the Alps. And to find someone—"

"Every year two of us hike to this hutte in mid-August to retrieve our mother," interrupted Thalia, "and it takes us a few days to convince her to come back with us. This year has been especially stressful for her." She shot a glance at Clio. "Which is why we think she's settled farther away and why she will cling especially fiercely to the mountains."

"It's not necessary to tell," Clio said, her voice clipped. "Remember, Papa—"

"They need to know," said Helene. "The more information they have, the better."

"And it's not as if it's private anymore, Clio!" said Thalia, pushing her plate away. "The whole world knows about it." Thalia frowned as she looked from Jim to Ambrose. "Before her trip this summer, our mother learned many things about her husband, our father, that she hadn't known before: that he has had a series—is that the word? sequence, succession?—of women. The way some men collect butterflies, fine wines, whatever—Papa collected women. They call it 'serial adulterer' in English. I read the expression in an English newspaper last week. It's disgusting." Shaking her head, Thalia rose from the table, removed one of her boots, and pulled her socked foot underneath her as she sat back down.

Jim glanced at Ambrose, whose brows were knitted together.

"But the thing that broke Maman," Thalia continued, sipping her wine, "the reason we think that she is not in the lower Alpine chalet where she usually stays in the summer and is hiding out somewhere else where we can't find her was that she found out from the press, *from the press*, as did *we*, that Papa recently had a child with one of the many women, apparently a Russian model. A baby girl."

"The press? Why the press?" Jim asked.

"Small detail," said Thalia. "Our papa is Yves Castellane, minister of the interior, who just announced his bid for the presidency."

• • •

MONSIEUR ACOLAS THREW A LOG INTO THE FIRE-place nearby and prodded it with a wrought-iron poker that had been resting against the wall.

"We're running out of time," said Helene. "Thanks to Thalia, who told Father when we still had cell reception that we couldn't find Maman, he's sent a helicopter up here daily to scour the peaks for her. He desperately needs her back for the press shots and all the publicity."

Jim had been surprised over the past few days by the regularity of the helicopter's presence in the area. Ambrose had guessed correctly that the chopper was on a search mission, but they hadn't suspected that the sought-after party was in hiding.

"I overheard a group of hikers," said Clio, tilting her chin to her left, "complaining about the noise. I don't think they'll vote for Papa if they know he's the reason—."

"Father," said Helene, addressing Jim and Ambrose, "cannot tolerate things not looking right to the world. He'll do anything to get our mother back—but it's really himself he is trying to save."

"Papa's search mission has seen no trace of her," said Thalia. "The last call I got before we lost reception was Papa demanding that I give him Maman's location so he can send the helicopter to retrieve her. He thinks we know where she is but aren't telling—"

"Thalia! You *wouldn't* tell him," admonished Helene.

"If it means saving her from freezing to death in the

blizzard that's forecast, yes, of course—I would push her into Papa's helicopter."

Helene frowned and dug her fork into her stew, but did not lift it. "I would *never* do that, even if she were freezing to death. Papa doesn't deserve her, and she's better off without him. It was hard enough for her to get away this time. She should never go back to him. I want her to be safe, but not back in Papa's cage—especially now that he'll parade her around by his side in front of the gawking press as if nothing has happened."

"I can see the headlines," said Thalia, spreading her arms to hold up a pretend newspaper. " 'Presidential Candidate's Wife Escapes to the Alps. If His Wife Cannot Live with Him, Why Should We—for the Next Five Years?' "

Jim rose to fill Thalia's and Helene's glasses with the remaining wine.

"We've had no contact with her for more than two months," said Helene. "She probably has no idea about this freak snowstorm that's coming our way."

"I agreed to Helene's Find-Hikers-to-Find-Maman plan to save her from Papa before we knew about the impending snow," said Clio. "At this point, I think we should do what Thalia has suggested from the beginning and summon the Swiss Air Ambulance. Our mother is strong enough to weather Papa, but snow in the Alps is another thing altogether."

"But don't you see?" said Helene, looking into all of their

faces, but gazing at Jim longer than the others. "The rescue service will take her back to *him*, you know he's paid them off not to listen to her wishes, but only to his. We want to save Maman not only from the snow but also from her marriage. Please, let's give her one last chance to come down the mountain on her own terms and get on with her life. Give her the option to escape what awaits her if she returns to Father."

Now it was Thalia's turn. "Ok, Helene, we get it already!" She turned her bright blue eyes on Ambrose and Jim. "Since you two were likely planning on going in Maman's direction anyway, all we're asking is that if you see our mother during your hike, that you could persuade her to join you and descend the mountain with you, offering her an alternative to the helicopter exit. I have a feeling that *you*"—was that Thalia's long leg that brushed Jim's under the table?—"could convince Maman. She responds well to lovely people."

She was now leaning so close to him that their arms were touching. Her perfume wafted around him.

Jim looked over at Helene. She had turned her chair away and was looking intently into the fire. An Italian from the neighboring table was trying to catch her attention.

"Before we get too distracted," said Thalia, dipping her hand into her knapsack, "I have a photograph of Maman. It's not that good, but it will give you an idea. Oh yes, and while I'm at it, here's, where's my card, oh here it is."

Jim took the business card from Thalia, gave her his and

looked over her sweet-smelling shoulder. The roses . . . The faded photograph showed a woman with long, dark-blond hair falling over one eye. She was laughing.

"Her name?" Jim asked.

"Calliope Marie Castellane," said Thalia.

"Calliope," said Ambrose, "the muse of epic poetry and the inspiration for *The Odyssey* and *The Iliad*. Now it's all making sense. Thalia, the muse of poetry. And Clio, the muse of history. Helene . . ."

"Not only do you know your Alps, but you also know your Greek muses," said Thalia. "I'm impressed."

"Helene," continued Ambrose.

"The muse of men," Jim interrupted, "'whose face launched a thousand ships . . .'"

"Bravo," said Thalia, clapping her hands.

"Back to Maman," said Clio. "Today is . . ."

"Friday," said Ambrose. "Unfortunately, I have to leave by Sunday morning. I have to be back in Paris by Monday."

Jim didn't think; he just said the words: "I'll do it."

Helene turned to him and smiled. It was as if the sun had dropped into the darkness, a rainbow after a rainfall, the colors shimmering in the mist.

"Jim, the Bernese Alps . . ." began Ambrose.

"My flight back to New York is next Wednesday," said Jim. "Ambrose, you and I were planning to hike up the Col du Brochet tomorrow anyway, and return on Sunday. If we haven't run into your mother by Sunday, Ambrose will point me in the right direction. If I don't find your mother

by Tuesday, I'll continue my descent. As soon as I'm back in Gstaad on Tuesday night, I'll contact you to let you know whether my mission has failed or succeeded. If I don't find your mother, you can call in the Swiss army."

"Very funny. Jim, it's never advisable to hike the Alps alone, especially for someone with no experience . . ."

"Does one need experience to walk? So far, the trails in these Alps have been very well-marked."

"You don't know the Wildhorn," said Clio, sitting back in her chair and darting a *told-you-so* look at Helene. "Jim, these are your last few days off after what sounds like many years of hard work. You should enjoy a good hike without searching for a woman who's determined to be lost. Not only that, but the snow could come any day. And waiting for you to tell us whether you have found her would delay the rescue service's search."

"If they're hiking the Col du Brochet anyway," said Helene, "there's no harm in looking for her. Perhaps they'll be lucky and find her, and it's not as if Father will call off the helicopters."

"And if we find her within the next few days, then what?" asked Ambrose.

"You should bring her back here, to the Cabane," said Clio. "The descent is easiest from here."

"If we do find your mother, would you have something we could give her that proves we were sent by you and not your father?"

Thalia winked and laughed. "Bravo! He's great, isn't

he?" she said to Clio. She quickly removed the maroon velvet ribbon from around her neck. "Maman used to keep yards and yards of this velvet ribbon. Remember? She used it for everything that year, presents, shoelaces for her boots, belts, hair ribbons. We all have rolls of it. I use this piece as a choker. I would like it back," she said, smiling at Jim flirtatiously.

The ribbon was warm from Thalia's neck. Jim folded it carefully and placed it in his pants pocket.

"The dining room is closing," announced Monsieur Acolas, nearing their table. Jim looked around the room and saw that most of the tables were empty. He hadn't noticed the hikers leaving: were they already snoring on their thin mattress pads upstairs? The logs on the dwindling fire shifted.

"It would be best to depart at dawn tomorrow," Clio said, rising from the table. "Come, let me show you the map."

Ambrose and Jim followed her into the narrow mudroom with its cubbies neatly packed with overcoats, boots, hats, gloves, climbing gear, and trekking poles. On the far wall at the end of the room they stopped at the floor-to-ceiling map of the surrounding mountains, marked with a red arrow indicating YOU ARE HERE. Among the ranges closest to the arrow were La Pointe des Audannes at 2844 meters, Geltenhorn 3065, Le Sex Rouge 2893, Le Mont Pucel 3177, Le Six des Eaux Froides 2905, and Le Wildhorn 3248.

"Is there a smaller map that we can take with us on the trip?" Jim asked.

Clio looked surprised by the question. "We're paper-free up here in the Alps. Here are the markers along the way. It takes about six hours from here to get up to the Col du Brochet. I would then take the Geltenhorn pass down on the south side, here. You can stop for a rest and a bite at the Geltenhütte, a very charming chalet. This is a much safer route, and you'll avoid the ladder in the sky. And hopefully the snow."

"Ladder in the sky?" Jim asked.

"A twenty-foot hanging metal ladder alongside a steep cliff face. The ladder swings out from the mountain with the winds, and —" She looked poised to say something else but closed her mouth around the thought and nodded at them before walking back to the table.

"She doubts our abilities," said Jim to Ambrose.

"She's right to. We'll take our hike as previously planned and conduct a search along the way, but finding anyone on foot in this glaciated massif is a dream if not a joke. All I'm hoping for is some sun. Already, that's probably too much to ask."

When they returned to the table, Jim noticed that Helene's eyes had become moist. All the mirth had left the room; the fire had died out. The Italians had gathered on the terrace outside the dining room, and small specks of orange from their cigarettes sparkled in the darkness.

THREE

THE SEND-OFF

WAS IT THE HOWLING WIND THAT WOKE HIM, OR the intermittent snoring in the far-distant corner? The room was so bright that Jim thought it must be morning, but his alarm had not sounded. He made out Ambrose's form on the mattress next to his, his back moving to the rhythm of his breath. From the blue cast that fell over the sleeping bodies, Jim realized that the room was lit by the moon. The light was channeled from a very small window near where the sisters slept.

In his dream, his mother had been playing bridge, shuffling the deck with her long red fingernails and smacking her red-lipsticked lips. The stiff-haired women's bridge group at the dining-room table were generals detailing the

next military operation in an army camp, their legs crossed under the table and their calloused elbows above it. But what was *he* doing in the room? The puzzle pieces of the dream were floating away one by one. Jim had never spent any time strolling along the idle distance of a dream. In his life at the investment bank, even on weekends Jim was out of bed and into the shower immediately after waking, his dreams long buried with thoughts of the coming day.

A pale-blue string of light from the moon was suspended like a tightrope from the small window near his bed to the partition wall near where Ambrose slept. Whose breathing did he hear, with a little singsong to it? Thalia's? Or was it her younger sister's, Helene's? How amazing it was to be privy to a stranger's sleep, something that belonged solely to that person. The guttural snoring from the far corner overtook the gentle sound. How could anyone sleep in such a din, between the sleep talkers, the snorers, and the whirr of the wind barreling around this tin capsule?

Jim stood and glanced around the partition at Clio. He saw her eyes open slightly, then close. He could not see Helene or Thalia.

He thought of Sally and their now-canceled wedding-to-be. He imagined their passionate kiss at the altar—no, she would have given him a self-conscious, public kind of kiss, actually. He envisioned himself placing a piece of wedding cake on her tongue. He thought of her red freckles. Her bright-green eyes, how her hips moved when she

walked and . . . How far away from her he felt. He missed the way she tucked her hair behind one ear, how she winked at him in her way that said, *Go on, tell me how beautiful I am!* Thalia's flirtatiousness reminded him of Sally, the day they had met at a conference five years earlier. Sally had touched his thigh under the table, had swung her leg as restlessly as Thalia had. It ached somewhere inside him to think that Sally was no longer in his life. Was it possible to turn off love, like shutting the flow of water at a spigot?

Was that Thalia's voice whispering to him from across the room?

"Jim!" the whispering voice called. "I can't sleep, either."

It was Thalia. She patted her mattress, and he maneuvered around the sleepers to sit on the edge of her narrow bed. The scent of roses.

"I can't stop thinking of mother, alone and cold and the snow coming. Please let us know as soon as you find her, if you do, okay?"

"I will," he said.

Someone stirred in the bed next to Thalia's and turned her head. It was Helene. In the blue moonlight, her face looked like a child's. She did not open her eyes.

"Go back to sleep," Thalia whispered to her sister. "Now that I've seen you," she addressed Jim, "I'll sleep better."

Jim wanted to ask why, but he was afraid of disturbing the others. He rose and retreated to his mattress in the moonlight.

• • •

WHEN HIS ALARM WOKE HIM HOURS LATER, IT WAS darker than it had been when he'd been roused from sleep by the moon. Three men in the corner, rising quietly in the dim light, looked like souls levitating from dead bodies. Knapsack in hand, Jim followed Ambrose quietly down the ladder to the warm, yellow-lit kitchen below. Bread and cheese, muesli and yogurt, and a tin bowl of hard-boiled eggs were laid out on the buffet table for the early hikers. With a nod, Monsieur Acolas offered Jim a white mug filled with what looked like foamy hot chocolate.

Jim took a seat near the only window in the dining room. A speck of light over the mountains competed with a bright star for attention. How forlorn it was on this rocky plateau.

Ambrose joined him. "Found this at our communal sink," he said, placing into Jim's hand a slender white book tied shut with a maroon velvet ribbon.

"It has your name on it," Ambrose said, pointing to the elegant script in light-blue ink on a small note card slipped under the ribbon. Jim slid the ribbon off to reveal the title and author: *Alcools* by Guillaume Apollinaire. Two pages in the middle of the book were each marked with a small sprig of light pink heather. The poem on the first page was titled "L'Adieu."

"You don't waste any time, do you?" Ambrose said, looking up as he chipped the shell off his hard-boiled egg. "What is written there, on the left?"

"This part has been translated." Jim read aloud:

> "I've plucked this sprig of heather
> Autumn is dead, you will remember
> On earth, we will see no more of each other
> The smell, the scent of time, sprig of heather
> Remember, I wait for you forever . . ."

"That's it?" Ambrose raised his eyebrows.

Jim nodded. "Another poem has also been marked, but only with a small exclamation point next to its title, 'Clair de lune.' Translate it, will you?"

"You certainly made an impression! I need my coffee for this:

> Smooth

"No . . . more like 'sweet-sounding' . . .

> "moon on the lips of the mad
> The orchards and towns are greedy tonight
> The stars are like the image of bees,
> Of this luminous honey that

" . . . That—'degoutte', I believe in this sense, it means 'drips'

> "from the vines,

For now, all sweet in their fall from the sky.
Each ray of moonlight is a ray of honey
Now hidden, I tell of the sweetest adventure
I fear darts of fire from the bee from the north
That places these deceptive rays in my hands
And takes its moon-honey, honeymoon
To the rose of the winds."

Ambrose closed the book and handed it back to Jim. "Who do you guess?"

"You have to ask? Thalia kicked me under the table on several occasions, was leaning into me all night so that I'm still smelling her perfume, gave me the ribbon around her neck and asked for it back, and last night, while you were snoring, she said she would sleep better after seeing me."

"All three sisters seemed pretty smitten with you."

He remembered Helene's curious, searching eyes that seemed to grow more luminous when she spoke to him.

"I suppose not the eldest," added Ambrose, "but even she cast a twinkle in your direction."

"She doubted me from the start. Justifiably—she was worried about my inexperience. She's not invested in Helene's rescue mission. I'm guessing that neither is Thalia, really."

"I thought I overheard one of the sisters talking about an engagement? Could it have been Thalia's?"

Jim picked up the book again. "In this poem, I think

Thalia is the honeybee who, I believe, would deflower me if
we stayed here one more night!"

"Want to postpone our trip a day?"

Jim laughed. "Why do I still feel the need to be faithful
to Sally?"

"A true Midwesterner, Jim. Straight as an arrow. Something our world needs more of."

After they washed their dishes at the small tin sink in
the corner, Jim followed Ambrose to the mudroom.

"Five years together, and it's as if Sally and I shared the
same DNA," Jim said, lacing his boots. "I can tell you anything you want to know about her: This is how she slept
last night. On her side, curled up, her hands like this." Jim
tucked them, prayerlike, under his chin. "It's as if when she
sleeps, she hides her wings underneath. She looks like an
angel. Sally, lovely, kind, and yet . . ."

"She decided to go off with Mr.-Higher-Up-on-the-Pay-
Scale."

Ambrose picked through the trekking poles in the bin
next to the door, reciting a checklist as he did so: "Water,
food to last four days, if you decide to stay that long, though
I think we should both return after tomorrow, rope, flashlight, knife, compass, first aid, extra socks, gloves, rain gear,
tarp, blanket, trekking pole." He filled his canister with
water at the sink and chucked Jim one of Monsieur Acolas's
famous brown bags of delicacies. Last night the other hikers
had raved about the sorrel-and-chicken-filled baguette.

"The Castellanes are," Ambrose added in a low voice, "if I'm correct, a very ancient French noble house from the ninth century. They've been involved in government since then. How interesting to have met them up here, and how unlikely. While you were gazing into the fire and daydreaming about Sally, I learned from Clio that their mother is a de Bonnin de La Bonninière de Beaumont, an equally important French aristocratic family."

"How—"

"It's my business to know who's who," Ambrose said. "Despite the French Revolution, a lot of art still resides in the castles of these families, and the auction houses keep a close eye on who owns what masterpieces."

"I can't find my pole. I didn't use it to get up here . . ."

"You'll need it where we're going." Ambrose was at the door.

"Can't argue with that—oh, good, there it is." Jim untangled his pole from the jumble.

He turned and cast a glance up the ladder in the center of the room. He half hoped that Thalia would be there to blow him a kiss or whisper "au revoir" with her honeyed French accent and pronunciation that stumbled so pleasingly on consonants.

No such luck. He threw his knapsack, with attached blanket and tarp, onto his back and closed the cabin's thick wooden door behind him.

In the burgeoning light of dawn's early rays, Ambrose stood waiting at the nearby post with yellow signs pointing

in four different directions. It promised to be a sunny day.

"Sex Rouge?" Jim asked, tapping one of the signs with his pole.

"Sorry to disappoint, but it was originally spelled *Scex*— it's the name of a species of deer, now mostly extinct."

"With your vast wealth of useless information, I'd have thought you'd have come up with something more titillating."

Ambrose chuckled as they began to hike in the direction of Col du Brochet, ascending a narrow ridge of natural stepping-stones into the cavernous shadow of the mountain.

"WAIT," SAID AMBROSE AT A TURN IN THE PATH, "I almost forgot." He dropped his pole, removed his knapsack, and got down on his knees. "I watched a hiking group do this earlier this morning. I had forgotten that it's Alpine tradition to say a prayer before you start a new hike."

Jim looked around him. The faint sunshine at their backs now illuminated the white mountain cap ahead of them and the craggy, rocky cliff below. To their left, the path fell off to a shadowed shelf that resembled the cratered surface of the moon. "Why don't you pray for both of us, a twofer."

Gradually, they began to ascend, single file, up the jagged incline. When Ambrose rounded the bend ahead of him, Jim heard him gasp. A few steps later, Jim realized why. Ahead of them stretched what looked like miles and

miles of a white boneyard, with no end in sight—and no distinct trail. How, around a single random corner, could the terrain of a mountain change so dramatically?

"I've heard about this, but I've never encountered it," Ambrose said. "It's called *lapiaz*—it's caused when the surface freezes and then thaws. Maybe over the span of a few centuries. Keep your head down. Hikers have been known to fall into the crevices."

"The one death a day in the Alps . . ." said Jim.

"Once we cross this, we'll hike about sixteen miles mostly uphill northeast toward Le Col du Brochet. I'm guessing it'll take us about two hours to walk this part, then three to four hours, depending on the terrain and altitude, to crest the Col du Brochet. Perhaps, along the way, we'll smell Madame Castellane's perfume."

The slowly rising plateau ahead of them resembled a garbage heap of calcified bones. Each bone looked as if it had been chewed and licked clean over centuries. Jim crouched down for a closer look at the sun-bleached latticework. He took a two-euro coin from his pocket and dropped it into the crevice. No sound: they were standing over the black hole of the earth. He shuddered to think of Thalia's mother. What if she'd slipped and fallen into the mountain, and that was why the helicopter had failed to find her? He'd been a fool to give the sisters hope that they'd find her.

"Ambrose!" Jim yelled to his friend, who was far ahead, picking his way across. Ambrose stopped and turned.

"There's got to be another way!"

"There *is* no other way. Look for a red marker," Ambrose shouted back, waiting for Jim to catch up. "There's the first one. Tuck your pole under the straps of your knapsack. You'll need both hands for balance."

The red marker ahead was as faint as a thermometer reading.

"Now I know why you got down on your knees," Jim said as he joined his friend. "Where's the warning sign with the skull and crossbones?"

"You're not in the US of A . . ."

"Why didn't the sisters warn us of this? This is down-right dangerous."

"Nothing new to them," Ambrose said. "If you've come up this high, you've had to deal with a lot of nature's hand-me-downs. Can you step it up a little? At the rate we're going, we'll be adding our own bones to this graveyard."

"I can't see the Parisian wife of the minister of the interior making this place her home for the summer months," said Jim when he next caught up to Ambrose.

"Clio asked us to check out a few caves in the region," said Ambrose, "but I agree—not only is this rocky plateau formidable, but it's also too open for someone in hiding, es-pecially with a helicopter searching overhead."

Jumping from one surface to the other, to the other, to the other, head bent, Jim thought of his first day of work, a week from Monday at Wolfe, Taylor. The work space they had shown him was, appropriately, labeled the "inner

sanctum." His desk was one among thirty, not unlike his mattress in the sleeping room at the Cabane. The firm occupied the fourth floor of 535 Madison Avenue on Fifty-Fourth Street, where, unfortunately, the endless corridor of buildings along the avenue blocked most of the natural light. Even the coveted corner offices were dark.

Ambrose stopped. "I can't see the next marker."

Swiftly moving clouds, like marching troops, had invaded the morning's blue sky. Jim pulled his water bottle from his knapsack, drank, and scanned the boneyard horizon.

"Break to get our bearings," he said.

"Agreed, pathfinder," said Ambrose.

They found a flat, smooth ledge and removed their knapsacks, drank water, and snacked on Swiss sausage and cheese from the Acolas lunch bags.

"If this mountain were a man," said Ambrose, tapping the rock with his trekking pole, "then this surely would be his ribcage. The markers are placed relatively closely, so I'm confused that we can't see the next one. Have I taken us off the path? You remember, Jim, I have to leave tomorrow morning. I have to sell the Bronzino that will send Zoë and Thierry to school next year."

"See that cave over there?" Jim pointed. "I don't think I would have seen it if we hadn't stopped. Let's check it out. Who knows, we might come across the female hermit whom the sisters mentioned last night.

"What would she eat up here?"

"What would she *do* up here?"

"That we shall discover if we meet her or madame."

Ambrose adjusted his pack and unzipped his jacket. "Thalia told me something about her mother's childhood that I'm still digesting."

Jim tapped his walking pole on the lapiaz.

"Where was I when you were having *this* tete-a-tete?"

"We were in the buffet line. Apparently, when Calliope was a young girl she was driving with her parents and her brother from Paris to their home in the Loire Valley, with the parents' best friends, a husband and wife, driving behind them. When they stopped to get gas, Calliope's mother suggested that she switch seats with her friend in the other car. Her friend took Calliope's mother's place next to Calliope's father. After driving a ways, the father realized that the car with his wife and his friend was no longer behind them. He pulled over and waited. Of course, there were no cell phones back then. They retraced the road, suspecting a flat tire or dead car battery. Finally they went on toward the chateau, thinking that Calliope's mother, who knew the area well, had found a faster route."

"Ambrose the confessor. People tell you everything."

"Calliope's mother and the monsieur never showed up—not that night, not the following day, not the following week, not the following month. It wasn't until months, *months*, later, after an insane amount of alarm, panic, and searching, that Calliope's mother called to announce that she and her best friend's husband were madly in love and had driven off the map."

"Ouch. That must have been brutal on the children."

"Not to mention the husband."

"Calliope, abandoned by her mother. The apple doesn't—"

"Clio told me that her mother said it would have been better for them all if the couple had been in a car accident."

"Harsh. Did they divorce?"

"Calliope's mother eventually returned to her husband, but only after her lover had died."

"Do you think there's a lover in *this* story?"

"The daughters would have told us, wouldn't they? Oh, voilà, thank God, I see it, I see it, there it is!" Ambrose stood and pointed to the sliver of red stick on the ridge above them. "Great idea of yours, my pathfinder friend, to stop and rest. I think the only way we could have seen it is from this vantage point." He rose. "Let's check out that cave. Do you hear that groaning sound?"

A herd of steinbock, the antelope of the Alps—there must have been fifteen of them—stood less than thirty feet away on the ledge below them. The low-hanging mist from the clouds must have obscured them only minutes before. Now, in the full sunlight, Jim could make out the ribbed design on their horns that curved backward like Indian chiefs' feathered headdresses. The valley that Ambrose labeled the Iffigtal opened up far away and beneath them, in the form of shapely, rounded patches of green separated by glimmers of silver rivers.

Jim would have liked to stop and take a photograph, but

Ambrose was already far ahead of him, hopscotching right and left. Jim could tell that his friend was anxious about crossing the lapiaz before dark. After an hour, Ambrose stopped at the entrance of a cave, one of the thousand yawning mouths of the mountain.

"Hermitess!" Ambrose called.

Hermitess, tess, ess, ss, s, s, the mountains mimicked. Jim switched on his flashlight, and the beam pierced the stale-smelling darkness of the cave. It was cold and pitch-black inside.

"No one home," said Ambrose, returning to the light.

THE SUN WAS AT THEIR BACKS AS THEY RETURNED to the white expanse of bonescape.

"The next marker!" Jim yelled ahead to Ambrose. "I've cracked the code."

"While no one mentioned how dangerous it is to climb through this mind-numbing heap of sediment," said Ambrose when Jim caught up to him, "one of the Italian hikers did tell me not to miss the mountain lake near the col. The lake is situated on one of the highest elevations in the Northern Hemisphere."

"I would jump into it now," said Jim, removing his Windbreaker and tying it around his waist.

"Listen," said Ambrose.

Jim heard a pounding, a rushing of water, steady, but fluctuating in tone from one moment to the next. It was like

different sections of an orchestra playing simultaneously, a symphony of horns, clarinets, and trumpets accompanied by distant drumbeats. Had they climbed into the larynx of the mountain?

"Waterfalls," said Ambrose. "We're at the Col d'Aiguille. See the peak sticking up horizontally, like a needle?"

Perspiring from the heat of the midday sun, the hikers crested the double-fanged ridge and stood back in amazement. In the vista ahead, the large, shimmering, glacial lake looked like a mirage. Eight, nine, ten, eleven waterfalls—Jim lost count—cascaded from the cliffs into the clear, azure-blue lake below. The sharp peak resembled the prow of a ship steaming toward them.

"Rainbows!" yelled Jim over the roar of the water.

Rainbows, hundreds of them, arched one after another across the falls.

"It looks as if you can walk over them to the other side of the lake," said Ambrose, at Jim's side.

After hours of hiking over atonal mountainscape, the ribbons of colors refracting off the sparkling lake were almost blinding. A fringe of color also lined the lake's edge, the first sign of plant life Jim had seen in days. The patterns of wildflowers dotting the rock faces reminded Jim of a similar template of stars that had decorated the sky the night before. He felt in his pocket for the velvet ribbon.

At the lake's edge, they ate lunch on a large, flat rock. "It's hard to believe that *this* is on the other side of *that*," said Ambrose, gesturing toward the lapiaz with his water canis-

ter. "We're at a higher altitude than we were at the Cabane."

"If I were Calliope, I'd pitch my tent here," said Jim.

"There's no protection from the sun up here," said Ambrose, looking around as he packed the remains of lunch. "I'm burning up as we speak." He removed sunblock from his knapsack, slathered it on his face, and handed the tube to Jim.

The path diverged ahead of them, narrow lines curving around either side of the lake.

"Which way, pathfinder?" Ambrose asked.

"I don't see a marker, but the path to the right looks more trodden." Jim pointed. "Tell me why we're the only hikers up here."

Ambrose did not hear the question over the pounding of the falls. They hiked the eastern slope near the lake's edge for the next three hours, the rock face smoother and the path clear. Freed from the need to concentrate on each footstep, Jim's thoughts wandered. What a luxury it was to let his mind go, unleashed from the logistics of work and daily life. He and Sally had shared the opinion that reflection was an indulgence; people who spent too much time thinking about the past could only get stuck.

After a week of hiking, however, he'd changed his mind. Running away from thoughts or creating busyness so there was no time to reflect struck him now as an act of cowardice. Reflection could very well be the sunlight needed for a human's photosynthesis.

Jim had obviously missed a few red markers on the

ELIZABETH BIRKELUND

landscape where Sally was concerned. Why hadn't he seen the breakup coming? When was the moment that she had changed her heart, her mind? Later, it came out that she'd told her parents a month before she'd let him know. A month! The wedding invitations had already been sent, but the reception room at the Plaza, the cake, the staff, the preparations had needed to be canceled ASAP, she'd said. She'd had to tell her parents immediately, but her fiancé? She could never find the right time to tell him.

"So you decided to tell me over the phone?" he'd asked her. He could feel fresh anger mounting as he remembered.

"I wouldn't have been able to handle it if I told you in person," she'd said meekly.

She'd been pretending when they'd laid a picnic in Central Park only a few days earlier. He remembered her laughing, pouring him wine, acting like their future together was as clear as the water in the sailboat lake. He'd asked a few questions about the wedding preparations, but she'd said she didn't want to talk about it, that a groom shouldn't know the details. They had kissed, made love back in his apartment. And yet by that point she had already moved on to his replacement. How could such a small body carry such duplicity?

AFTER ANOTHER TWO HOURS, JIM PAUSED ON A DIRT path at a small crescent of white beach lining another interconnecting lake, not far from the entrance to a cave. He

52

watched a furry hyrax disappear under a rock. Ambrose was far ahead.

"Ambrose!" Jim motioned for him to come back. "It'll be dark in a few hours and this looks like a good place to sleep."

"Our own petite Saint-Tropez," said Ambrose at his side. "I thought we'd be at the Col du Brochet by now."

"Picking our way over this beast's ribcage slowed our progress."

"Tomorrow morning we'll get an early start. I'm guessing we'll hit the Col du Brochet an hour into our hike. After that, we'll start our descent down to the Geltenhütte. Monsieur Acolas told me that we'd find a dangling metal ladder nailed into the mountain there that will shorten the hike to Gstaad by six hours."

"The famous Ladder in the sky. You have to hold on, or there's a *real* shortcut to the bottom," said Jim, laughing.

"Hey, where did the sun go?"

"Looks like rain," said Jim. "We'll need cover."

At the mouth of the cave, they dropped their knapsacks and unfurled their tarps and blankets.

"Five years ago, the last time I was up so high in the Alps," said Ambrose, gazing at the view ahead of them, "there was snow on almost every mountaintop. Now you can see it only on a few distant peaks. It's as if these mountains are old men losing their white hair. One day only the crevices will retain the snow, and then not even those."

"Wilderness evaporating before our eyes," said Jim. Wilderness was the moon—or a woman's heart. Sally's.

"Hallo, bonjour!" Ambrose shouted into the cave. The darkness swallowed the sound.

"She's not up here, Ambrose," Jim said. He settled his tarp under the cave's upper lid. Ambrose unpacked the wrinkled brown paper bag of nuts, dried fruit, and their dinner of sorrel and chicken.

"Do you think we're on a wild—"

The distant drone of the helicopter far below them interrupted him. The rumble faded into an echo as quickly as it had appeared.

"As if on cue, eh? I was asking myself the same question." Ambrose spread his dinner on a napkin. "Finding a woman in the Wildhorn seemed a lot easier with all that wine and beauty in our midst. I agree with you. Calliope is probably camping down by the side of the Iffigsee, way below the Cabane, with a view of grazing brown cows. We might very well catch a glimpse of her on our descent."

"I'll be taking the longer way down."

"As I've told you—"

"I need this time on my own, Ambrose, especially before I go back to work."

"Go soul-searching in the lowlands, my friend, not up here, where no mammals dare tread."

"These are well-marked trails—"

"The lapiaz pass?"

Jim stowed his plate and fork and dinner leftovers and

lay down. Despite the tarp and blanket, the damp chill of the cave floor pressed into his skin. "We'll discuss this in the morning."

Ambrose stared behind him into the black maw of the cave. "I'm half-afraid the hermitess will find us up here. She could be spying on us from inside this cave. Hear that?"

"Bats?" said Jim.

"I would have preferred the sandy Saint-Tropez," said Ambrose.

"Wet, but bat-free."

"And warmer than on the edge of this mountain's carapace. The temperature has dropped."

"I hear her voice in the rain," said Jim.

"Whose?"

"Some say Italian is the most beautiful language, but I would argue that it's French. There's an intimacy in the way the French say things, like *chez moi, chaleur, amour, Bonheur . . .*"

Thalia's voice was like the rolling hills of the lowland Alps. Helene's was like a gust of wind in a sail, held there only briefly. Sally's voice was high in tone and had a scratchy quality that was sexy: he missed it.

"I thought I would hear Sally's voice for the rest of my life."

"This is your journey to forget Sally."

"Five years of loving her. And then you tell your heart, 'Sorry, wrong recipient! Delete!'"

Sheets of heavy rain—or was it sleet?—began to drop

suddenly from the edge of the cave roof, and the men quickly rose and pulled their tarps deeper inside.

Jim knew that he and Ambrose shared the same concern: how they would find their way tomorrow if the sleet turned into snow and the mountain path was covered.

Between yawns, Ambrose began to tell the story of his standoff with a ten-foot elk while on a fishing trip in Wyoming: he and the elk glared at each other for half an hour . . .

"Then?" Jim asked.

Ambrose whistled in his sleep, and Jim found himself counting the seconds between each exhalation. He readjusted his position on the cold, rocky, uncomfortable surface. Every night, he thought, transformed a person in a small way, with the dreams and the tossing and turning of thoughts in the rolling water mill of the mind. Sleep was not a break from life's continual sweep. In it, you were still living life, seeing things you would never see come morning, and it could age you as quickly as daytime.

FOUR

THE ALCHEMY OF A MOUNTAIN

"MAYBE THEY KNOW SOMETHING WE DON'T," said Ambrose. "They must have closed down yesterday or the day before." They were standing before the boarded-up rustic chalet at the summit of Col du Brochet. Unlike the tin Cabane des Audannes, this chalet was adorned with classic Swiss wooden balconies and some of the summer's leftover pink flowers at the windows. Wooden planks covered the two front windows.

After hiking under clouds that now stretched like a white sheet of ice over the sky, Jim had expected to find this chalet, which he'd heard was a charming Alpine gem with a commanding position over the glaciers, with its doors open and fellow hikers spilling over benches and picnic tables outside.

"These chalets don't usually close until mid-September," said Ambrose.

They ate their midmorning snack at one of the picnic tables that no doubt provided an awe-inspiring scenic overlook on a clear day. Now they saw only layers of gray upon gray. Jim had never imagined so many combinations of grayness.

"We'll take Monsieur Acolas's shortcut," said Ambrose, squinting at the familiar yellow signs and pointing in the direction of Gstaad, eight hours.

"I've decided to take this route"—Jim pointed—"to Geltenhütte, southwest. On my way I'll look for the mysterious Calliope."

"You know that the Swiss Air Ambulance actually *trains* people to rescue stranded hikers or skiers in the Alps—" began Ambrose.

"Ambrose, we've been through this."

"Jim Olsen. I've never known you to be this obstinate. Take a man off his job, set him down in the Alps, and you never know what could happen. I'm guessing that you want to prove something to the ladies in the hutte."

"Maybe." Jim honestly didn't know, himself.

"You're aware of those clouds? White, powdered fortune cookies with strips of paper inside that all say 'snow'?"

"They've been following us."

"Come back with me, Jim. It's not sensible or smart to hike alone in these conditions."

"I promised—"

"Jim—"

"The path is clearly marked, Ambrose. Ten-dollar bet that I beat you down!" Jim patted his friend on the back. "Really, I'll be fine. Give my best to Stephanie and the kids."

"Text me as soon as you arrive in Gstaad. I will be waiting," Ambrose said.

After a good-bye hug, Ambrose disappeared around the bend of the shale path. "Safe travels and bon voyage!" His voice trailed off.

"You too!" Jim yelled back, though he realized that his reply was probably lost in the thickening mist.

NOW THAT HE WAS ALONE, JIM FOUND HIMSELF walking faster. He would not call it panic, but it was something close, an alertness that he imagined he shared with the mountain mammals seeking shelter from the coming storm. Based on his summers working in the paint department at Manny's Hardware and Paints, he would categorize panic in the same color family as anxiety: red, but possibly a deeper hue. He recalled the metallic taste of anxiety before giving presentations to a room of thirty or more executives. This hike along the open-jawed terrain of the Alps could never be as threatening as those thirty-odd steel-edged minds sharpening their grist on his every word.

The path he hiked was composed of slippery, shattered

scree—layers and layers of shredded slate. With no Ambrose or mountain views to distract him, Jim hiked forward, but found himself looking back.

He was seventeen years old, arriving for the first time at Princeton University. He'd never visited the college—the trip east was too expensive, and who needed to see it? Princeton was his father's boss's alma mater, and it was the college Jim's parents had chosen for him as soon as he'd entered the sixth grade. When Jim had dropped his only duffel bag on the shiny wooden floor of his freshman dorm room, his hometown friend, Tommy Murphy, a junior on the lacrosse team, had rushed in to welcome him. Thankfully, Tommy had showed the naive Midwesterner the ropes and invited him to team parties at Cottage, an eating club.

But Jim was quiet by nature. Among his convivial new friends, Jim considered his self-restraint and reticence a personality flaw. He'd never learned the art of talking, as his competitive sister had (everything she undertook was motivated by the desire to outshine her younger brother) from their fussy, loquacious mother. Rather, he'd intuited from his father that talk was idle and worth little. It could even cost you your integrity. The dialogue of the men of the family was interior, like these barely whispering mountains.

Jim stopped to remove his fleece from his knapsack. Had nature decided to hold its breath? It was so quiet. Or was this break in the howling wind the pregnant pause before the snows? The clouds were regrouping and gathering above.

Where were the hikers, the yodelers, the sheep and cow-

herds? Jim would welcome even the relentless chop of the helicopter. What if the sought-after Calliope had been located? What if it snowed? What if the barely perceptible path upon which he walked disappeared into miles of endless slate scree?

Enough with the what-ifs, he told himself, pulling on his fleece and returning to his fast pace. This mountain, the Wildhorn, was about *whatness.* The sheer verticality took his breath away. Jim Olsen from the flat prairie lands couldn't stop looking up and up and up and up. Even if nothing else was moving, surely this *mountain* was alive, yearning, incessantly heaving upward to touch the clouds. It inspired awe, fear, and humility. This sensation of being literally in the clouds, in a land of vertical suspension, made him feel more alive than, yes, come to think of it, he ever had in his life.

He was walking so quickly now that he almost missed the signpost to the Refuge de Geltenhütte: elevation 2759 meters, four hours southwest; The Wildhorn 3247, four hours north, the direction he'd come; Le Sex Rouge 2893, six hours east; and The Arpelistock 3035, five hours south.

Four more hours? His watch had stopped long ago. Had his walking slowed? Was that the smell of . . . snow? Well acquainted as he was with frigid Midwestern winters, Jim had never known snow to smell. It was as if these mountains hungered for it, impatient for its release. As Jim continued in the direction of the Refuge, everything he saw along the way suggested snow: the white sky, the white patches on faraway peaks, the sparkle ingrained in the granite mountainside,

the deafening quiet. Why hadn't Ambrose, king of preparation, thought of packing an ice pick? Jim's legs devoured the
mountainscape in huge, lunging bites.

At a pass between two sharp-edged ridges, Jim stopped
to drink and eat. The traverse he'd been treading looked
so faint in the distance that he wondered for a panicked
moment whether he'd been following a trail made by steinbock. How could a trail taper off and disappear? The Swiss
were a reliably predictable people.

He threw on the next layer, his Windbreaker, and donned
the gloves that he'd told Ambrose he'd never use. His fingers
were almost numb. All around him, the mountain inclined
into peaks of jagged rock. He crouched down. One of his heels
was bleeding again, despite the Band-Aid he'd stuck on that
morning. A trace of a trail, then nothing but gray-black scree
in the distance. Ambrose and Clio had been right. Who did he
think he was to tackle this black-eyed mountain solo? Should
he turn back, retrace his steps? He felt for his flashlight in the
knapsack, his only weapon. He'd been hiking five hours since
he'd stopped for lunch. He would need to find a place to sleep.

The evening darkness encroached from all sides. He would
live with uncertainty that night, and in the morning, with the
sunrise as his compass, he would recover his bearings.

THE SECOND SOLO DAY WAS SIMILAR TO THE FIRST.
He failed to find a marked trail and feared he was walking
in circles. The snow had still not arrived, but Jim sensed it

in his every bone, in the bloated clouds, and the pregnant silence.

Someone please speak. A steinbock, a bird, a breeze, a helicopter. Someone remind me of life! Would he get out of here alive? What about his job? Maybe Calliope's helicopter-heavy-handed husband would rescue him *and* her. What if he had hiked out of helicopter range? He cursed himself for every act of foolishness that had led up to this moment.

That night the temperature dropped dramatically, and the slight breeze that had developed late in the afternoon grew into a howling wind. Jim would have liked to light a fire for warmth, but how could you build a fire with rock?

When he woke in the night he thought he heard water splashing, and he wondered if he had accidentally wandered near the waterfall of the legendary Grotte aux Fées. One of the hikers at the Cabane had told him about this miracle of a waterfall inside a mountain—more than 250 feet long.

He would locate the trail to Gstaad the following day. When he was hiking with Ambrose, time had seemed limitless, but now it was closing in on him. He needed to get back to New York in time to start his new job. He could not risk being one day late. But risk what? Would they fire him if he was one day late? *Yes*, he heard. It was Sally's voice. "Go away," he told it.

But the words surfacing from the distant splashes were French, the voice in tune with the falling water. So much breath in a voice. Something about it soothed him. He called out the names of the Castellane sisters as if they were his

family: "Thalia, what man are you pursuing? Clio, are you happy to be among your children? Helene, are you sleeping well tonight?" He remembered how childlike her face had looked in the moonlight that night in the Cabane. "Calliope, mother, mirage, meanderer, did you realize when you lost yourself that you would lose me as well?" He doubled up the blanket and pulled it to his chin.

With dawn nowhere in sight, Jim decided to drain his valuable flashlight battery to light a page of the book of poetry Thalia had given him. Although he didn't understand most of the words, he repeated one line aloud in the glow of the flashlight as the snow began to tumble like white down from a comforter above, as the wetness began to seep into his clothing, as the world he did not know changed into another world he would not recognize. Appropriately, the poem was titled "La blanche neige"—"The White Snow"—and the line that Jim repeated was "Les anges, les anges dans le ciel"—"the angels, the angels in the sky."

He thought he heard a faint echo of footsteps, someone walking along the once-dry riverbeds that were now drinking in the snow. Perhaps it was another lost hiker, he mused to himself as he drifted off to sleep. Perhaps it was Madame Castellane.

FIVE

VALASIAN, MOUNTAIN FARMER

WAS THAT THE SOUND OF A FIRE CRACKLING? HE
was dreaming. He could feel its warmth. But no! His clothes
were cold and clammy. He remembered the snow, appearing like a prowler in the night. He opened his eyes slowly.
The dimly lit sky hovered so low that Jim felt he could touch
it. The snow had stopped. Thank God. And yes, that was a
fire! Not far from where Jim lay, a man hunched over flickering flames. The man's face was creased and marked like
the bark of a tree. His hair was thinning, gray and white.
He wore a brown jacket that was too short for his long torso;
it rose up from his waist as he bent. His pants were a darker
shade of brown, stained in many places and ripped at the
knees. The skin on the back of his neck was stretched so

thin that Jim thought he could see through it. Was he in the presence of a ghost?

Jim scrambled to his feet and rubbed his sore back. "Bonjour," he said.

The man stared stonily at him, shook his head, grunted, and returned his gaze to the fire, prodding it with a crooked twig. He dug his hand into his pocket and, without looking up at Jim, held out a wedge of cheese and a small sausage.

"Thank you," Jim said, taking the proffered food and sitting down on a boulder near the busy little fire. Monsieur Acolas's soggy brown bag of food had lost its appeal the previous night.

Speaking felt strange. "Jim Olsen," Jim said.

The man stirred the fire.

"Valasian," he said in a deep voice.

"Valasian," Jim repeated. Last name or first name? Maybe both.

Valasian looked like an extension of the mountain: his face was the same shade of gray. Tattered long underwear peeked out from his dark brown trousers.

"I'm looking for the trail to Gstaad," Jim began hopefully.

Valasian kept his gaze focused on the fire. He did not speak.

"I need to get to Gstaad today to catch a plane tomorrow from Geneva to New York City."

Did this old man not understand him, or did he refuse to respond?

Jim asked if the man had seen a woman in the area? Aha—a reaction from the stone! The man frowned, shifted his position, and then returned his curtained eyes to the fire.

In broken French, Jim explained that the woman's three daughters had sent him to find their mother. To illustrate his story, Jim removed the now crushed and damp maroon velvet ribbon from his pocket and held it out.

The old man's slits of eyes opened wide. He grimaced, rose, and gestured for Jim to follow him. They walked around a small hillock, and Jim stumbled when he saw the orange-pink shimmer of dawn reflected on the white cover of the formerly gray-locked mountain. The morning had been ignited.

Was it 6 a.m.? How inadequate a measure hours and minutes were to mark the passage of time in the Alps. You couldn't swallow 6 a.m. as Jim now drank in the pink lure of sky; you couldn't inhale 6 a.m. and feel it become a part of you, as he did with the yellows, pinks, and oranges that swelled into him from the rocky, shimmering backbone of the mountain. The colors on such a palette had texture, even sound.

Extending his bony fingers—the joints reminded Jim of potatoes left too long in a cupboard—the old man pointed downward, into the valley.

"Aha," said Jim. "Will you please show me how to get there?"

Valasian limped back to his fire, his head angled toward the mountain. Everything about him, Jim noticed, tilted to

one side, giving the impression that he was on a ship listing portside.

Valasian stamped out the fire and, with his crooked forefinger, gestured for Jim to collect his things. He walked briskly ahead, treading unevenly on the loose shale rocks.

"The trail?" Jim yelled ahead as he followed Valasian over the slippery snowfield. Despite the views of the green valley patchwork below, it was cold away from the fire, and Jim shivered in his wet clothes. Not a person nor an animal nor a signpost did they pass, nor a word did the two men speak as Jim followed Valasian through the midday hours— not even when they both stopped to gaze up at the sound of the helicopter. Jim guessed that the search had been renewed now that the clouds and snow had passed. He felt relieved.

Valasian squinted up at the buzzing insect in the sky, shook his head—a persistent habit—and turned to walk in the opposite direction. Jim followed. Was the old man avoiding the chopper, too?

Valasian stopped to peer over a cliff overhang. Without a word of warning, he disappeared. Drilled into the rock ledge at Jim's feet was a thick rope secured to a rusty metal ring. Looking down, Jim caught sight of Valasian's crooked body rappelling to the bottom of a deep ravine. He tugged on the metal ring. Why should he trust this old guy? This was no ladder in the sky, it was just a rope. Abandoning his trekking pole, Jim grabbed the frayed cord, and grateful for his gloves, slid down. Landing in the ravine, he was

surprised to see that the valley around him was untouched by snow.

NEXT, VALASIAN POINTED TO A SPLIT IN THE SIDE OF the mountain, a hole about four feet wide. With surprising agility, the old man lifted himself up into the wide fissure. He looked like a man in a circus stuffing himself headfirst into a cannon.

"You've got to be kidding," Jim said.

With a deep breath, Jim followed his guide *into* the mountain wall. With Valasian's boots in his face, Jim slithered along inside the dark, damp tunnel, wondering once again whether he or this newfound companion had lost his mind.

It was frigid inside the mountain, and it smelled of mold. After some time, the tunnel began to slope. Jim heard water rushing, and then felt the tug of gravity. He dug the toes of his boots into the wet rock but failed to get traction. Before he knew it, he'd been dumped like a waterfall out of the guts of the mountain, plunged into a body of glacial water. When he popped up, breathless, he saw a waterfall streaming beside him. He was swept along in the turbulent current, his extremities numb in the freezing water, his knapsack wet through. He whipped his head around in search of Valasian and caught a glimpse of the old man climbing onto the riverbank behind him. Using all his strength, Jim swam across

the current and pulled himself up onto the sharp, rocky shore about thirty feet downriver from Valasian.

"Thanks for the warning, old man," Jim said as he joined Valasian on a rock slab. Valasian resembled a nearly drowned rat: the little hair he had was matted down along his ears, and water dripped from every part of him.

Jim detected a ray of mirth in his guide's blue slivers of eyes.

"I suppose this was the faster route, if we don't die of hypothermia," Jim continued. He rubbed his hands together. "If I'd known we were going swimming, I would have protected my knapsack."

A drop of lake water hung from the tip of Valasian's nose. Jim pulled off his gloves, T-shirt, fleece, and Windbreaker and squeezed the cold water from them. Valasian glared at Jim's bare chest with a look of disdain.

"For God's sake, it's just us up here," said Jim, laughing. He imagined his mother's face screwed up into the same knotted scowl.

Despite, or perhaps because of, the shock of the plunge, Jim found himself shivering and laughing at the same time. Had he ever appreciated the presence of another human being as much as he did this older man? Had he ever felt so refreshed? Every cell in his body vibrated with new life.

Jim drank in the green that carpeted the sloping mountain. Valasian pointed to something in the distance. It looked like a chalet with a bell tower. Beside it was a dark wooden

barn and an oval-shaped lake. In the late-afternoon sun, the lake looked spangled with gold and silver.

Valasian nodded to the chalet, his face unyielding. No cues, no clues, no information. A hermitess could live in such a place, as could Madame Castellane.

Valasian pulled his jaw up square to Jim's and gestured for Jim to don his wet shirt. Jim obeyed. Valasian took a seat on a nearby rock and closed his eyes, clearly waiting for Jim to depart—Jim had grown fairly fluent in the old man's silent language.

"Thank you," said Jim, wondering whether he should dip into his pocket for a tip.

"*Allez*, go!"

A handshake seemed too casual for this dignified man of the mountains. Jim bowed his head. Valasian nodded back.

Keeping the bell tower in view, Jim picked his way through a small copse and slid down a cliff face to find a lightly worn path that wound in the direction of the lake. As he descended, he caught glimpses of the bell tower behind this rounded hill, that grouping of cedar trees, this mountain boulder. It was as if the chalet were beckoning him closer. Listening for the tinkle of a bell, instead Jim heard the distant strobe of the helicopter, blasphemy in the peaceful setting.

Landing a chopper would be a challenge in this area. The chalet rested at the very top of a peak, among many other narrow mountain aiguilles. The only unbroken plane

was the lake, which had now lost favor with the sun. In the silver shadow, the shining lake resembled a mirror.

As he attempted to mentally reconstruct Calliope's face from the faded photograph, Jim slipped and cut the fleshy part of his thumb on a sharp ridge. Cursing, he tore off a strip of his T-shirt and tied it around his finger.

Despite the more challenging terrain, the chalet continued to draw him like a magnet. A narrow trail bridged a crevasse easily two hundred feet deep on either side. A tightrope across a chasm. Jim felt dizzy. Was it the altitude? But this peak lay far below the Geltenhorn and the Cabane des Audannes. Blood loss? The T-shirt tourniquet crisscrossing his thumb was soaked. He slipped, caught himself, and watched the displaced slate crumble as it hit the canyon below. He dropped his head to his chest until the dizziness passed.

Once he'd crossed the canyon, he threaded a slope of brambles, scratching his arms and legs, and then heard—was that finally the bell? A tinkling bell! What a welcome sound. He clambered up a steep hill and glimpsed the bell tower of the little chalet higher up on another peak. A flock of small white birds burst into the sky, balloons heralding his arrival.

He was immediately overcome by the smell of wild roses, a sweetness that he could almost taste. Roses in the Alps? He thought of the sprig of heather in the book of poetry, of Thalia's flirtatious advances, of Sally's beleaguered disavowals, and he climbed faster. Enough of Sally.

Relying on the tips of his fingers and boots, he hoisted himself up the precipitous rocky crag in front of him until he ran out of cracks in the mountain face. He paused, his heart pumping madly as he lifted his head to examine the ten-foot vertical sheet of granite above him and the bell tower above that. After inspecting the rockface, he finally spied a small notch to his left. He glanced down at the exposed drop and across at the ice drapes of the Wildhorn Massif in the distance. He took a deep breath. With his left hand, he reached as far as he could, got a finger-grip on the notch, and with a loud shout "Ahhh," threw himself in one bold motion, one leg after the other onto the top of the cliff. When he lifted his head, he saw the chalet with the bell tower and the brown wooden barn beside it. The bell tinkled in the light breeze.

Not far from the chalet, he spotted the silhouette of a woman.

SIX

THE CHALET OF OWLS

FROM WHERE HE STOOD, THE WOMAN DID NOT look like the mother of three daughters, nor did she resemble the image Jim carried in his mind of the legendary hermitess. Valasian must have led him to a younger woman of the mountains, a huntress. A braid ran down the middle of her back, the end of which was tied loosely with a ribbon. She wore a white T-shirt, a vest, riding pants, and boots, and a small quiver of six arrows hung carelessly from her back. Jim advanced behind her quietly, as if he were a spy. She was within fifteen, now ten feet. She, and now he, faced a circular target with a yellow bull's-eye at the center. The target was tacked to a hay bale about ten strides away.

"Don't move," she said in a voice that was rich and

deeply accented—a dancing, playful voice, warm with the last drops of sunlight.

Jim stood motionless. Kestrels chirped above him. The wind stirred the woman's hair, and wisps fell from her braid. The world was vibrant in the moment, heated by the last glimmer of the sun.

She drew the arrow back in one fluid motion and then released it. The arrow hit the target an inch off the center of the bull's-eye and vibrated there in its certainty.

Still the woman did not turn around.

"What took you so long?" she asked.

Jim looked behind him. Was she addressing someone else?

She reached behind her, her elbow pointing up in the air for a brief moment, and extracted a second arrow from the small leather pouch on her back.

"It took you longer than you expected," she said, threading the arrow into the bow and slowly drawing back. Her French accent was fused with a British one. Her voice resembled all the sisters' voices in his head. It was her: Calliope Castellane.

With surprising swiftness and in one move, she turned and pointed the arrow at him. The arrow's target was his heart. Had Calliope's solitary existence transformed her into a madwoman? A lock of light-brown hair fell over her eye.

"Yes," he said. He didn't move. She was more beautiful than in her photograph. Her cheekbones were more pro-

nounced and higher, her nose was a straighter line—but it was her large, intense blue-green eyes that demanded attention.

She laughed, then twisted her body back in the direction of the target and released the arrow. In the dimming light, he could see that she'd missed the bull's-eye by only a fraction. As she retrieved her arrows, he noticed that the ribbon that held her braid was identical to the maroon velvet one that Thalia had given him from around her neck.

From the picture the sisters had shown him, he'd expected an attractive older woman of forty-nine, but here, now approaching him, was a woman in full bloom, with a rosiness in her cheeks that spread down her jaws. She was, as her daughters had described her and as the photograph had suggested, the physical embodiment of her daughters. He noticed the high cheekbones of Clio, but in her mother, more refined; the blue eyes of Thalia, in her mother, deeper set and more intense; the stubborn defiance in Helene's chin, in her mother's face, more pronounced.

"Now it's your turn," she said to him.

He noticed a thin line of perspiration above her lip as she handed him the bow. She reached behind her back and offered him an arrow.

He tried to still his ricocheting mind. The last time he'd shot an arrow, he was twelve years old at Camp Chippewa in Wisconsin. He stood perpendicular to the target, as she had, and placed the arrow on the shaft of the bow at eye level. He

squinted down the spine of the arrow and pulled back the string, trying to ignore the throbbing in his thumb; he'd lost his T-shirt bandage during his climb up the ledge. He was about to release the arrow when he heard her laugh, an extended throaty laugh. He pointed the arrow to the ground, then turned to see what she found so amusing. Was she distracting him to rattle his concentration? She *was* distracting, that was undeniable. Her eyes were now the gray blue of the nearby lake at dusk.

He returned his focus to the target.

She laughed again.

"The last time I did this—" he began.

She did not let him finish. "Then it's fresh in your memory."

It was Thalia's voice, but lower in pitch, more assured, more worldly, if a voice could be such a thing.

He turned back to the target, relaxed his fingers, and released the arrow. Where had it landed? It had not even hit the board.

"You were not *fuckising*," she said, her accent confusing him for a moment.

"No," he said to her, "I was not *focusing*. How did you know to speak to me in English?"

She left his side to gather his errant arrow from the rocks far to the left of the target. How had she seen where it had gone? When she returned, she surprised him by taking his arm and guiding him up the small incline toward the chalet.

Her audacity reminded him of Thalia's dauntless arrival at his and Ambrose's table at the Cabane.

"You haven't answered me," he said, feeling like a petulant child.

"You Americans are so obvious," she said, and laughed. "How could I not hear your exhalations that carried on the wind?" He remembered yelling out as he was throwing himself over the vertical rock face. She covered her ears. "Now all I can hear is your breath! You've walked far today."

She was making fun of him.

"I'll show you your room, so you can change out of your wet clothes. We also need to properly bandage your thumb." Her English was as flawless as her daughters'.

"I am Calliope," she added. "You?"

"With all your listening, it's a wonder you don't know my name. Jim Olsen."

In response she again took his arm, this time more formally, as if they were about to step onto the dance floor. Her body moved smoothly, rhythmically beside him. She led him past a small garden of green vegetables and herbs to the open door of the small chalet. He paused on the threshold to inhale the fragrance of sweet roses and looked up to see, amid the gnarly brown vines, a profusion of pink and white. The bell in the small tower rang in the evening breeze.

"Your daughters . . ." he began.

"Have sent you here to fetch me . . ."

He nodded. He hesitated, his hand fingering the velvet ribbon in his pocket.

She laughed again, and she was the photograph Thalia had showed him, her head tilted back, her hair falling across her eye.

What spell had the mountains cast upon him? Only the night before, he had been ready to consider himself part of the one-death-a day-in-the-Alps statistic.

"My daughters don't realize that I'm at home here," she said, unlocking arms with him. "I'm more at home here than I am anywhere else in the world."

He'd only just met her, but he could tell that it was true: she looked as if she belonged on this threshold of roses. How luminous and rose-colored she was, in contrast to the melancholy blue dusk that beckoned nighttime.

"It looks as if you've been hiking for many days," she said, cocking her head and studying his thumb, "but the Cabane, where I believe you met my daughters, is only half a day's hike away."

Not possible!

"You must have come down the scenic route. Take off your boots. You're limping! Here, sit here." She pointed to the tree stump just outside the door of the chalet. He removed his boots.

"Your socks, too!"

He stretched out his aching and blistered feet and bleeding ankle.

"This chalet looks as if it's from another era," he said,

peering inside at the blackened beams lining the ceiling.

"It's what's left of a Benedictine monastery, I'm guessing from the sixth century. It's amazing that the chalet and the barn have endured since then. I think the Benedictines chose this spot because the land here is unusually fertile for a mountain peak."

Her accented, lilting voice slowed down time. In New York City Jim had learned to talk fast, rush through conversations, finish people's sentences, and wait vigilantly for opportunities to prove his intelligence and superiority. Sarcasm and skepticism won you extra points. But in the presence of this elegant woman in such eternal mountain surroundings, edginess seemed hollow.

Still, he had a flight to catch tomorrow, Wednesday. Walking in circles had cost him a full day. Even if he left with Calliope first thing in the morning, they would only get back to the Cabane by the midday. On Thursday they would arrive in Gstaad; he would leave Calliope on her own and contact the sisters to let them know that their mother was safe from the snows and her husband. He would then catch the afternoon train from Gstaad to Geneva and just maybe make it to the Geneva airport in time for a 6 p.m. flight back to New York. But that was pushing it. Luckily his first day of work was not until Monday. Since his ticket was nonrefundable, he'd have to pay for another full fare back to the States.

"Your anger, your agitation, I can feel it."

"You caught me planning—"

"The pass of perpetual snow." She pointed to the small gap between twin white snowcapped mountains above them. "It's one of the most difficult passes in this part of the world. At any point during the year, there might be seven to eight feet of snow up there, but in the winter the drifts can reach more than forty feet. French and German pilgrims still cross it on their way to Rome. Back in the day, the monks who lived here offered them food, medicine, and rest.

"Come inside, you look like you could use a little of all three. How hungry you are," she added, as if in an afterthought.

He was famished.

INSIDE THE CHALET, SHE WAS ALL MOVEMENT. SHE lit two candles in the dark wooden interior, stirred the contents of a pot hanging by a hook over a fire, stoked the fire, and disappeared somewhere into the darkness at the far end of the room. While she was gone, Jim gazed around in amazement at the chalet's interior. Two copper pots and a pan hung above a wide wooden trough that served as a sink, and a red-and-white checked cloth, similar to the ones in the Cabane des Audannes, covered the small table that was set for two. Thick red napkins had been placed at the center of each pewter plate. Tin cups took the place of glasses. What was the spice in the pot that filled the room with a sweet, earthy aroma?

"You were expecting me for dinner?" he asked when she reappeared.

"Again you're surprised!" As she laughed, the ribbon in her hair fell to the ground and her braid loosened. Jim was quicker to reach the ribbon, and she took it from him playfully. Instead of tying the ribbon around the bottom of her braid, she held it up to her neck and, elbows raised horizontally, tied the ends together.

"Valasian must have told you," he said, but he doubted that the old man had a cell phone or that there was cell service here. Perhaps he'd taken a shortcut and beaten Jim to the chalet to warn her.

Was that music coming from the room where she'd been? He recognized the tinkling bell, but it was accompanied by a low-pitched throbbing sound.

How had she brought all these supplies—the pots, pans, plates, napkins, forks, and tablecloth—to this remote peak? She bent down, lifted a floorboard, dipped her hand into the opening, and removed a dusty black bottle. Holding it, she approached Jim and stared up into his eyes.

"You didn't believe me when I said I heard you coming."

"No," he said.

She closed her eyes as she handed him the bottle.

"Is this wine?" he asked.

She turned from him to tend the fire. Only after a long pause did she answer.

"You may not believe this, either. It's from the Benedic-

tines' stash, possibly left behind a century ago. This is the first time I've filched, but I would call a dispatch in the form of a messenger from my daughters a special occasion."

Jim pulled out the Swiss Army knife that Ambrose had given him at the beginning of their hike and, after several fumbles, managed to pull the cork from the bottle using the tiny corkscrew. He poured black syrup into each tin cup.

"Could use a little opening up," she said, raising the cup to her long, elegant nose. He noticed a slight bump in the middle of it. She laughed, the creases next to her eyes deepening into upside-down crescents. Reflexively, he laughed with her. For this woman, to laugh seemed as easy and thoughtless as taking a breath.

"To the Benedictine monks," he said, raising his glass.

"To your arrival," she said. She smiled over her cup as she sipped. She placed the drink on the table, and without warning, she'd tossed another log onto the fire and returned to stirring the pot. Even when she wasn't moving, she vibrated like a flame dancing in the wind. Like Thalia had.

"Sit down, please," she commanded.

He obeyed and sat down on one of the two tree-stump stools at the table, his knees scraping the top of the log table. He heard the mysterious sound again; again, he tried but failed to place it. A moaning of sorts grew into a chorus of cries, only to fall away to a murmur. The lament arose from the wall on the opposite side of the fireplace.

"What—" he began.

"Tomorrow," she interrupted, "I'll teach you how to shoot an arrow. My falcon, Dalí, and I will."

He remembered Clio's derisory comment to Thalia, that she was always playing a game. Possibly she had inherited this trait from her mother. "Excuse me. Did you say your falcon named Dalí?"

"Doubting Jim, I shall call you. I've been sharing my residence with Dalí and many other fowl friends, mostly owls. They're the ones creating the sounds you are working so desperately to identify," she said, nodding toward the back of the chalet.

Owls? A falcon? Surely she was making it all up. Weren't owls solitary creatures? Would so many owls remain in such close proximity to a human?

Calliope vanished into the back of the chalet again. When she reappeared, she placed a small tube of antibiotic ointment and a bandage on the table. She pulled her tree-stump stool beside his and studied the slice on his thumb. After she gently spread the ointment and secured the bandage over the wound, she smiled triumphantly, as if the wound had healed immediately, thanks to her careful attention.

Back at the fire, she slid her hands into thick red oven mitts, removed the cast-iron pot from the hook over the fire, and, arms wilting under its weight, placed it on the small table. Her face—how quickly its expression changed—grew serious as she lifted the lid under his nose. He closed his eyes;

the steaming scent was of fish and the unidentified sweet herb, perhaps licorice or anise. When he opened his eyes, she was ladling brown fish, carrots, tomatoes, and thinly scalloped potatoes onto his pewter plate.

"What kind of—"

"Brown trout. The lake is full of them. I shoot them, and Dalí plucks them from the water."

Alpine Disney. Before he could tell her that he knew she was joking, he noticed his hostess bowing her head. When she looked up, her eyes were glistening. The glow of candlelight rippled around her face.

She lifted her fork and brought a piece of fish to his lips.

"It was a beautiful fish, shiny and full of zest," she said sadly.

The fish melted in Jim's mouth; the potatoes tasted of sage—and anise, he decided, was the herb. Everything smelled so fresh, as of wildflowers.

Jim tasted the wine. It was heavy with resin, very acidic and faintly sweet.

"Dense, isn't it? Hmm," she said. "It tastes faintly like blood."

The same thought had crossed his mind.

The flames from the candles wavered, and Jim felt a cold draft on the back of his neck. He touched the velvet ribbon in his pocket.

"Three beautiful women asked me to convince their mother to leave the mountains before the snows," he said.

A gust of wind from the direction of the door extinguished the candles and left them in semidarkness. He rose

to take the tapers to the fire to light them, but she placed her hand on his arm and shook her head.

"Our last candles. We don't need them when we have this fire."

He heard the bell tinkling outside and felt more cool air funnel into the room.

"Anyway, I find candlelight a little sad," she said.

A melancholic *whooooo whooooo, hooooot, hooooot* from the wall behind the fireplace punctuated her words.

Sally loved candlelight, but only with the lights on. He was always turning off the lights, and she would turn them back on. "Why do people not want to see everything they can?" she would ask.

He strained to see Calliope's expression.

"The owls sense you," she said. "They're louder tonight than normal; they'll leave soon."

"For the night or for the season or forever?" Jim was not certain he spoke the words aloud. After the day's hike, the frigid swim, the perilous rock climbing, the filling trout stew, the Benedictine brew, and the dim light, he'd begun to feel groggy. What if Calliope had drugged him?

"Which wars were raging the last time someone sipped this wine?" he asked so he would stay awake. He swirled and peered at the viscous black liquid in his cup.

"Everyone thinks the Alps are peaceful, but for centuries these mountain peaks have echoed with gunshot exchanges between the Oberland beer-drinking northerners and the southern vineyard owners."

"In peaceful Switzerland?"

"In your tranquil Switzerland, haven't you heard the life-choking sounds of a helicopter penetrating our hours of light?"

He moved quickly to change the subject.

"I was lucky to have met Valasian."

"How *fonny*!" she said, suddenly laughing.

"What's so *fonny*?" he said, feeling himself the subject of derision. He remembered how Thalia had pronounced *funny* as *finny*.

"You believe in luck!" she said, a smile on her lips as she dipped her fork into the stew.

"Excuse me?" he said.

"Luck," she said. "*La chance. La fortune.* A primitive concept, *non*? But one moment—where is Dalí?" she called out. She jumped up from the table, opened the door, and peered outside. The cold air startled Jim awake.

"I can't see anything: no sun, no moon, no Dalí. My fierce and noble hunter has left today: I feel it in my bones. Au revoir, *mon* Dalí," she called into the blackness.

"Luck," she said, returning to her stool and leaning across the table as if she were confiding a secret, "is the religion of a man without imagination."

Could there be anything worse?

"For example," she said, standing and retrieving something from the darkness. She bent over the table. "Did luck bring you this?"

In the dim light, he could make out a small basket con-

taining what looked like half a baguette and three rounds of cheese.

"Your daughters think you're starving," he said.

"They should know their maman by now," she said. "Try this one." She pointed to one of the cheeses.

It melted in his mouth like butter yet had a sharp, tangy bite.

"Chèvre from the farm in the adjacent valley, and, of course, the ever-present Emmentaler, and an Alpkäse. Gabriel brings it from his mother's pantry once a week."

"Gabriel?" He knew it: her Alpine lover . . .

"My friend, a fifteen-year-old goatherd."

"And in the winter, your friend returns to the valley? Are you aware that there are warnings of an early snow—"

"Up there, yes." The flame from the fire sparked, and in that moment he noticed her dainty chin pointing upward. "At the Col des Sybelles and the Col du Brochet. Instead of hollyhocks budding for the last time, as they are in my garden now, at those passes the crystals are compounding— large and lustrous crystals, more faceted than any diamond. At certain times of year, crystals fall from the clouds—and in different colors."

She leaned her elbow on the table, rested her knuckles against her chin. "I witnessed it once with my *grand-père*. We called it *rainbow snow*, a snowstorm caught in a rainbow. I don't think I've ever seen anything more beautiful: red, blue, green, yellow jewels dropping from the sky, some as big as a pea"—she made a small oval with her forefinger and

thumb—"some as small as a fleck of gold." She pinched her finger and thumb together. "It was as if nature was having hallucinations. On second thought, it was like witnessing nature while she's dreaming."

"Sounds like the first sign of hypothermia."

"Did *you* grow up in the Alps, monsieur the expert?"

Without waiting for a reply, she rose from the table. Did she ever sit still?

"I have something very special for you that you must tell my daughters about, something I've been conjuring all afternoon. Please don't move, not an inch. I wonder if you'll also consider *this* to be luck!"

It was too dark in the chalet to see where she'd gone. If he completed his mission tomorrow, she, not he, would be describing this night to Thalia, Clio, and Helene. He would be on a flight back to New York. But even if they left early and hiked to Gstaad by the end of the day, even then it would be pushing it to catch a flight out of Geneva by tomorrow night. He would have to pay full fare for another flight on Thursday.

The last embers of fire illuminated what looked like a glaze of frost in the far corner of the chalet. He threw another log from the small pile in the corner onto the dying flames and listened to the residents hooting. This little chalet would be an icebox before long.

Ice house. His grandfather Ocean Olsen had once been locked in one back in Norway, the Old Country—or at least that was the story he'd told his impressionable

six-year-old grandson. He was found blue and frozen, all but his eyeballs. They were able to save him, hot-blooded Viking that he was, but the picture in Jim's mind of moist blue eyeballs in a frozen blue body had remained with him all these years. Grandfather Ocean's family had hauled in a good income exporting ice to England, but his grandfather left that and the fjords behind when he immigrated to the New Country. What he had kept and passed on to Jim were his descriptions of the vast Norwegian mountain cliffs, valleys and fjords.

This, Jim decided, *this* was his heritage: craggy mountain peaks, lakes that floated on the top of the world—not the flat plains of Illinois. No wonder he felt more alive here. On the perilous cliffs of his trek earlier that day, he'd felt as if the sky had held him up by the back of his shirt and suspended him in the blue light.

Where had Diana the Huntress gone?

"*Et voilà,*" he heard as she glided back into earshot. She'd been away so long that the room had lost its luster. She placed before Jim a pewter plate bearing what looked like a white model of an archipelago.

"*Île flottante,*" she announced as she took her seat and pushed the islands around with her fork.

"How did you—" he began.

"Don't inquire," she said, and the *q* seemed stuck on her tongue. "It's also called *oeufs à la neige*. Eggs in the snow, which might be more appropos," she added as she hopped up and stoked the fire.

He closed his eyes as he tasted the soft custard with the stiff, honeyed meringue crust. He had never tasted anything like this soft, sweet melting on his tongue. Like snow.

She laughed when she returned to the table. "You have a dollop on the tip of your nose!" She tapped his nose gently, and he joined in her laughter.

They ate the remainder of the melting islands without speaking. He listened to the bass notes from the owls, the occasional clanging of the bell in the tower, and the high-pitched whisperings of the wind outside.

"Before you sleep," she said finally, rising from the table and taking his plate, "I'll introduce you to your bedfellows."

"I thought we were alone," he said.

She threw back her head to laugh once more, and her eyes shone in the darkness. Helene, yes, Helene had the same laugh.

"You are *fonny*, Jim Olsen! One is *never* entirely alone," she said. "Follow me." She bent over the small, crackling fire and lit the candle stub.

He stood and could hardly lift his legs to walk. Calliope of the Wildhorn *had* drugged him, with her wine dregs and perfumed eggs in snow.

All the better, he thought as he followed her into the barn that was attached to the chalet.

AT FIRST GLANCE, IN THE LIGHT OF THE CANDLE, HE counted twelve of them: twelve sets of blinking yellow-orange eyes; twelve gray-and-beige feathered bodies with

heart-shaped white faces. Most were perched on a beam near the ceiling of the barn, and some were in the rafters.

As they entered, a large owl flew silently out the open door at the end of the room. *Whoosh*. Its wingspan must have been five or six feet. Another fluttered its feathered wings as if it were compressing and expanding the bellows of an accordion. Rotating its head, it blinked down at them. Jim could make out a few smaller owls in the corner, roosting on thick nests of hay. This room was warmer than the firelit room in which they had eaten dinner; Jim noticed that the gaps in the logs that formed the walls had been stuffed with hay.

What a sound! An orchestra of low, muted exhalations— soft, rounded, sweet, muffled, measured, and tinged with indescribable melancholy.

"They own this place," she whispered. "They allow me to take up residence here."

"How about in the winter?"

"They'll leave soon. Can't you feel it? I worry about the little ones."

"Unlike you," he said, "they don't believe that summer will last forever."

She disregarded his words and stepped farther into the barn.

"I thought owls were solitary birds," he whispered, stepping beside her.

"I did, too," she said in a low voice close to his ear. "In my time here, I've learned that they're monogamous crea-

tures. If their mate dies, they'll die faster than they would from starvation or dehydration. Like us, they also communicate with facial expressions. Look over there."

She lifted her candle to the corner. Four smaller owlets ruffled their feathers; their round blinking eyes looked accusingly at the intruders.

"A late brood. I'm guessing that's why this group has stayed here so late in the season. I've named the owlets: Hildegarde, Catherine of Siena, and Teresa of Ávila. Oh, yes, and then there is Hamlet, the smallest of all. Stop staring, Jim: you've made Teresa freeze and compress her feathers so she looks like a tree branch. Yes, Teresa, a man is in our midst, sent by my daughters to take me away."

She raised the candle and met his eyes as if to challenge him. He did his best to match her look: defiant and deeply knowing. She returned her gaze to the owlets.

"I hope they forgive me for naming them. They have such different personalities. I've recorded their behavior in a journal . . ." How he loved the way she pronounced that word, *j-our-nal*, the *o* and the *u* intimately touching, grazing each other.

"Just as my *grand-père* taught me," she continued. "Like a good ornithologist, I record their habits, their flight patterns, their relationships."

Another of the larger owls flew out the open barn door. Its flight was noiseless and weightless, like snow falling in late spring.

"Called to the night hunt," she murmured.

They heard a sharp shriek and lifted their heads to the owl on the beam above them.

"That is Hrotsvitha," she whispered. "The name in Saxon means 'strong voice.' Hrotsvitha was a tenth-century dramatist who wrote plays about powerful women. Yes, Hrotsvitha, this is our guest for the night. Most of the owls will be gone all night and will return only at dawn. Hrotsvitha, why are you still here? The big men are gone. The rest usually wait for her to go, and then they follow."

Hrotsvitha raised her feathers, snapped her bill, and shrieked again. One by one—whether because of the human disturbance or the direction of the tenth-century-dramatist owl, or because the perfect moment of velvet darkness had arrived outside—they departed, ten owls swooping above them out the large barn door into the night. All except the four smaller owls in their straw nest.

"I'll miss them when they're gone for the winter," she said.

Jim was about to protest that she would not be here in the winter, either, that they were leaving together in the morning, but he suddenly didn't have the strength.

Calliope closed the barn door softly behind them.

"Your room is here," she said as they retraced their steps into the small chalet. He could tell that the room she offered him was hers. On the bed, composed of neatly stacked hay, a sheet was drawn; a comforter decorated with pink flowers was rolled at the bottom. A round of hay served as a bedside table. He spied some books on it, but in the faint light of

the candle he could not make out the titles. A small, square, paneless window, through which cold air blew into the room, had been cut crudely from the log wall. In the candlelight he noticed curtains nailed to the top of the window and tied in bows with the telltale maroon velvet ribbon.

"And you will sleep . . . ?" he asked.

"Your outhouse is the mountainside." She disappeared without a sound, like the owls into the darkness.

He undressed, dove under the comforter, and was asleep before he could take notice of the sounds from the baby owls in the barn nearby; before he could think about the ribbon around Thalia's neck, then around her mother's; before he could imagine what Sally was doing that night in New York City; before he could picture his grandfather in the fjords of Svalbard, sailing around the white archipelago that looked like the floating-islands dessert; before he could wonder if this woman of the mountains had drugged him with the hundred-year-old wine of the Benedictines or if, with her clear blue eyes and her voice like the silver streams of the mountains, she had awoken in him a sense that life could offer more than he had ever thought possible.

SEVEN

BEEKEEPING

HE HEARD SINGING, THEN THE CHORUS OF HOOT-ing. From the small opening that served as a window, a soft rosy light filtered into the room. Jim's eyes were drawn to the half-moon in the sky, lightly outlined with what looked like a halo.

He could not understand the lyrics, but Calliope's singing voice was like smoke filling the room slowly, changing the air around him. As he lay under the comforter, which was so light it defied the laws of gravity, he recalled the dream that had been so vivid moments before. He'd been kissing his ex-fiancée in a cave, and as they kissed, as many bats flew out of the cave as there were stars in the night sky. An infinity of bats, one darting after another, so that the sky was black with them. Then Calliope entered the cave, and

like a sorceress she touched one of the bats, and all the bats changed into butterflies.

The melodic singing drew closer but was interrupted by a long, drawn-out cough. Jim had not noticed her coughing yesterday. He looked out the window. She was hanging laundry—sheets, lingerie, a long white nightgown—on a clothesline. Her slim body weaved in and out of the laundry, so that he could never see more than a part of her at any time.

He found his clothes, folded and warmed from the sun, outside his room next to his knapsack. He dressed, and on his way out of the room stopped to look at the two books on the bedside table. One was a tattered hardcover titled *The Cloud of Unknowing*; the other a coffee table book, *La dame à la licorne*, showed a photograph of a medieval tapestry depicting a maiden framed by the unicorn on one side and the lion on the other.

He could not resist returning to the window for one more glimpse of Calliope's dance among the billowing sheets and clothing. She looked like a woman at sea amid the sails of a ship. She wore the same riding pants, long boots, and T-shirt as the day before, but the morning was warm enough for her to leave off her vest.

"May I carry your basket?" He sprang up to surprise her.

"Yes," she said, not looking at him but handing him the basket as if she had been aware of his presence from the moment he stepped outside. He followed her and the strong scent of roses into the house.

"Place it there. We'll take care of it later, as now we're going beekeeping." She said this as if she were singing a nursery rhyme. His stomach growled, but he ignored it.

"It involves a short walk. Afterward"—she coughed discreetly into her elbow—"we'll have breakfast."

"You have a cold," Jim said. "We have to—"

"A change-of-season cough," she interrupted him and laughed, her hair falling across her eye. "Let's go, Mr. Man-with-a-Mission."

He grabbed his boots.

"No boots for you," she said.

"I will help you pack up—"

When he looked up, she was running ahead of him down the hill toward the lake. He rushed to catch up with her. The meadow grass was surprisingly soft beneath his feet.

"I suppose our packing up will have to wait," he said, breathless, when he caught up to her. "May I?"

In the crook of her arm she carried a tin bucket with trays, a large fork, and a wooden spoon.

She smiled up at him as she handed him the bucket.

"The Benedictines," she said as they walked side by side, "left these tools and the framed hive. All I had to do was entice a swarm to start living here in early summer. Rubbing beeswax inside a hive will attract a queen. Et voilà, one fell for the trick. She's been quite prolific, even now, into the fall. Have you ever seen a swarm of bees? It's like in the cartoons, this bubble of black. If you're careful and if you

remember that slowness is genius, you can stick your hand in the middle and you won't be touched."

She cupped her hands to the small trickling waterfall to their right and raised them to his lips. The water was cold and refreshing and smelled of her roses.

"In the old days, they used smoke to distract the bees while the beekeepers removed the honey. The smoke calms the bees and masks the alarm pheromones released by the guard bees, but in the end the confusion caused by the smoke takes a toll on honey production."

He spotted a few bees in the distance.

"Those are the drone spies, alerting the queen of our presence. The queen is inseminated about this high in the air." She stretched her arm above her head. "This ensures that only the fastest and strongest can pass on the best genes. If she can help it, nature never settles for second best."

A short walk from the waterfall near a cliff side at the edge of the lake, she turned to him, lifted a white gauze veil from the bucket, and placed it over her head, then pulled on man-size, camel colored leather gloves that covered her arms up to her elbows. Jim scanned the horizon for a hive and saw, nestled into the mountain about twenty feet away, an indentation and the swarming of hundreds of bees.

"Stay here," she whispered to him. He lost sight of her white veil in the swarming blackness. A few times he saw her arms moving, as gracefully and slowly as if she were a dancer in *Swan Lake*. How was it possible that the bees did

not detect her presence? The dance of the beekeeper, the prowl of a tiger on a night watch, the glide of a spider along its web. She hummed a melody.

She returned carrying a rectangular wooden tray draped with honeycombs. In her veil she looked like a priestess, and he thought of the hermitess. Some drones hovered around the top of her veiled head; it was as if she wore a crown of bees.

She nodded at the bucket, and he brought it to her. Using a flat metal tool, she scraped the combs off the wooden frame and into the bucket.

"We'll have fresh honey for breakfast," she said as she removed her gloves. "Our queen has had a fertile summer. Did you know she can lay half a million eggs in her lifetime of three years? And we humans think we are productive!"

She offered him her gloves.

His look was a question.

"Your job is to return the tray into the slot. The secret is patience and fearlessness, and moving as slowly and guile-lessly as the moon rising in the night sky. I will coach you as you go."

He bent down as she placed the veil over his head.

"Slower!" she called to him as he moved toward the black swarm.

"Feel around the inside of the recess in the rock face," she directed from afar. "For the place where the tray fits. Do you feel it?"

"No," he said as calmly as he could. It was hot under

the veil, and bees were bumping into and around his veiled head, his eyes, his nose, and mouth; the buzzing made him feel claustrophobic. A few bees that had penetrated inside the veil tickled his eyelashes; one was perched on the tip of his nose. He wasn't breathing. He felt a drip of perspiration along his cheek. It stopped at his jawline.

"Close your eyes," he heard Calliope say, her voice a melody above the din of buzzing bees. She was beside him without a veil, the bees covering her: she was black with bees. He obeyed. He pushed his hand inside the hollow space and felt a sharp angle that he identified as the slot.

"Slide the tray onto the slot very slowly, like you would a baking tray into an oven," she said. He'd never slid a baking tray into an oven, but he had seen his mother do so, roughly, impatiently.

"Keep your eyes closed," she murmured.

The buzzing was so loud and intense. The bees were in his ears and eyes as he placed the tray on the track. Weren't they supposed to be *outside* the veil? Perspiration trickled down his neck and collarbone. Everything was tickling, moving on his skin. As he removed his hand from the slot in slow motion, a bee flew into his glove. When it stung his hand, he jerked his arm back. Pressure bore down on his arm, and he felt burning up to his shoulder.

"Fire in the house," she said calmly.

She took his gloved hand and retreated a few yards with him in a slow dance. If there had been an ax in the bee-keeping basket that he glimpsed near his feet, he would have

used it to amputate his arm. The searing pain! Her fingers were like spiders speeding up his arm to catch prey. She removed the glove from his burning hand and arm and gently brushed away the bees. A thousand knives stabbed his hand, wrist, arm, and shoulder. He felt light-headed, and his knees buckled. She caught him just before he fell and helped him slowly to the ground.

"Taste this," she said.

She placed a wooden spoonful of honeycomb into his mouth. He sucked the honey. The sweetness was like a jolt of caffeine. His skin tingled, and he no longer felt faint. As Calliope bent over him and began to pluck the stingers from his arm, he again noticed the delicate bump in the bridge of her nose.

"Do they die after they sting you?" he asked, hoping Calliope's voice would distract him from the pain. She shook her head, coughed into her elbow, and, with the wooden spoon, covered his reddening, ballooning hand, arm, and shoulder with the sticky honey.

"Now you'll feed me to a bear," he said.

She did not laugh. She made a sling of the white veil and tied it around his shoulder. His hand had doubled in size; he must have been stung at least fifty times.

"Are you still in pain?"

"No," he said, though he winced from the burning sensation.

She knelt so close to him, he could feel her breath on his cheek.

"You're still in agony," she said, "yet you say the pain is gone. Why?"

She searched for something in his eyes. Tiny beads of perspiration collected above her lips.

"You don't have to do that with me," she said. "No, you mustn't do that with me." She covered her mouth with her hand as she coughed again.

She helped him to his feet and led him by his other arm to a bend in the mountain path, where an outcropping of rocks lay beside a trickling waterfall. She cupped her hands in the water and brought them to his lips.

"It's tempting to cool the burning with cold water, but we need to keep this honey on your arm," she said. "Today you've received an excellent dose of the inoculation. Good beekeepers should be stung at least twice a season, but now you are many seasons ahead."

Seasons . . . How would he ever convince this queen bee to leave her sunlit hive?

"This afternoon, after breakfast, you and I will be leaving," he said. "Your daughters—"

She cut him off. "Ah, Gabriel!"

IN THE DISTANCE A HEAD BOBBED ALONG THE MOUNtain ridge below them, then disappeared. When the figure finally emerged in full view, Jim saw that he was a young boy of about fifteen, that in-between age when the body has not yet caught up to the size of the hands and feet. He

had thick eyebrows, small brown eyes, and a wide nose that looked as if it had been broken. Everything about the youth looked like it was going to burst. His shirt was uncomfortably tight under his arms; his pants were too short. Stubble protruded from his large chin. A shock of black hair fell over one eye, and he didn't bother shaking it aside. He had a bag slung over his shoulder.

"Not only are your daughters convinced that you have no food, but they also think you're entirely alone in these Alps," Jim said.

"Gabriel!" Calliope greeted the boy, smiling and kissing him on both cheeks as he embraced her. Gabriel's darting eyes rested on Jim and his sling. Jim felt the boy's curiosity, then distrust, then anger in quick succession. He did not hide his feelings well.

"Gabriel, voilà Jim." He loved how she said his name.

Gabriel spoke to Calliope in a gruff voice, refusing to look at Jim.

"He wants to know if you're staying with me. Gabriel's family owns the farm below the lake."

It looked like Gabriel would slug Jim, bee-stung arm and all.

"No, Gabriel, I won't leave with him!" Calliope said slowly. "I'm trying to teach him English," she said to Jim.

Gabriel grabbed the honey-dripping wooden spoon and the bucket as if this were his daily chore. He rushed ahead of them and jumped from rock to rock along the mountain path toward the chalet.

"The voices of the river are so loud today," she said to Jim as they passed a gurgling stream. She looked at him with her sparkling eyes. "What's the river saying to you?"

"The river," Jim said as he paused to gaze into it, "is saying very clearly, 'Jump IN!'" Which he did. How soothing was the numbing-cold mountain water on his still-throbbing arm, and how liberating it felt to follow an impulse!

She laughed as she and now Gabriel, who had doubled back, watched Jim swim in his clothes against the strong current that pushed him from the center. Above him on the ridge, Calliope began to sing, and Gabriel joined her and belted out the refrain in his cracking voice.

> L'amour est enfant de bohème,
> Si tu ne m'aimes pas, je t'aime
> Mais si je t'aime, prends garde à toi
> Si tu ne m'aimes pas,
> Si tu ne m'aimes pas, je t'aime
> Mais si je t'aime, si je t'aime,
> Prends garde à toi!

The part of the song that Jim understood went something like: "If you don't love me, I love you, but if I love you, if I love you, watch out!"

He lifted himself onto the riverbank and with his good hand, wrung the water from the bottom of his shirt and pants.

"Your swim has cost us much honey," she said from the

overhang above the stream, where she and Gabriel sat with their legs dangling.

She took the bucket from Gabriel and carried it to where Jim stood. "While I reapply your honey balm, let's hear *your* song."

First archery, then beekeeping, now singing? Was he, like Hercules, required to use skill, talent, and ingenuity to prove his worthiness? Would she then consent to accompany him down the mountain? Or was she baiting him solely for her amusement?

"I don't sing."

"Did you just say you don't sing?"

She tilted her head so her hair fell over her eyebrow, the way it did in the photograph the sisters had given him, and then translated for Gabriel. Gabriel laughed, and she laughed, too.

"You say that as if it's a religion," she said, coughing and laughing again.

"Laugh all you want," he said. "I haven't practiced since elementary school."

She threw up her hands and laughed again. "Does one need practice to look out of one's eyes?" she said.

Addressing the sky, she asked, "*What* have you sent my way?"

As a young boy, Jim had participated in the school chorus; he sang in the shower, where his voice sounded good and where his mother or sister couldn't hear him or

tell him to stop. During school plays he volunteered for the offstage jobs, stage manager and lighting technician. Grateful to remain in the dark, he enjoyed guiding and shining the lights over the faces of the kids who were the stars. And here was Gabriel, in full adolescence, belting it out, despite the fact that his off-pitch voice cracked over and over again.

"Does no one sing where you come from?" she asked.

Neither she nor Gabriel heard his response, as the two were scampering up the mountain toward the chalet. He followed them through a sunburst of white flowers that he hadn't noticed earlier. He heard her cough again and realized that he'd been listening for it, registering its frequency and depth. He would use her illness as a reason for them to depart the following morning. He had already missed his flight that day, and it was too beautiful to leave.

EIGHT

TELL ME YOUR STORY

THAT AFTERNOON, WITH HIS BACK TO THE WARM
Alpine sun, Jim plucked weeds from the soil of the thriving
vegetable garden of Calliope Castellane.

"*Pas mal*, not bad," she said, standing over him and cup-
ping a tomato with her palm. "We'll have a *dîner magnifique*
tonight. But first, a swim."

She was calling to him and laughing and throwing off
her clothing as she darted ahead like a deer down the hillock. Her white shirt whipped Jim in the face; then came her
riding pants, then her black-and-pink lacy underwear, all
smelling of lavender. Her undressing was as natural as water
flowing down a riverbed. Her skin was a pigment in the natural landscape, tanned an even gold. Jim collected what fell

in his path as he ran behind this woman, now wearing only her boots, the laces flying behind.

When he reached the lake, she was in the shimmering ripples, beckoning him in. He removed his clothes and walked gingerly among the sharp rocks lining the lake. How had she maneuvered such terrain so quickly? She dove and resurfaced like a seal and appeared at his side, and guided him to a sandy path into the lake. The frigid water soothed the itching that he now experienced instead of pain on his hand, arm, and lower shoulder.

"Doesn't it feel divine?" she said, her face bright above the shimmering.

"Yes," he said. "Your lips are blue."

"So are yours," she said, laughing and diving again.

When he could no longer feel his extremities, Jim swam to the shore and called to her to dry off with him. When she finally emerged, he found himself unable to look away. *Thalia's mother*, he repeated to himself, as if in reminder. In the bright sun, her slim, tanned body looked half of her forty-nine years. When he offered her her shirt, he noticed that she was trembling from head to toe and her teeth were chattering.

Instead of putting on the shirt, she carried it to a flat granite slab and lay down in the sun, as if taking her place on a towel at a beach. Jim lay beside her. The sun felt like it had weight.

"Jim," she said, propping herself up on her elbow and then coughing into her hand.

"Yes?"

"Now is a good time for you to tell me your story."

"What story?"

"*Your* story, of course," she said. "Of who you are."

"No," he said.

She sat up, hugged her knees, and looked at him as if in wonder, then laughed. Her nudity was as natural and easy as the wildflowers in the field nearby. Sally turned away every time she undressed, as if he might be disappointed by what he glimpsed. But Sally had a beautiful body! What was it that made a person modest? Calliope was as free as anyone he'd ever met. Her freedom was inspiring. He followed her eyes to gaze into the endless blue sky.

"Your story," she said.

"Why do you need my story when we're in your fairy tale?"

She turned quickly to look at him, her eyes narrowed.

"Where Calliope," he continued, "doesn't have a cough, and she'll reside in the Alps for a summertime that extends into a year. You *do* know that snow is predicted, and that we're leaving tomorrow morning."

She laughed. "Give me another name if I'm in your fairy tale . . ."

"Calliope is perfect," he said.

"No, it isn't!" She leaned back on her hands. "I reject it. Calliope the muse, or rather the concubine—"

"Inspiring people is a gift—"

"Not a gift: a curse! I'm wilting under the weight of others' egos. My childhood bedroom at Bellerevoir was covered wall-to-wall in murals of the nine Greek muses. Those paintings now hang in the corridors of our house in Paris. When my daughters were born, I named them after muses: Clio, muse of history—and how amusing, she's a natural historian. She still prefers history books to any other kind. Thalia, the muse of comedy—et voilà, she's my outspoken actor, though more dramatic than comedic. And Helene: Helene is the muse of centuries, of course, the woman who inspired the Trojan War. How I regret their names! I wish I'd named Helene Eleanor, after the most powerful woman in the High Middle Ages, queen consort for more than fifty years. Yes, Helene would be fit for such a part."

She coughed and looked as if she would cry.

"You've distracted me with me. Nice job, Monsieur Jim. Now tell me your story, so I can properly name you!" she said.

"Only if you accompany me back to the Cabane tomorrow morning," he said.

She closed her eyes and did not speak for some time.

"Perhaps," she finally said, "if you tell your story, I'll consider doing what you wish."

A weakening in her resolve . . .

"We'll leave tomorrow morning."

"Your story!"

"It's not much of a story," he began, "even if I speak in the presence of a muse."

She did not respond. She could have been sleeping; she was that still.

"I left my family at eighteen when I went to college, hoping never to return. I went to business school, worked in the summers at an investment bank with few opportunities to see the light of day, was hired by the same investment bank after I graduated, worked in the investment bank for six years with few opportunities to see the light of day, climbed my way up the ladder to managing director, was planning to marry a woman whom I loved and who I thought loved me, was fired from my job during the recession because I was dispensable when I had thought I'd been indispensable, and was fired by my fiancée, who found me dispensable as well. Then I found another job, less money, lower rank, that starts next Monday, which is why I have to leave tomorrow morning, no matter what, and with you. Et voilà, as you would say, that's my story."

She frowned and reached for her shirt.

He'd disappointed her. From her shirt pocket, she plucked out what looked like a fluffy ball of cotton.

"I collected these owl feathers this morning," Calliope said, holding them out to show him. "I knew they'd be useful, but I didn't know for what. Watch this."

She rolled the feathers into two balls and pushed them into her ears.

"I can't hear. *Now* tell me your story."

He squinted and watched a cloud pass quickly, high above.

"I have all day," she said.

"I was born—"

"Everyone who tells a story is born!"

"I thought you couldn't hear."

"I could hear *that*. I can't hear much, though."

"I was born in Illinois," he persisted.

"I should wear these all the time," she said languidly, touching the white feather balls. "My hearing is too acute."

She coughed into her arm.

"Okay, I'll make it easier," she said. "Tell me who *I* am."

"I don't know who you are."

She sighed dramatically. He was a worthless adversary.

"You're compelling, intriguing," he began. "You're fully alive. Fully aware of your surroundings, though not of the coming snows . . ."

He felt like a poacher as he stole a glance at her. She was in rhythm with everything around her: her inhalations were the passing of the clouds overhead, her skin the movement of the wind rippling on the surface of the lake. The sun made her eyelashes look golden. He spied a drop of water on her chin.

"When I met you," he said, looking up at the sky, "it was as if my boat had capsized, and I'd hit freezing water. I slipped into an unknown world and stopped breathing." He thought of his waterfall dousing with Valasian. "But then,

as if by a miracle, I popped up and gulped the fresh, watery air."

"Your story begins," she said, smiling.

AND THEN SUDDENLY THERE IT WAS: THE RUMBLING. The slicing. The buzzing.

"Let's go," she said, standing, coughing into her arm. She struggled into her shirt and ran along the rocks to the place where they'd discarded their clothes and boots. He would never get used to the speed at which she did things, her lightness.

She perched on a rock ledge and was dressed in seconds. It seemed as if she were always waiting for him, waiting for him to understand, for him to follow her, to wake up, to sing, to tell a story, now to pick his way among the sharp rocks to where she stood. They raced past the waterfall up the hill, through the freshly weeded garden, into the shadow of the chalet; the chopper rounded the mountain peak above the lake just as they dashed inside.

"Your husband?"

"His pilots."

"How can they *not* suspect this charming little chalet, with its orange pom-pom curtains in the windows and your telltale ribbons?"

"It's tough to land anywhere around it . . ." she said, breathing heavily and then coughing into her elbow.

From the covered doorway of the chalet, they watched the chopper approach.

"They've tried to land on my stargazing rock over there, but it's not big enough—here, take this basket—and there's a seven-hundred-foot drop on the other side. Those clever Benedictines, finding this insurmountable peak . . ."

"But the lake—"

"To land on the lake would be challenging for even the best pilots." She led him into the garden. "The mountain juts out there, can you see?" she said.

"Yes. Why can't you convince your husband to leave you alone—"

"You don't know him." The copter veered to the west. "Their daily hour-long search is over." She sighed. "They're returning to their master, like puppets on a string. How well I know their drill."

The buzzing of the helicopter waned in the distance. She walked into the garden, knelt, and peeked under a thick undergrowth of leaves. She pulled one, then another shiny purple eggplant from the vine. He carried the basket to her.

She looked up at him with brimming eyes. "We'll have ratatouille tonight."

She dipped from plant to plant, filling the basket with ripe tomatoes and zucchinis. He helped her pull beans from a vine strung up on hooks along the wall of the barn. On the way inside the chalet, she stopped at the rose-decorated threshold. The clouds had passed from her brow.

Nothing could interrupt this gentle, unassailably lovely moment.

For some reason, he bowed. The last time he bowed might have been to a dancing partner—no doubt taller than he, late bloomer that he was—at the dreaded Miss Marsh's Dancing School, where his mother circled the dance floor, inspecting manners.

In response, Calliope curtsied.

NINE

THE SEARCH PARTY

IT STARTED AS A PURR, LIKE THAT OF A LARGE CAT, then swelled to a lion's roar. Jim was sifting the residue from the honeycomb when she ran up to him, clutching her wooden spoon stained red with ratatouille. Calliope had been wrong. The search party had not called off its pursuit for the day. Perhaps the pilots had spotted them running along the lakeshore. The grinding sounds from the rotor blades intensified as they watched the copter make a beeline for them.

"The lake! They've returned, with an amphibious helicopter. They must have seen us. Quick. Stamp out the fire. I'll hide our ratatouille. About a mile up, there's a cave from which we can watch them." She turned, spoon still in hand. With her other hand, she lifted from a corner of the room

a hammer and a bunch of long, thick nails. "Board up the front door with these. We'll leave by the barn door."

She was the general, a tactician who had been planning her exit strategy for months.

"Leave the owlery open."

The green-and-gray chopper, a spotlight at its tail, hovered over the lake. Jim stamped on the fire and covered the last embers with a thick gray blanket that she threw to him. She hid the pot of ratatouille under the floorboards in the place where she'd found the Benedictines' wine.

"Meet you in the garden," she said, darting into the barn.

Jim quickly boarded up the chalet door, as instructed. In the garden he found Calliope throwing her bow and quiver of arrows onto her back. She carried an owlet in the palm of her hand.

"He was the only one left! 'Amlet. Allez!" she yelled over the stuttering of the helicopter.

At first he thought she'd named the baby owl Amulet, for protection or good luck. But after she repeated the name again, he remembered that she'd named the feathery ball in her palm after Shakespeare's Danish king.

They sprinted into the open and down a path to the edge of a forest. They passed a sea of wildflowers, a sheet of colors that he would not have imagined possible. Earthbound rainbows.

Once they'd doubled back to reach a higher path, they were sheltered by the shadow of the forest. Her bow and small pouch of arrows swung back and forth on her narrow

back. In the green sweater that she had thrown on before their departure, her beige pocketed vest, her loden green riding pants, and her boots, she could have been mistaken for Robin Hood.

An eerie silence fell. They peered out from the edge where the forest ended.

"I preferred the noise," she whispered.

He heard the muffled sound of Hamlet's hooting in the pocket of her vest.

They approached a slick rock face. "The risk is that there's only one way to get up and down. If they find us, we'll be cornered. But the cave is dark and deep, and it stinks of rotting. These men won't have the stomach for it."

The mountain face was steep and disfigured with indentations and crevices, so toe- and fingerholds were easy to find. He followed the sound of Calliope's coughing above him. Once he'd climbed to the flat surface above, he saw her leaping over what looked like a wide chasm. She hadn't stopped to pause, as he did now, at its edge. Calliope took risks like a person with nothing to lose. He planned his jump with more calculation.

"I see them." She was out of breath when he joined her at the edge of the cave. From her quiver of arrows, she pulled out her canister of water. With an eyedropper, she satisfied the restless and mewing owlet. An eyedropper!

"Over there," she said, nodding her head in dismay at the two men who were climbing the hill toward the chalet in the distance.

"They're pulling the boards off the door. You could have done a better job, eh? They'll see my curtains, my ribbons, the preparations for dinner. They'll take photographs; my husband will know then, for sure." She turned her face away to muffle a cough in her elbow.

"It was such a lovely place to live." Her face was transformed in sadness, her youth stolen.

"We were leaving tomorrow morning anyway, remember? No matter what, it would have been impossible to weather the winter up here."

"Please don't say the word *impossible*. 'In Français, impossible is not possible.' An old French adage. How can you talk about winter when my head is swimming with wildflowers? Have you ever seen so many?"

Like a wilted wildflower refreshed by the lightest rain, she sprang back to life.

"Early September in the mountains," she added, sighing, "is the season when Earth has won, and the award is this massive garland of congratulations."

"Look," he said, pointing.

The men were skirting the border of the chalet. As she predicted, they were taking photographs and barking into radios.

"After they leave, we'll gather our things and hike to Anzère," she said. "It's a darling Swiss town on the path to the Iffigsee. I visited once as a child."

"They're carrying something."

She squinted. "One of my curtains," she said.

"They're coming in our direction," he said.

A breeze stirred the feathers of the sleeping owlet in her hand. He'd forgotten about the small creature.

"That path leads to Gabriel's house, and I've instructed Gabriel, and also Valasian, many times to tell them that I have taken up residence in Lauenen, the town below."

"But the ratatouille—if they find it, they'll know you're nearby."

"I trust my friends. And don't forget, we have the cave's nasty smell on our side, and that skull," she said.

"Skull?" He turned and caught sight of a white object just inside the mouth of the cave. He crouched down. It was so small; it must have belonged to an animal, or a child.

"According to my grand-père," she said, "these caves were formed in the Pliocene or Miocene Age, three to four million years ago."

Jim moved away from the cave opening. He would be sick from the smell. Rotting cheese was an apt description.

"One winter," Calliope continued, "Grand-père took me and my brother to the ice caves of Eisriesenwelt in Austria. Maybe"—and she looked him over as if she were looking at him for the first time—"yes, maybe one day one of my daughters will take you to see the ice formations. They are nature's living masterpieces, as they change shape constantly, drip, drip, drip. *That* is a place where the art *belongs*. Don't art museums sometimes feel like graveyards?"

He heard a fluttering sound inside the cave and turned

his head. The opening reminded him of the pupil of an eye, drawing in the light.

"Come away." She touched his arm lightly and guided him to the edge of the cliff, facing west. He was relieved to feel a breeze in his face.

HE'D HEARD THE TERM *ALPENGLOW*, BUT THIS WAS the first time he'd witnessed it. The enormous bowl of the sky was lit from below by the amber light of the setting sun. The few snowfields nestled inside crevices in distant peaks glowed a deep mauve.

The men were back in view. She leaned on the mountainside and stroked Hamlet's feathers as they watched them.

"Why are you doing this?" he asked her. "Why are you hiding, running away?"

"Get a divorce, you say. You don't know my husband."

"No, but . . ." How could a woman of such competence feel so trapped?

"He's running for political office."

"It's 2008. You can protect yourself."

At the corner of the cave, she began to part the thick webs. Her nose was red and her cheeks were flushed.

"Do you think I haven't already tried to extricate myself from his web?" She shook her head, then suddenly threw back her head as she laughed. He loved when she did that. It was like a fresh start to everything.

"*Web*, an apt word; they're everywhere up here in these caves. Look," she said, laughing, "they're in my fingers, my hair. Help me, Jim! I'm stuck!"

He slid the viscous strings of web from her hair. One caught on her shoulder and he gently lifted it from her shirt. She continued to move through the webs.

"My husband thinks he can disguise his webs of manipulation. If he doesn't wake me at all hours of the night to persuade me to stay—the exhaustion technique—he'll spread a cloak of charm so thick around me that I won't be able to move. He'll laugh with me, at me, seduce me, punish me, curse me, diminish me, intimidate me, confuse me, distance himself from me to the point that I don't exist for him (what I call the Gulag treatment), make me think I'm crazy so that I can't trust myself, scare me with his physical strength—all of this, interchangeably, inexhaustibly, until I lose myself again and again to him. He's a master, like that big spider up there, waiting for the fly to stop for just one moment . . ."

She placed the owlet on the cave floor and began, with one of her arrows, to strike at the webs, pulling them down one after another.

"In a moment of clarity," she said, coughing, "after all those endless years of battling, of trying to make him see things from my perspective, I realized that this person, my husband, had *no* conscience, and that no matter what I said or did, nothing would change him or his mind. He is more immutable than this mountain."

She closed her eyes as if it hurt to keep them open.

"If I go back to him now," she continued, "he'll charm me yet again, into my addiction. I'm a junkie—is that what you call it? A junkie for his evil. Evil! You might think that word is too extreme, but it's not. Being up here in the clear mountain air allows me to see things as they are. If I return to him, which I will not, I'll be preserved in formaldehyde as Yves's pretty political spouse, or rather, as he says to me tête-à-tête, his 'stupid *fucking* idiotic wife.'"

She paused and pointed southwest. Valasian was aiming an arrow at a steinbock with large antlers. He missed, and the herd dispersed.

"Valasian is a great shot. He doesn't usually miss. He's distracted. That sound—do you hear it?" she asked, turning deeper into the cave.

He detected a low rumble that sounded like the New York City subways when they pass underneath the pavement.

"It's like a heart throbbing, like the cave is alive," she said.

Jim had lost sight of the two men, but now he spotted them on the ridge below.

"They're talking to Gabriel," she said. "Gabriel will be asking them for a ride in the helicopter. Gabriel, tell them what we practiced, that the bell-tower chalet has been abandoned for years and that a French lady went down to the town of Lauenen. *Shhh, mon petit hiboux.*"

"How far to Anzère from here?" Jim asked.

"Not more than four days if we go at a good pace."

"And to Lauenen?"

Ambrose and he had started their hike from Lauenen two and a half weeks ago. "Lauenen is only a six hour hike away; that's where they should look first, if they believe Gabriel." Gstaad, if he remembered correctly, was a short bus ride from Lauenen.

"So the Cabane des Audannes is closest, half a day's hike as you told me when I arrived?"

Her eyes fluttered.

"Yes, but . . . I'd rather go to Anzère." Her eyes were fixed on the men. "Yves expects me to retreat to the Cabane. He's paid off— Wait, *shhh*— *Merde,* it's not possible! They're headed in our direction."

She drew him back from the ledge of the cliff. "They'll see us," she whispered. "Come, into the cave."

THEY NAVIGATED THROUGH A DENSE ARCHITEC-tural mesh of spiderwebs, shaking the sticky silk threads from their fingers as they went. A blue-black bat flitted outside the cave and disappeared.

Calliope took his hand in hers and pulled him into a far corner of the cave. Hamlet hooted and hissed.

"I can't, won't, believe that Gabriel failed to tell them I was in Lauenen," she whispered.

Gabriel had shot Jim enough jealous glances for Jim to guess that the adolescent boy would rather Calliope be

discovered by her husband than spend any more time alone with Jim. The stench inside the cave seemed alive—or recently dead, rotten or rotting.

They heard men's voices.

"*Shhh,*" she whispered to the hissing owl.

The men called out to each other in French. Jim couldn't understand. The owlet hissed loudly. Did it smell the bats or the pilots?

The men paced the terrace ledge outside the cave.

"Regardez ce vieux crâne," came a voice. Look at this old skull.

"Madame," they laughed. Calliope poked Jim in the ribs.

Jim turned his eyes away from the glare of the flashlight that hit the cave floor not far from them.

"Comment il empeste dedans ici. C'est fétide!" How it stinks in here. It's disgusting.

He felt her fear, a trembling within her disciplined stillness. Her body was clenched, ready to spring if necessary. He guessed that she was calculating how quickly she could reach her bow.

She suppressed a cough. The owlet hissed. Jim held his breath.

"Écoutez," one man said. Listen.

Calliope's hair fell against his arm as she moved her hand to stroke the little bird. The owlet hissed again. Calliope coughed again, loudly this time. It was impossible the men hadn't heard.

Then it came: a shrill screeching sound combined with

a thundering from deep inside the cave, louder and louder. Calliope was so still. Was she breathing? The noise erupted from the black hole of the cave behind them, and Jim jumped back instinctively, pushing Calliope against the cave wall, shielding her. A thick black mass of bats—that's what they were—flew over their heads as if it were one monstrous creature, thumping and flapping and blacking out the cave's entrance. Its shape resembled a stingray with cyclopean wings.

"Les chauve-souris!" one of the men yelled, his voice strained. Bats!

"Allez!" yelped the other. "Sortons d'ici!" Let's get out of here!

They waited for the sound of the men's voices to recede and that of the thundering bat wings to dissipate. She was the first to move. Outside, blinking in the twilight-infused air, she coughed into her arm until she cried.

"What if I could *promise* that your husband would leave you alone if you returned to the Cabane des Audannes with me?" Jim asked.

"I wouldn't believe you."

"A restraining order."

"He'd kill me if he couldn't contain me."

"Calliope," he said, looking into her large eyes, the color of the blue-green-gray expanse of evening around them. "What are you saying?"

She turned away from him and sat down on the edge of the cliff.

"I'm an impediment to his career," she said. "Underneath all his charm, I suspect that he hates women. You don't know what he's capable of—those men might have come to push me off a cliff. 'Wife of minister of interior took one step too many.'"

"You're sounding paranoid."

"You sound like *him*. 'You seem unstable,' he would tell me anytime I disagreed with him. 'Isn't there something you can take for that?' A drug that will make you surrender every ounce of independence to your husband!"

Was her mind healthy? The thought came to him swiftly, like the screeching of the bats moments before. Who would come so far away to live in isolation? What if her politician husband was right, and Jim was falling under the spell of someone who was not well, who had concocted this story . . .

"I have a hard time believing—" started Jim.

She rose and walked to the other side of the cliff ledge. He followed her. The stench was thick there, and he felt dizzy.

"You, too," she said calmly, stroking the owlet's feathers. "Rationality is a delusion. *Everyone* is blind! Isn't that right, little one," she said, bringing the owl to eye level. It twisted its head, raised its feathers, and snapped its bill. "Too bad," she said, addressing Jim, "you missed the helicopter ride to the bottom. I'll be going on my way now."

She placed the owlet in her pocket and, at a run, jumped the chasm they had crossed on the way there. She turned to begin her descent down the cliff face. The white scarf

around her neck, which he hadn't noticed before, glowed in the blue night.

"Wait," Jim said breathlessly, joining her on the other side of the chasm. She did not look up but continued to make her way down the side of the cliff.

The helicopter revved its engine and lifted off the lake, sending ripples into the water and into the empty, darkening sky.

"They'll be back tomorrow," she said once he'd joined her at the bottom.

"We'll hike to the Cabane des Audannes at the crack of dawn," he said.

"One thing you should know about me," she said, "is that I never go back the way I came, and that's the way I came. Never. My grandfather's principle. There's a sign to Anzère over the next cliff. I've seen it. But I'm going back to my chalet for the night. Wait. Valasian is near. He sees us up here. Back up. There, there, little owl."

"Hiding from everyone. Is that your grandfather's principle, too?"

Even in the faint light he could see the contemptuous expression in her eyes. He'd crossed the fine line of familiarity.

She sped ahead hidden by the cliff, along the border of the dark copse of pine trees, toward the chalet. Some light had appeared in the north, where the moon was rising. When they finally reached the chalet, breathless, everything was as they'd left it except for the boards torn off the entrance door and one other detail: the window just inside the door was missing the curtains with the orange pom-poms.

TEN

GRACE

CALLIOPE PLACED HAMLET ON THE TREE-TRUNK stool just inside the door and lit what was left of the candles on the table in the small room. She lifted the pot of ratatouille from under the floorboards and hung it on the hook over the tamped-down fire. From a replenished supply (Valasian must have been to the chalet after the men had gone), Jim fetched logs and revived the fire.

He walked with Calliope to the barn. It was cold in the large space, and there was no trace of the owls, even the younger ones. Neither she nor Jim spoke; they returned to the flickering firelit room, the ratatouille, and candles. Calliope sat on a stump and fed the baby owl with the eyedropper.

"This will be our last supper here," she said, staring into his eyes. "At least, *my* last. Jim, you are welcome to stay, or

you can return to your Cabane des Audannes tomorrow morning, as that is what you wish to do, or you can come to Anzère with me. The train from Anzère to Geneva takes three hours. Everyone is free to do as they please, rule of the house. Come and go, no guilt, no burdens, as free as the owls." She coughed into her elbow.

"*That* owl is not exactly free," he said, nodding at the small bird.

"Not now, but one day he will be, won't you, my hesitating Hamlet. He doesn't know his capacity for freedom yet, like so many of us." She lifted the bird to eye level to look at it. "We die without knowing how truly free we were. I suppose that if we never knew freedom in life, God gives us the chance to know it in death: the ultimate liberty."

She placed the pot of ratatouille on the table and ladled the vegetable stew onto their pewter plates. Sitting across from Jim, she bowed her head.

"Will you please say grace?" she asked.

Jim's parents were not grace sayers, but he remembered a short prayer he'd learned at a friend's house as a child.

"Bless this food to our use, and us to thy loving service. Amen."

She burst into laughter. And laughed and coughed and laughed. Hamlet raised his tufted ears.

"You ridicule me," he said.

"*Non, non,*" she laughed, "I am sorry, *non*, you speak grace like . . . like a child . . . in a child's voice."

"It's your turn to say grace," he said.

She closed her eyes, bent her head, and raised tightly clasped fingers. "Bénissez-nous, Seigneur, et la nourriture que, grâce à Votre libéralité, nous allons prendre. Amen."

"Amen to whatever you said," Jim said.

"*Bon appétit*," she added. "But wait!" She jumped up from her chair. "On our last night, we must have a final blessing from the Benedictines."

Jim took the black bottle that she lifted from under the floorboards. With his jackknife corkscrew he yanked at the cork as he had done the night before, to no avail. She removed an arrow from the quiver that she'd hung on a hook at the doorway and pressed the dart into the cork.

"*Merde*," she muttered. "This really *is* the last supper," she said, shaking her hand back and forth quickly. "Blood and wine."

"You need a bandage."

"*Non*, it's fine."

He stood, placed the bottle between his legs, and pulled. Finally the cork gave way. He poured the thick black syrup into their tin cups.

"To your Chalet of Owls," he said, raising his cup to her.

"*La maison des hiboux*," she said, her eyes closing as she sipped. "To Jim." She lifted her glass, her eyes meeting his. "To finding yourself lost in a place where the straight path has vanished. Dante starts his journey through the *Inferno* like this. But for you, I think, deviating from the course won't be such a bad thing at all."

Neither spoke for some time. A soft darkness filled the

contours of the room. The quiet bound them together as if they were discovering a new place. In the dim light, he noticed that her cheeks were flushed. He rose from his seat to touch her forehead.

"You have a fever," he said. "We should have left this morning."

"Please don't ruin this last night," she said, dropping her eyes to the table.

THE RATATOUILLE WAS SWEET AND EVENLY TEX-tured; each vegetable had a distinct taste. Calliope was an excellent cook.

"These Alps shape the contours of my mind," she said suddenly, looking up at him. Did she speak in such poetic rapture in her daily Parisian life, he wondered, as she bought a baguette or a round of Camembert at the local market. "As a child, I pretended they were God's Gothic church, thrust up from the ground especially for me. Up and up and up, they would draw my eyes to what really mattered. This is the place that tells me that everything about life—for instance, even this little wildflower—is meaningful."

She pulled a Queen Anne's lace wildflower from the bouquet in the glass jam jar at the center of the table and twirled the stem, the flower spinning like a pinwheel.

"Do you have a place, somewhere in the whole wide world—or it could be inside you—a place that calls to you?"

"Are you like this with everyone you meet, asking these

unusual open-ended questions? Or is this what happens when you seclude yourself for a few months?"

"What do you mean?" She cocked her head to the side.

"I mean asking things that no one else asks."

She laughed and shook her head. "Does no one ask about your inner desires and passions? Or is everything in America evident, open, and obvious?"

Jim took a deep breath and struggled against her question. He could not remember a time when anyone had been interested in what he really thought, what he wanted to do with his life, who he really was underneath the crisp cotton shirts and well-tailored suits. It was enough for his parents to follow his progress up the ladder to East Coast financial success. All other life questions were moot. Sally shared his parents' neighbor-envy. "My friend Allie and her boyfriend just rented a house in Montauk for the summer," she had said in the tone of a complaint. "Why don't we do that?"

Calliope was waiting for him, her eyes on his as if they would never let go. Then he saw it, as if it were at the forefront of all his thinking, as if it had been there all his life. Sea, wide expanses of sea, waves crashing on a beach. It was a mottled gray-and-blue day; pieces of blue were falling out of the sky as if out of a puzzle. The wind blew a dappled pattern in the sand. It was cold and barren and open, and no one, no one, could put a claim on any of it. He told her his vision.

"Your belonging . . ." she said.

It was the view of the North Sea from Norway, the

view he'd never seen but had pictured from his grandfather Ocean's many fondly recalled descriptions.

" . . . often becomes your longing," she finished.

"I shut my heart," he said, "after . . ." He stopped. What was he saying?

How ridiculous to think that he could actually "shut" his heart. To resist the hurt of heartache, of Sally's rejection, of his career's misadventure, of his alienation from his family, of his father's daily disgraces. Distraction worked pretty darn well. But for how long can you turn off a feeling?

"It's true," she said. "So often, we choose to deceive ourselves. I know I—"

They heard a sound in the barn, a scuffling and scurrying. In one swift motion, Hamlet rotated his head 180 degrees.

"The owls are back. I'm hoping that one of the mother owls will warm up our fledgling," she said, taking the owlet and rising from the table.

"When and where will they go?" he asked as she headed toward the barn.

"It's almost a full moon tonight. I thought they'd left for good. They've been ruffling their feathers for a week now; I feel their restlessness. It's too cold in the barn, and they've sensed the intrusions—first you, then the pilots. Many have already left. I'm not sure where they'll go, probably somewhere in the lower Alps. They might leave tonight at their usual hunting time and return again in early spring. We'll depart as well, but in the first flush of dawn. You'll go your

way tomorrow to the Cabane and work your way back to Geneva and New York. I'll be heading to Anzère. I'll pack food and water for each of us. And I recommend that you dress warmly." She coughed.

"I took your warm bed," he said.

Either she did not hear, or she did not care to respond.

"Come with me to say good-bye to the owls," she said.

As they entered the barn, he felt as if the otherworldly moaning emanated from his own lungs.

"C'est moi, mes hiboux," she whispered to the owls. "It's me."

The flame of the candle in her hand trembled.

"I'm worried about your fever," he said.

They heard movement above them in the rafters, and they turned and watched as, in the dim light, one by one the owls took flight and disappeared out the barn door. Soft-feathered wings into the silent night . . .

"Au revoir," she whispered. She coughed, and he noticed how much deeper the cough had become. "I will miss them."

She turned to face him, her eyes watery in the candlelight. "Thank you, Jim, for your courageous efforts on behalf of my daughters, for taking your mission so seriously. One of my daughters and you, I can see it very clearly . . ."

She hesitated as if she wanted to say more.

"Yes?" he asked.

She quickly turned toward the door and stepped back into the chalet, taking the little light in the room with her.

ELEVEN

DREAMS AND FEVER

IN HIS DREAM HE WAS DIPPING HIS FINGER INTO the muddy Benedictine wine, and with his wine-wet finger-turned-paintbrush he was drawing a line down Sally's aquiline nose. Along her almond-shaped, blue eyes, the top of each cheekbone, around her sharp chin, her collarbones, her luscious breasts . . . He finished with a dot on her belly button. In the moonlight, the wine paint sparkled.

When he woke, he wasn't sure if he'd dreamed of Sally or Freyja, the Norse goddess of love and battle. As a child, he'd cherished the colorful depictions of Freyja in her red cloaks battling fire-breathing dragons in a book of Norse myths that his grandfather Ocean had read to him.

But *was* that Sally's chin in the dream? Jutting out sharply, as if in bold opposition? No, it was Helene's! Were those Sally's

eyes? No, Thalia had such clear eyes, like a blue day with no clouds. Whose face had he been painting? Whose breasts? Something in the dream had been disturbing. What was it?

He heard the clanging of a pot, and Calliope's cough. The morning light was streaming in opaque white strips through the small window. The mountain sky was a stamp of blue. He dressed and walked into the makeshift kitchen. Calliope stood at the fire, a wooden spoon in her hand, which she lifted as he entered. Her wand.

"Bonjour," she said, smiling.

"Your cough is worse," he said.

She laughed in the light way she had. She wore her white T-shirt and her riding pants and the velvet maroon ribbon around her neck. Was the shiny hue in her rosy cheeks caused by the fresh mountain air, or by her fever?

"You look as if you could gobble down three of these," she said as she flipped an omelet in the pan.

"More logs," he said. He wondered how many hours she'd been awake.

"No more logs," she said, intercepting his movement toward the door. "We leave as soon as you've eaten, you to the Cabane and I to Anzère. I've packed food for each of us, and even for the owlet; the garden is nearly empty. We'll pick up water as we go. They'll be here soon."

He heard a hooting and saw the fledgling owl, eyes blinking, on the stump.

"Yes, sadly, the brood left Hamlet behind. I'll bring him with me and hope he'll take flight along the way.

"Stand aside," she continued, sliding the omelet onto his plate. When she was finished cooking the second omelet, she led the way into the garden with her plate and forks and napkins for the two of them.

The bright day had that crisp feel of autumn to it. He sat next to her as she bowed her head and closed her eyes, and he said inside himself the first authentic grace he had said in his life—praying that he could convince Calliope to come with him to the Cabane.

"Did you dream last night?" he asked.

She laughed. "One dreams every night in these mountains!"

"More likely it's the Benedictine wine that makes you *think* you're dreaming."

"Tell me what I dreamed."

He would make it all up.

"Okay," he began. "You dreamed that you were in a place where there were many doorways, but for some reason you couldn't escape."

"Many doorways," she said, tilting her head and looking across at the mountain peaks. "That could be the piece of the puzzle that went missing. Yes, very possibly. Thank you, Jim, for completing the picture. Now it's my turn. *You* were dreaming of a fire raging—where was it, in a barn, in your grandfather's barn?" Was she right? He'd dreamed of painting Sally, or Thalia—or Helene actually, but there had also been something violent, something that caused him to startle awake. Dreams were grab bags. A blazing fire was

vaguely familiar, but wasn't everything? Had he dreamed twice in the space of a night?

"In my dream," she said, "I was drunk—no, I wasn't really, I was pretending to be drunk. I'm not sure why, perhaps because I was trying to escape from the place among doorways that you just described. I was slurring my words. I stumbled and deliberately fell to the ground. I was *not* intoxicated; but I *acted* as if I were." She stood, balanced the plate on her head, and then stumbled on purpose and caught it.

"Most people drink to escape," he said. "*Pretending* to drink to escape: I'm learning that that would be *you*."

She resumed her seat next to him. "*Your* dream?"

"I was painting my ex-fiancée's face—and her breasts, actually—using your Benedictine wine as the paint and my finger as the brush," he said.

She smiled brightly. "How did she look after you painted her?"

He remembered the deep-set, clear blue eyes that did not blink, Thalia's eyes; the long, aquiline nose, Helene's chin. He was so confused.

He would not tell Calliope. "She looked like Freyja, the goddess of love and battle," he said.

"Who?"

"Norse mythology."

"How could she be goddess of both?"

"As a child I asked the same question. Freyja introduced desire into the world, which causes war; the two will always be intertwined."

"Life appears so complicated, but voilà. It's so simple. The two sides of a coin can never be separated."

"Freyja," he said, "loved her husband, Óòr so much that when he went on long journeys, she cried red and golden tears that turned into amber and gold when they fell to earth."

"How sweet," she murmured. "Sadness appearing in forms from the physical world."

She sighed and pushed her hair behind her shoulders. "I'm sorry that this will be our last meal together, you and I, such lovely new friends." Her hand shook as she lifted her fork. She placed it back on the plate.

"This is no change-of-seasons cold." He placed his palm on her forehead. "Your forehead is burning. By the sound of your cough, you've probably got bronchitis, if not walking pneumonia. You need antibiotics."

"The mountains are my antibiotic."

"You're coming to the Cabane with me this morning," he said. "We will find a first-aid kit there, hopefully with some antibiotics."

She narrowed her eyes. "As I've told you, I'm hiking to Anzère. You forget: I know the mountains better than you. We separate after breakfast." She placed her untouched plate on the flat rock slab between them. "I'm sad to leave this, my refuge."

"You've made it home."

Her sorrow was at once so powerful that he dropped his fork.

"I say good-bye and thank you to this house," she said, turning to look behind her at the door to the chalet, "that has held me in such happiness."

"Eat something," he said. "You have a vigorous day of hiking ahead of you."

"No time," she said. She rose, took his plate from him, and walked back into the chalet.

HE STOMPED OUT THE FIRE. NO NEED TO BOARD UP the front door this time. She pulled her bow over her shoulder and her quiver and small knapsack over her back. The owlet peeked out of her vest pocket as she raised a handkerchief to her mouth. She coughed at the exact same time that the chalet bell tinkled as the door closed behind them.

"We part here," she said. "The route to the Cabane is around that bend," she pointed, "much easier than the way you arrived, by way of the steep aiguille. Jim, I'm so happy that we've shared these last days of summer together." Her body looked about to wilt.

She kissed him on each cheek and then took off at a run down the hill toward the lake. He could no longer see her, but her cough trailed behind her.

He hesitated.

It was Thursday. To get back to New York for Monday's first day of work, he would have to catch a train from Anzère to Geneva on Sunday morning at the very latest. Calliope had said that it could take four days to get to Anzère. They

would have to sprint. How many times had Jim readjusted this schedule in his mind? Somehow, sticking to a schedule was impossible on the Wildhorn. Or maybe this was Calliope's magic?

Another cough echoed up to him, ricocheting against the craggy folds of crust and rock, and his dream became clearer. He *had* been painting Helene's chin, her high cheekbones, and her breasts.

"Calliope," he called, running after her. He could not leave her alone.

When he caught up to her, she turned to him and laughed. She seemed so much frailer than she had the moment he had first seen her only two days before, arrow stretched across the bow.

"Jim, are you playing the hero in your Norse mythology?"

When they reached the banks of the lake, they filled their canisters with water and balanced on rocks that looked as if they'd spilled from the mountains above. Jim almost fell in, then caught himself.

"I'm glad you came to your senses," she said. "You will adore Anzère."

She gazed at the sun-dappled lake. He could tell that in her quiet way, she was saying good-bye. To the lake, or to her reflection in the lake?

When they heard the machinelike purr in the distance and saw the copter's dark shadow staining the mountain behind them, they accelerated their pace along the narrow

path. Whisking the clouds in its path, the chopper flew above the trail in the direction of the Cabane des Audannes.

"I just had a vision," she said, panting, after an hour of strenuous hiking. He slowed his pace to walk beside her. Her face was pale. "I saw the hermitess." She pronounced the word without the *h*, as *ermitess*. "Valasian told me that she lives in the north-facing cave on the other side of a mountain of gray scree, and now I realize that this is the mountain, right here. She's so very alone." Her eyes widened.

"Isn't that the nature of a hermitess, to be alone?"

"I'm sure even you know, Jim, that there is aloneness, and then there is loneliness. *Les deux solitudes*. One is a soul complete and still; the other is a restless and hungry person crying out to be fed by another."

They could no longer hear the helicopter, and both knew it must have landed. Calliope began climbing a steeper, less visible path. If Jim did not think of some way to divert her, they would be stopping to see the female hermit for who knows how long and then hiking for four more days to Anzère.

"We're so close to the hermitess that we cannot *not* pay her a visit."

"Calliope, your cough—"

"My grandfather and I ran into her years and years ago on one of our high Alpine climbs. She was walking with a stick along a mountain ledge, and she seemed so happy. I think it's the only time in my life that I have witnessed bliss."

"If I were not on a tight deadline to get back and if you were healthy, it would be a joy to visit her. As it is—"

He plucked a bluebell growing at the edge of the rock.

"This has snow on it," he said, offering it to her.

"It's the morning dew!" She placed it against her forehead and sighed. "Snow is too much on your mind," she said, and she licked the moisture off the flower as if it were a miniature ice-cream cone.

"Look," she said, pointing to a small marmot that they must have frightened from its hiding place. The small, furry animal carved a path along the flowers, creating a rippling effect in the meadow of wildflowers. The massive cliff of the Wildhorn above them, with the sun bouncing off the granite, looked like a sparkling chandelier in the sky.

"I see Valasian." She stepped onto a large rock to catch a better glimpse. Valasian appeared over the ridge of the nearby copse. He had a way of emerging from nowhere, wherever he and Calliope were. It was as if they lived in a small village. Jim was grateful to see the lanky figure of the old man.

He was beside them within minutes. His face looked thinner than before; the skin under his eyes was puffy. His clothes smelled of smoke.

He spoke to Calliope in French, using his arms to express exasperation.

Jim understood that the "men" had set the chalet and barn on fire. The two buildings were still burning as they spoke. Only now did Jim notice that the old man's wiry eyebrows were black, as if singed by flames.

"A fire, no . . ." She shut her eyes and melted to the ground. "He would know that would be the worst . . ." She covered her face with her hands. "No . . ." She coughed into her handkerchief.

She lifted her head and looked blankly ahead. "My brother," she said in a whisper, "died in a fire when we were young. I was saved, but he wasn't able . . . " She coughed deeply. Both men knelt beside her, as if their bodies were buttresses of a Gothic cathedral. Valasian's head was bent.

A fire. Calliope had told Jim that he'd dreamed that a barn was burning, and now he recalled the dream. He'd been painting Helene with the wine, and she'd suddenly told him to stop because she smelled smoke. Indeed, the owls' barn was burning, and Helene was crying, her tears red stains on her pale face. That was it. She was screaming that her mother was inside. Flames were bursting through every orifice of the wooden barn. He had to get her out. That was when he woke.

Valasian talked quickly, drawing circles and lines with his hands. Jim understood that the old man had tried to convince the pilots that the chalet was his, but they hadn't believed him. He'd tried to stop them from setting fire to the chalet, had tried to extinguish the flames, but one of the men held him down. They asked repeatedly where Calliope was, and he told them he didn't know.

To escape the pilots, Valasian began talking to himself and raving like a madman about the hermitess, how she held

the secrets of the universe in the folds of her gown. Finally he was able to get free.

"Valasian," Calliope said, looking up with tears in her eyes at the old, tired man, "I thank you from the bottom of my heart."

"Where will you go?" Valasian asked, in English this time, the creases in his brow like a crevice in the granite mountainside.

"Anzère," she said. She stood and dusted off her pants. "Over those mountains, but first we'll visit the hermitess. It's on our way. Please come with us."

"Anzère is too far," Valasian said in English. "The snows come tomorrow. Early snow. Bad at the pass to the south. Audannes is better, half-day walk."

Calliope responded in French, and Jim guessed she was explaining to the old man who cared so much for her what she had told him earlier—that his worries were unfounded, early snows were rarely dangerous, and Anzère was farther south. She suppressed a cough and sneezed.

"Madame," he said. "You are very sick."

She handed Jim the owlet wrapped in her sweater. "Will you excuse me?" she said.

They watched her pick her way to the edge of the copse and disappear inside.

"No Anzère," said Valasian in broken English. "It is too far, and you will have difficult and cold mountain. With snow, impossible. You are not prepared."

Valasian quickly and gruffly conveyed to Jim that he

would give Calliope and Jim other directions that were unfamiliar to Calliope, and tell them that it was a shortcut to Anzère. The path would start in the direction of Anzère but would eventually cut east, toward the Cabane. If they did not stop often, they could arrive at the Cabane later that afternoon. He would have accompanied them, but he was already delayed in sweeping the mountain of livestock before the snow arrived.

"The hermitess?" Jim asked.

"No!" Valasian shook his head. "Go to the Cabane now. Her cough," he said, pointing at his throat and looking in her direction. "She is very sick."

Valasian removed a scrap of paper and a pencil from his jacket, placed them on the large, flat rock in front of him, and sketched the hike east and south across the pass to arrive at the back entrance of the Cabane. He showed Jim the route as Calliope walked up slowly from the forest.

"Valasian is showing us a shortcut," Jim said when Calliope approached.

"To Anzère?" she asked.

"Valasian says we'll see only one sign along the way, the one toward Col des Eaux Froides"

Valasian spoke to her quickly in French, pointing to the lightly trodden trail ahead of them. Jim understood that he was emphasizing that they should take the fork to the east—he looked meaningfully at Jim—to arrive in "Anzère."

"I don't have a compass," Jim said.

She laughed in a way that made Jim nervous. "*I* am your compass, Olsen!"

She had never called him by his surname. Her voice sounded strange; she was elongating her words.

"I realize that this is hard to imagine," said Jim, "but what if even you cannot see the sun through the clouds?"

"Allez, *assez*! Go!" Valasian ordered them.

Valasian's eyes bore a hole into Jim's.

She coughed. "Such fuss over a little cold."

From the bag he carried, Valasian lifted a loaf of brown bread, two apples, and a wedge of cheese. He handed them to Jim who added them to Calliope's supply in his knapsack.

"Before I, or we, go anywhere," Calliope said, "I'm going to visit the hermitess. Valasian, you have told me she lives up there." She pointed to the right, where the skies had been muzzled by gray clouds.

The old man shook his head. "No. It will snow there tomorrow."

"But this is today!" she said.

Calliope lifted her elbows and untied the maroon velvet ribbon from her long neck.

"Valasian," she said in English, "when you visit Gabriel and his family, will you please give him this?" She held out the ribbon. Thalia had learned the trick from her mother. Valasian bowed.

"Do not stay long," Valasian addressed Jim, his face stern. "If the helicopter finds you, that will be better than the snow."

"Valasian!" she scolded, visibly wincing. "Jim, don't listen to him."

"*Vite*," he said. "Go quickly."

The old man hesitated, and Jim guessed that he was waiting for his own gift from Calliope. He fixed his eyes on a patch of green moss growing on a nearby rock.

"This is not a good-bye, Valasian," she said to the old man. "I will return next summer. You have been my godsend. Thank you for keeping my fires always burning, for the local news, for the food, for your protection."

She hugged him. She opened her knapsack and lifted out a gold chain with what looked like two lockets dangling from it.

"No, madame," he said, backing up, shaking his head, and blushing.

"Valasian." Calliope's voice grew serious. "This is for you. My grandparents' faces. See?" She opened each of the back-to-back lockets on the chain to show Valasian the miniature photographs inside.

"It is fitting that you have this, so my grandparents will now be as much a part of the Wildhorn as you are. It will make me happy to know that you have it."

She held the gold pendant out in front of her. Valasian dropped onto one knee and bowed his head. He was a knight receiving a dubbing. She coughed into her handkerchief, then laughed, lowered the chain around his wrinkled, brown neck, and secured the clasp. He kissed her hand, then stood.

"Merci," he said.

"He," said Valasian, lifting his chin toward Jim as he retreated, "knows the way. Go before the snows."

"See you next year, Valasian!" she said.

"Go!" he yelled, staring stone-faced at the ground. "Go!"

PART TWO

THE WILDHORN

TWELVE

THE HERMITESS

THE GREEN PASTURES AND WILDFLOWERS HAD given way to a gradual ascent up a sea of broken gray shale. The mountain was a dragon that had shed its scales. Sharp pieces of Wildhorn detritus lay scattered randomly, layer upon layer.

"Her cave should be just on the other side of this, on the north face." Calliope was breathless. "What a barren place she chose."

"This is too far off our path," Jim protested, but she continued to march resolutely ahead of him, coughing into her handkerchief every few strides.

The sky was now a milky white, the temperature had dropped, and floating mist shrouded the rocks to either side.

Jim imagined that this was what it must be like for fish, gazing flat-eyed upward through the water's surface.

The hike up the north side required full concentration, as the slivers of scree and slate were slippery and the ground uneven. After an hour, Jim stopped.

"This is too long a detour. Your cough is getting worse, and it's getting colder. We need to get back to the trail—"

"I see it." She pointed to a small cave halfway up the mountain wall. "Just up there."

From where they stood, the dark chamber looked like a lopsided eye in the mountainside.

"Hold Hamlet, will you?" she asked when they'd reached the vertical granite wall. He had almost forgotten about the bird. She placed the owlet on top of Jim's knapsack, then took hold of a rope that dangled nearby. Jim traced its origins to a hook protruding from the top of the ledge.

"Valasian must have attached this rope to carry supplies and food to her," she said, her voice wavering as she shimmied up the rope with a strength that he would not have imagined in her slight figure.

Jim held the knotted rope still. Once at the top, she swung her legs over the upper ledge. Jim followed, the owlet in his knapsack, wedging his boots against the glistening rock face, listening to Calliope's cough above him. He disliked this detour as much as Valasian did.

"How did the hermitess get up here without this rope?" Jim asked once he'd cleared the ledge.

"She came as a young woman," Calliope said, taking Hamlet into her hands, "and she'll leave through the back door that is paradise, and become a young woman again." She coughed into her handkerchief.

At their new height, he could see a foreboding white shroud of mist pierced by a crown of mountain peaks. He should never have acquiesced to Calliope's request to visit the hermitess. Why had he let this sick woman determine their fate? He would take the lead on the next leg of the journey.

"You're skeptical about our hermitess," she said as they neared the entrance to the cave.

"I'm skeptical about your health," he said.

They covered their noses immediately and simultaneously. She removed a candle and matchbook from her pocket and lit the candle. The owlet hissed.

"*Shhhhh*, 'Amlet," she said, stopping quickly, holding Jim back.

"The smell of death," she whispered.

The odor was not as rank as that of the bat-infested cave, but it was sour.

They found the old woman propped up against one side of the cave, her head of long white hair collapsed onto her chest. One of her dull-gray eyes was open, the other shut. *As you go to death*, Jim thought, *perhaps there is always one eye turning back toward life.*

Had she resisted Death, fighting tooth and nail as it

sucked the air from her lungs? As she was swallowed into nothingness, was her mind reaching for the wildflowers of her youth, the white giggles of edelweiss?

"By the looks of her, she must've died more than a week ago." Calliope handed Jim the candle. "We can't leave her like this."

The dead woman wore a sack of gray fabric; her bare ankles and feet were swollen. A wooden bowl and spoon lay next to her fingers, along with an empty metal cup and an untouched loaf of bread that looked as hard as the rocks outside. No rodent or insect had found it appetizing. Fear in the form of adrenaline rushed through him.

Calliope sank to the body and pulled the long-white-haired head into her lap. With her delicate fingers, she closed the woman's open eye.

Jim worried that they were losing daylight outside the cave and that the temperature was dropping. Aiming the candle at the cave walls, he noticed that they were scalloped like the inside of a shell. As in the sea, as on land. There were markings on the wall: simple stick figures came into view. *Not possible.*

Wherever Calliope was, there were miracles. Had the hermitess painted them? He walked closer and deciphered waving lines: a river; stick figures with objects in their hands; animals in motion, some resembling reindeer. The shape of a flame—or was that a fish in the sky?—and the contours of the mountains. Hadn't Calliope told him that her grandfa-

ther thought the mountain caves dated back to the Pliocene or Miocene Age?

Calliope gestured to him, and Jim placed the candle on the cave floor and took the dead woman's ankles. It repulsed him to feel how loose the skin was. Together, they moved the hermitess's body so that it lay flat. The body was light, as if the person within had left her skin behind. Calliope arranged the woman's bloated arms, then found a blanket in a dark corner. She shook it out and spread it over it—over her. Calliope placed her hands together in prayer and pressed her lips to the bone-white forehead.

"Valasian will bury her," she said. Her cough echoed throughout the cave.

OUTSIDE, IT FELT AS IF THE SUN WERE WEARING OUT. Clouds blurred the outlines of the mountains. They descended the rope quickly and began hiking in the direction that Valasian had indicated. Despite the challenge of hiking this trail of slippery and loose slate, it was a relief to gain distance from the cave.

He walked to the rhythm of Calliope's stride and her cough, and neither of them spoke. The hermitess's death had left a stamp of gloom. The landscape was colorless, and the mountain under the gray sky looked hard-eyed and deserted.

Even if they kept up their brisk pace, they would not

reach the Cabane des Audannes by nightfall. The visit to the hermitess had cost them two hours of daylight.

At dusk, Calliope began to drag her feet. Jim wished he hadn't abandoned his trekking pole. When they stopped to rest, she fell into his arms, holding out the owlet for him to take.

"Bacon in my knapsack," she said, her voice hoarse.

He lowered her gently onto a slab of rock and found a small container of bacon in her knapsack. He placed the bacon near the agitated, blinking owlet, and it pecked greedily.

"Can you make it a little farther, Calliope?"

"Yes," she said, smiling as she unwound her shoelaces.

"Just a little farther."

"Yes," she said as she lay down on the rocky plateau.

There would be no more hiking that day, he thought.

"Were you ever here in the snow?" he asked her as he spread the tarp. Saying the word *snow* felt forbidden, as if in saying it he would give it permission. Over the last hour, it had been at the edge of Jim's every thought.

"Only once, with Grand-père." She opened her eyes and smiled up at him. "It was a rainbow snow, but I still think my grand-père made it come especially for me." She was a little girl again. "We were usually back in school before the snows arrived."

Jim dug into his knapsack and offered her some bread and cheese. She waved it away.

"You want to hunt, eh, mon 'Amlet?" She lifted the vig-

orously flapping Hamlet above her head. "Nature is finally calling you hers.

"Fly away!" she commanded. The owlet's eyes were orange lanterns in the gathering dark. It stared at her motionless as if it were a sulking teenager.

Jim was hungry, even if she was not. He ate slowly and tried to entice Calliope with small bites, but her interest was elsewhere, her energy fading.

As she curled up under the blanket next to him, Jim considered how the managing directors at Wolfe, Taylor would greet his failure to appear on the first day of his new job.

"Too many words," Calliope was murmuring in her drowsiness. "You mustn't trust them. Poison hides in words.

" 'I love you,' says my husband to his mistresseses," she continued, slurring her words in her fatigue. "He says it to this one and that one, and also to me and also to you.

"Too many loves in the world," she said. "A plague of loves: sexual love, romantic love, married love, adulterous love, family love, friend love, love *platonique*, love lost, love found, young love— No, no more words. Please! No more loves!"

She coughed. He placed his cold hand on her burning forehead.

"Do you still love him?" he asked.

She answered as if she were completely lucid. "How can you love someone who is able or likely to cause physical, mental, or emotional injury? How can you love someone who doesn't cherish anyone or anything?"

He thought of himself, of his work, and of Sally's look of sadness when, so often, he said he was too busy to make plans for the weekend. He'd kept her waiting at a restaurant for an hour on her last birthday. He couldn't help it; he was under a work deadline. Now, reflecting back, he wondered, could he have helped it? Could he have told his colleagues, "My fiancée is more important"?

"How can you love someone," she said, her voice groggy again, "who gives his body and takes others' with no thought of the spirit within them? How can you love someone whose integrity is corruptible by his own unsatisfying excuses, someone who has never attached any consequences to his actions? Can love exist without trust?"

"You're planning to leave the marriage."

"Enough about me! Jim Olsen, you, whose true north is your heart, must find someone whose compass is as fixed as yours. That I can see now very clearly. Yes, that I can see."

Would Sally have said that Jim's magnetic north was his heart? More likely she thought that his compass needle pointed to his version of success: getting to Princeton, getting to Harvard Business School, getting the first job, getting Sally. As his peers were getting, so was he. He would not be left behind.

"Helene." Was Calliope speaking in her sleep, or was she awake with her eyes closed?

"The electricity went out in Paris the night Helene was born. My hospital room overlooked the Tour d'Eiffel, and voilà, the moment she was born, all the lights on the tower

went on: *ping, ping ping, ping.* That is Helene, *la lumière*, the light. Lives are short, with a few moments of epiphany. That was one—the moment when Helene was born and the lights returned to Paris—and now the lights are on again, with us, even in this blacked-out city of rock."

No stars, no moon, no light tonight, and Calliope was shivering. He placed his jacket around her shoulders, but that did not stop her shaking. Every inhalation required strength.

When she was fully asleep, he placed his ear to her chest. He doubled up the blanket to cover her and tried to warm her with his body, negotiating the sharp contours of the mountain floor. What if he took a wrong turn tomorrow, if they got lost, if she could no longer walk and he had to carry her? What if it started snowing before they arrived at the sign for the Col des Eaux Froides and they found it impassable? The image of the dead hermitess filled the gaps in his thoughts.

Calliope's eyelids fluttered, and he wondered if she was dreaming of the burning barn or of the dreaded helicopter, of Anzère or her daughters or her life in Paris. He felt for Thalia's ribbon in his pocket. It was no longer there. He felt a strange panic, as if a part of him had been lost.

THIRTEEN

WHITEOUT

THEY'D BEEN HIKING A STEEP ASCENT FOR TWO hours. Calliope had tripped and fallen several times. Her lips were blue, and when she spoke, her teeth chattered. Perspiration covered her forehead and cheeks—a glistening, like dew at dusk instead of dawn. Her gasps and wheezes were punctuated by the hooting noises coming from the owl in her pocket.

Jim whispered to himself, as if he were repeating the refrain of a song, "Please don't let it snow."

He encouraged Calliope to drink from the almost-empty thermos. They would have to find a river or waterfall within the next few hours. But Calliope refused to drink.

"I'm cold," she said, "and hot."

When he brought what was left of Valasian's bread and

cheese to Calliope's lips, again she turned her head. Her face looked as pale as the cloud cover.

"'Amlet," she said, feeling around blindly in her knapsack. She handed the dropper and water bottle to Jim.

"I should have fed *you* like this," he told her, as he squeezed the liquid into the owlet's beak.

She lowered herself to the ground as if in preparation for a long night's sleep.

"We can't stop here," he said.

"Time to sleep," she insisted.

The ascent sloped into the dispiriting distance for as far as his eye could see. He guessed they had three more hours of hiking to get to the Cabane, but Calliope's stopping along the way could delay them another hour.

He removed her knapsack, bow, and quiver of arrows and tied them onto his knapsack. He wrapped the blanket around her.

"I'm going to carry you," he said, squatting down to where she lay. "Place your arms around my neck."

She lifted her arms, then dropped them as if they didn't belong to her.

"It's too hot," she mumbled, nudging her head into his chest.

He lifted her and the restless owlet in her pocket off the ground. Despite her pallor, her skin was on fire.

Within minutes, she was asleep in his arms. It made for slow climbing. About an hour into the hike, Jim stopped to rest. He looked up and saw that the great blue eye of the

sky was closing. And then it began to snow—thick, wet flakes.

"Damn!" he yelled. Calliope stirred. He placed her gently on the ground, untied his tarp, wrapped it around her, and lifted her once again. She felt lighter. Was she disappearing in his arms?

By now he should have seen the sign to the Col des Eaux Froides. He had memorized Valasian's drawing. They should have crossed the pass an hour ago. Had he walked in the wrong direction without knowing it? He should have carried a compass, like every other hiker.

Everywhere he looked, he saw gray and now wet gray and black. He was hiking through Death Mountain instead of Death Valley: the black-rock interior of the Wildhorn.

Calliope stirred in his arms. "Tell me the truth, Jim," she whispered, looking up at him, her teeth chattering. "We aren't going to Anzère. This is the way to the Cabane. You know it, and I know it."

If only he could lie to her.

"I can see through you," she said, looking into his eyes.

"I shouldn't have let you convince me to visit your hermit friend—"

"You lied to me, Jim. You!" She wrestled out of his grip, sobbing, and fell to the ground.

"Calliope. You can't do this alone," he said, lifting her into his arms, her lovely face wet with tears.

"If only I weren't sick," she said, her tears mixing with

the snow on her face. She coughed into the crook of her elbow.

"The hutte will be warm. If this isn't severe bronchitis, it's pneumonia. At the Cabane—"

"Don't you see? They're waiting for me there!" She kicked at him with renewed force. Jim caught her before she slipped to the ground.

"We could both die in these mountains," he said, gripping her tightly. "*Do you want that?*"

She turned her face away from him, her lips, firmly clamped.

They couldn't afford to waste the white light of day by stopping so frequently. As Jim trudged into the snow, he felt himself a part of the lonely, rugged landscape.

"I was in my chalet." Her voice was muted. She spoke as if she knew it was a way to keep a grip on consciousness. "Was it a dream? I heard growling outside. I ran to make sure the door was closed tightly. And it was, but a huge black bear pushed it open. Even as I panicked, I marveled at this bear's shiny, luscious black coat. I escaped into the next room and slammed the door shut, but the bear broke through! His claws were out; he wanted my honey. I fled to the window, and before I jumped out, I looked back. He was the most powerful and beautiful creature I'd ever seen."

She closed her eyes, as if she was picturing the bear again.

"Did you escape?"

"I don't know. I don't know. I don't know."

• • •

JIM GUESSED IT WAS LATE AFTERNOON WHEN IT HAP-
pened. The clouds became ghosts, the mist painting everything around him white. The opaque fog insinuated itself
everywhere, separating even Calliope from his view. The
horizon had disappeared. The white of the clouds had con-
verged with the snow at his feet. He could not make out any
contrasts in the space ahead of him. It was a whiteout.

He extended his hand and could not see his fingers.

"Jim!" she yelled in a thin voice. "Jim! We're sleepwalk-
ing in a cloud!"

In these conditions there would be no chance for a husband's valiant rescue, presidential candidate or not. When
Jim released her just a little, her knees buckled.

They had no choice but to sit it out. One move in the
wrong direction, and they could stumble off a cliff. Who
knew how long this snowstorm would last? Only an apple
was left from Valasian's and Calliope's food supply.

In the absence of visibility, Jim became keenly aware of
the sounds and sensations around him—the wind whirred
in a high pitch, as if nature's alarm was ringing in his ears.
Each snowflake pressed into his skin, branding him with its
imprint. Was he hallucinating?

He imagined the senior partner at Wolfe, Taylor pursing
her lips, rapping her fingers on her desk, wondering where
he was. She would refer back to prior e-mails about their
agreed first day of work. She would call Jim's cell phone and
e-mail him. How long would it take Jim's parents—and
Sally, if she cared; would she even notice?—his friends, to

realize that he hadn't returned on his scheduled flight? His mother would be angry, concerned that he would forfeit his job; his father would be busy placating his mother.

Calliope and he could die up here, tomorrow, three days from now. Why was he worrying about Wolfe, Taylor?

"HELLOOOOO!" he called out. The white monster ate his voice.

"We're in heaven together!" Calliope interrupted his dark thoughts. Finally, she was awake. "You and I, and the whiteness of rabbits' whiskers and the white feathers of swans. Thank you for hiding me in this white cloud from the *chop chop chop*, the black predator spider in this vast white heaven."

The snow began to dive at them in sharp miniature icicles. Now there was plenty to drink, and Jim tipped the filled water canister to her dry and chapped lips. He tried to feed her small bites of the apple, but she refused, so he ate most of it himself. His hungry eyes rested on Hamlet, then on Calliope's bow and arrows. He shivered at the thought. The owlet hooted only occasionally, and when it did the sound was a trembling *wwwwwwwaaaa . . . wa . . . wa*. The snow had matted down its feathers; it looked half its normal diminutive size.

Jim slid down next to Calliope and pulled the tarp, blanket, and his Windbreaker over them.

"Have we gone to a place where the white is the night?" she asked, as if he had the answer.

Calliope did not like her name, but she was true to it. In

less than four days since he had met her, Jim Olsen felt more himself than he had ever before, more capable and powerful. The muse had called on him to rescue her.

He listened to the icicles striking the tarp and found himself hoping for the sound of the once-dreaded helicopter. Without a moment's hesitation, he would offer Calliope to her captors in exchange for her safety.

WHEN JIM WOKE, THE NEXT MORNING, SATURDAY morning, soaked through and shivering, to the sound of Hamlet's hissing, he turned toward Calliope, lying on her side beside him. Her face was pale and lifeless. In a panic, he dipped his ear to her lips to listen to her breath and placed his hand on her cool forehead. Her eyes were closed, her breathing irregular.

"Calliope," he said gently, laying the backs of his fingers against her warm cheeks. Everything was wet: her hair, her cheeks, her lips, her body. She shivered in response to his touch, opened her eyes slowly, coughed thickly, and surprised him with a smile.

How could she smile when she could hardly breathe? He brought the thermos to her lips.

"Attagirl."

In the distance—what a relief—he was able to make out a path. The whiteout had finally lifted. Above them on the ridge, pockets of snow looked like white fillings in the black mountain teeth. He was glad he hadn't been tempted

to move during the whiteout; they surely would have fallen off the edge of the cliff only ten feet away. The chute was steep, and a cloud was nestled inside it.

Wildhorn, I will never underestimate you. I promise. Never!

A belt of clouds hung at eye level, and then another, and another, repeated as far as the eye could see. They reminded him of scene changes in a Kabuki theater: actors in the foreground and background holding clouds made of boards, rearranging the furniture of the skies.

"We can move again," he whispered to Calliope, crouching down next to her. The skin under her eyes was shaded blue, reminding him of the color of Calliope's lake at dawn.

Breathing took effort. Was the air thinner after a whiteout? Or had he grown weaker? Calliope's weight was now almost unbearable. He considered dropping the tarp and blanket, even the thermos, to lighten his load, but he decided against it. Calliope was barely conscious. The owlet peeped and hooted only seldom. Were the glint of sunlight and the majestic mountain views mirages? Would the shiny-nosed Monsieur Acolas bound from the front door of an imaginary hutte, offering to carry Calliope down the rest of the mountain? Or was he inside, stirring up a dinner of lamb stew, ready to tuck them into eiderdown comforters? Jim could almost smell the roasted garlic.

To keep himself awake, Jim regaled Calliope with tales of his Viking ancestors and his grandfather Ocean Olsen, whose legs were as strong as the trunks of oak trees. He told her about generational battles against the Frost Giants,

whose scattered bones became the mountains and whose blood fed the rivers, lakes, and seas. Jim had underestimated how many stories he could tell. They had been lying dormant for years.

Only after his stories were told, his mirages had dispersed, and the day had begun to discard itself did he see the saddle rising in the mist above the shattered ice-gray plateau. Valasian had told him that the Col des Eaux Froides was the highest point between the two valleys. Once they crested this pass, according to Valasian's directions, the path would lead them to the back entrance of the Cabane. The contour lines resembled an hourglass lying on its side. From where he stood, he could see snow blocking the pass.

He was sorry that the new crop of clouds had snuffed out what he imagined was a majestic view of the Bernese mountain range beyond.

"Calliope," he whispered in her ear. "We're almost there."

She shifted her shoulders, lifted her head on her tall swan's neck, and frowned, then nestled into him as if he were a down feather bed.

"'But all the gods pitied him except Poseidon,'" she recited in a slow and deep voice, "'who, stayed relentlessly angry with godlike Odysseus until his return to his own country.'"

"Am I Odysseus?" Jim asked, but she did not respond.

When they reached the peak that was a narrow gap in the mountains, Jim laid Calliope on the blanket to rest his

back and take a drink. He tried to cover her with the soggy tarp, but after three attempts that involved running after the tarp in the wind, he gave up and tucked it back into the knapsack. He pressed snow on Calliope's wet and warm forehead.

Mr. Politician Husband, collect your treasure!

For the rest of the dark afternoon, as Jim cleared a path over the pivot of the valley, as he strode with Calliope in his arms through the barren snowfields, Calliope said nothing. She slept; she coughed; she was feverish, then cool, and she did not stop trembling.

He imagined the Castellane sisters awaiting him in Paris: Clio's eyes narrowed at him in judgment; Thalia's flirtatious smile, perhaps more hesitant. Would she retract the line of poetry she had translated for him, "Remember, I wait for you forever."? It was the thought of Helene's softly yearning eyes that compelled him to walk faster.

FOURTEEN

CAPTURE

WHY WOULD ANYONE LOCK A CABIN ON ONE OF the most forlorn peaks of the Wildhorn Mountain? To keep out desperate, hungry, and stranded tourists in life-threatening snowstorms? Using his Swiss Army knife, Jim tried to break the locked door of the Cabane des Audannes while the listless Calliope asked inchoate questions followed by the refrain, "Jim, why here?" He had placed her sitting against the doorstep, and now she lay down on the wet gravel terrace beside it.

After giving up on his Swiss Army knife and bending two of Calliope's arrows, Jim finally cracked the lock. He carried Calliope, with the now-silent Hamlet in her pocket, into the icebox chalet and laid them beside the cleaned-out metal fireplace. Jim sprinted through the hut in search of

food, medicine, and something to light on fire. What had been a cozy refuge stoked with singers and hikers from all over the world, including the lovely Castellane sisters, was now a hollow shell. How quick the transformation had been. The seasons had shifted in a week's time!

The Swiss were neat and tidy; he would give them that. Jim's frantic rummaging produced a jar of gooseberry jam, a Toblerone chocolate bar, two sets of hand warmers, a first-aid kit complete with homeopathic medicine for colds and flus, aloe vera for sunburns, and a box of matches. No antibiotics. No wood for the fire. Not a scrap of paper to burn.

He scurried up the ladder and pulled down two mattresses and a comforter. He laid the inert Calliope and Hamlet on one mattress near the fireplace and placed the comforter over them. Using a steak knife from the kitchen, he shredded the other mattress and fed scraps into the fireplace. With the matches—thank God for the matches—he lit a fire. He filled pots from the kitchen with blocks of snow from outside and placed them on the stove top. He found the gas pipe under the cabinet, turned the lever to open it, and lit the stove. Outside the Cabane Jim spread out his red Blackhawks sweatshirt, logo staring upward, and used rocks to pin it to the holding wall. The area surrounding the cabin was large and flat, a perfect helicopter landing pad.

When Jim returned to the fire, he found Calliope mid–coughing fit, feeding pieces of chocolate to the bird in her arm. How could the scrawny fowl still be alive, and, more important, why would she feed it the little they had? Jim

was ravenously hungry. Before he could speak in anger, she raised her head and smiled at him, a smile so serene and innocent that his flash of rage melted away. They split the rest of the chocolate, and Jim spoon-fed her the gooseberry jam and the homeopathic pills. He tipped a cup of heated water into her mouth and watched the rosy color return to her cheeks. Her forehead was burning, her lips gray blue. As she was too weak, he removed her wet clothes and then his. He looked away in panic when he saw how her hipbones jutted out, how concave her stomach was. The owlet lay on its side as well, and Jim noticed that its trembling had stopped. Calliope fell asleep immediately, and he listened, sleeplessly to her labored breaths until the dawn approached.

ONLY AFTER HE FELT HER BODY BECOME RIGID DID he hear it—a faint trace of the sound he'd been praying for for days.

Calliope sat up, alert. "There's a storage cellar below— we'll hide there."

She was the commander in chief again, despite her sickness and fever.

Jim rose groggily, threw on his damp shirt, pants, and boots, and ran outside.

It was still cloudy, but the morning sun cleaved a bright path through the thick soup of ashen sky. Jim guessed it was 9 a.m. He must have fallen asleep just after dawn. He grabbed the wet red sweatshirt from the wall and began waving it in

the air, jumping up and down until he grew dizzy. It had begun to snow again—a little blizzard, but nothing like the thick white glue he had hiked through the day before. It looked like the black speck in the faraway skies was making a beeline toward him. Valasian must have told the pilots that they were headed to the Cabane.

"What are you doing?"

He turned at the sound of her hoarse voice. Calliope held herself up by the knob of the Cabane's outer door. With her other hand, she held the comforter to her body. He continued to wave the sweatshirt. She ran at him with what must have been the last strength she had preserved in her weakened condition.

"Stop!" she cried, her eyes too large for her face.

Now almost overhead, the helicopter was clattering, thundering. From where he stood, the blades and their shadows on the snow looked like the spikes on the back of a dragon.

She was screaming and coughing and crying, but he could not hear her. He rushed to her, holding her in a tight embrace as the chopper blew a tornado of snow around them.

"*NON!*" She was hitting him with her fists. "Let me GO!"

The chopper dipped and dropped and dipped, banking to the right, then the left, and then it rose up again as if on a string that would not let it down, its madly slicing blades trammeling the air above them. Calliope and he were in its

shadow. In its clutches. She was shivering from the exertion, her lips chattering and blue, her cheeks flushed dark pink.

"No!" she said, crying, close to his ear. "Jim, I beg you, take me to the cellar, take me. I beg you."

Why wouldn't the chopper land? It looked as if it was caught in a wind tunnel above them; its carriage was buffeted by the competing air drafts and snow.

She wrenched herself free from him with one last burst of energy and ran inside. He followed her down the stairs to the cellar. She knelt beside the thick metal cellar door and pointed her bow and arrow at him. He remembered the last time the arrow had been aimed at his heart. Then, he'd been part of a playful dance; now, she wanted to kill him.

"Open the door," she demanded in a quavering voice that he barely heard above the din of the helicopter outside. "I can't open the door by myself with that heavy padlock on it. Open it, or I will kill you.

"I will shoot you!" she yelled, pulling back the arrow on the taut bowstring. Her fingers shook. She was having trouble focusing.

"I will do it." She shut her eyes. "Even with my eyes shut. I will."

In a swift dash he grabbed the bow from her, avoiding the arrow that jettisoned up the cellar stairs. She bent her head onto her chest and began to sob. When she looked up, her eyes were filled with panic.

"'Amlet? Where is 'Amlet?" She struggled past him on

the stairs. "'Amlet, 'Amlet, where are you?" she called, looking frantically around the room.

From the starkness of the silence outside, they both knew that the helicopter had landed. The sound of men's voices punctured the quiet.

Jim approached her as if he were trapping a cornered wild animal. She struggled as he lifted her in his arms. After a few moments of kicking, her body went limp. Her eyes were bright, watery blue, and in what was left of her voice she whispered:

"I know, my American Galahad, that you alone could break the padlock on that cellar door, you alone . . ."

For a moment they were both convinced that he would do what she wished. Then he turned his face from her and carried her outside.

THE SNOW WAS FALLING GENTLY NOW. THE MASSIVE and unwieldy copter, its long tail lit at the end with a flashing light, rested on the stone terrace where not long ago Jim had watched the Italians gather for a smoke. Jim heard the engines revving, and the blades, which had slowed, now spun into a blur.

"'Nothing,'" she said in a strange, deep, clear voice, loud enough for him to hear above the windmill of noise and swirling snow, "'nothing is as dangerous as an ignorant friend.'" When he looked into her face, her eyes narrowed. "'A wise enemy is to be preferred.' La Fontaine always has the last word."

"I can't let you die, Calliope!" Jim yelled over the clamor, making his way around the copter.

"You are sightless," she yelled, and her warm breath tickled his ear. "You are blind as the ocean, yes, the ocean! Can't you see it? Look! Down below! The lights of a town, a short walk below! We could go—"

His eyes followed her pointing, trembling finger; the twinkling lights of the town below were surely a mirage that would disappear. Had Jim been so exhausted by the day's hike with Ambrose to have missed seeing the glimmering lights only a week ago?

The copilot appeared at Jim's side. He opened his arms. Despite the barrage of snow and sound, Jim noticed the man's bearded and handsome face. From one man to another. As Jim delivered her, he imagined Calliope's father doing the same: bestowing the prone Calliope as an offering to her husband.

"*You have betrayed me,*" she yelled out to Jim in staccato, short breaths.

Having deposited Calliope into the whirring chopper, the copilot, with snow in his beard, rotated his arms in large circles, urging Jim to join them.

Jim was tempted. He could ensure that she landed safely and that the ambulance dispatched her immediately to a hospital. But how could he look Calliope in the face after he had failed her, her daughters, and himself, by delivering her into the hands of her abusive husband?

"No," he yelled, waving his arms. "Go!"

"Allez, allez!" yelled the copilot.

"No," Jim yelled back. "GO!"

The rotor blades beat the snow-filled air like eggs in a blender.

"May they be safe," Jim said under his breath. "May they be safe."

Hamlet. When he found Hamlet, he would walk with the owlet in the crook of his arm, as Calliope had done, to the small town that Calliope had spotted below. His legs felt like lead and his back ached as he dragged himself into the cold and empty Cabane des Audannes. He listened for hooting but could only hear the clattering copter outside.

From the constancy of the sound, it seemed that the chopper had stalled and was not able to move forward. Perhaps Calliope had threaded an arrow onto the bow and was aiming at the captain.

He stepped into the mudroom and as he passed the map on the wall, he saw one of Calliope's arrows struck into it. The map was on the wall directly at the top of the cellar stairs. In her anger, had she struck her arrow into this map on her way up the cellar stairs? Or could this have been the arrow that had been intended for his heart and had missed? The arrow pierced the mountainous area half an inch from Anzère! Could she be that good?

At last he heard the engines of the chopper accelerate into a roar. He could no longer resist. He dashed out of the Cabane to watch the chopper transition from hovering to forward flight. Its nose pitched downward and it cut

through the white, falling sky, the victorious battle weapon bringing back the spoils of war. She was coughing just then, or crying. Or she was reciting a stanza from a French poem to the pilots. Or covering her ears with her hands, the way she'd done when she heard the helicopter nearing. How like a young girl she looked when she did that, her elbows raised to eye level, her forefingers delicately pressing into her ear canals.

He was sure she had pneumonia. She could die on the way to the hospital. It was unforgivable that he had not brought her back before the predicted snows.

"Whiteout." He said it aloud, as if he were explaining it to Thalia. The truth was that Jim had lost track of time; one day had melted into the next. Calliope's illness had slowed them considerably, as had the snow and their visit to the hermitess.

He listened to the faint drone of the chopper in the gathering stillness, trying to calibrate each diminishing decibel. He wanted to catch that moment when the hum of the chopper vanished. From mountain world, Calliope world, enchanted world, to . . . what?

Silence. The world had emptied itself out.

Jim walked around the outside of the Cabane. He spotted a path, now snow covered, that meandered around the jagged boulder down into the valley below. Calliope knew the mountain as well as anyone. Should he have listened to her? But what looked like a few miles as the crow flies could take hours, possibly days, by foot.

"Hamlet!" he called out.

A single hawk flew overhead. Jim remembered Calliope's reaction along the trail when she had seen a similar white-tailed hawk—she had covered the owlet from its sight with a swoop of her hands, quickly, deftly, as she did everything.

The town lights beckoned him. Her face, her tears, her words *You have betrayed me*, gnawed at him, as did his hunger.

After some time, he gave up his search for the owlet. The clouds were meeting again in the white congress of day. The snow was falling again, thick and fast.

She was gone.

FIFTEEN

LAUENEN

BELLS. RINGING IN HIS EARS. HIS THROAT WAS parched. Knives twisted in his stomach. He couldn't remember the last time he'd eaten. Or the last time he'd seen the sun. Where was he? What day was it? Why was he still trying to pry the whiteness from the sky? To wrench himself free from it. The smell of snow.

Jim checked beside himself for the owlet. He was in a bed. Dry, warm sheets. His body ached, his shoulders, his legs, his feet. He could feel his feet! Beneath the hunger pains, a vague, unpleasant sensation spread inside him, the empty echoes of a thousand dank, cold caves. Loneliness.

Sunlight penetrated the room through the white lace curtain. Why was the curtain drawn? He would let the sun in. Sitting up, he reached to pull back the curtain.

He lifted himself out of bed and limped into the bathroom down the hall. The wonder of a bathroom! He looked at himself in the mirror. He'd grown a beard. He spotted a furrow between his brows that he'd never seen before. The skin on his cheeks was red and dry and chapped.

It consoled Jim that Calliope had been wrong. The village that Calliope thought was an afternoon jaunt down the valley had taken him a full day and half a moon-filled night to reach. Marked by dizzying cliff walks—vertical descents that he'd had to maneuver on his backside and using two dangling metal ladders, the last of which he'd dismounted in the dark—it hadn't been an easy hike.

He shut his eyes and saw Calliope walking ahead of him. He watched her elegant ankles and her long, slim calves, and he heard her laughter in the wind, like stones skimming the surface of a placid lake.

Betrayal. No matter how hard Jim tried to convince himself that he could never have made the descent with Calliope in his arms, he knew deep inside that they could have prevailed. She would have encouraged him, one step after another. After all, she was Calliope, the muse.

But she would have been required to register at the hospital, or he would have had to do so for her. She would have had to reveal her closest kin. The news would have traveled quickly. The helicopters would have been assigned a new destination; the press would have been smacking their lips for fresh gossip.

It would have been better never to have found her, to

have returned empty-handed to Gstaad. "Sorry," he would have said to the sisters. "As you failed to find her, so did I." In any case, she would have been forced from the chalet by the pilots. Or would she have eluded them and hiked unde-terred to Anzère? With pneumonia? More likely, she would have entranced another, smarter, hiker.

Jim needed to know how she was. Where was his knap-sack in this tidy room of this tidy inn that a Good Samaritan had led him to in the middle of the night? He felt for his wallet in his back pocket and was relieved to find it. He re-moved two soaked five-hundred-euro notes, his credit card, his insurance card, and his driver's license. He also found a crumpled, wet business card embossed in peach-colored ink with *Éditions Gallimard* and below it, the name, Helene Castellane, hdcgallimard.fr. On the back of the card, he no-ticed some words written in blue ink that had blurred to-gether and were indecipherable. But hadn't it been Thalia, not Helene, who'd given him her card? Heaviness filled the empty spaces inside himself as he turned the card over in his hand. His mind was playing tricks on him. Or perhaps the sisters had been colluding, having fun with him, the naive American. Bait and switch. Sleight of mind and hand. Thalia flirts with you but gives you her sister's card.

His knapsack. Where was it? It contained his passport, his phone, his life! He stumbled around the room searching for it futilely, then lay back in bed. He had a dim memory of slipping down the slick mountain face in the darkness. Now he remembered. His knapsack had snagged on something, a

jagged mountain edge. Knowing that his passport was in it, he had tried with all his might to free it. He'd finally decided that he had no choice but to slip out of it. At the time, fearing that he would slide down the mountain to his death, it had seemed a small thing. He hadn't lost his life, but he *had* lost his identity, and his connection to the world. He'd also lost track of time. His new job. Again, he asked, what day was it?

He swept his wet Windbreaker from the nearby chair to check the pockets. Instead of his passport, he found the book Thalia had given him. He remembered placing it in his jacket pocket after seeing Calliope off, after . . . his *betrayal*. He'd planned to try to decipher the French words and take some solace from them as he walked (*ha!*) down the mountain.

The small book was soggy and torn in places, and many pages were stuck together. He opened to the page with the sprig of heather—miraculously still there—and the spine nearly broke.

He spoke the line, "Remember, I wait for you forever."

Desperately, he felt for the maroon velvet ribbon in his jacket pocket, but recalled that he had lost it along the way. He smiled to himself when he found instead one of Hamlet's feathers. Jim was grateful to the owlet for sparing Calliope the misery of his dying in her arms.

HE STOOPED TO DESCEND THE LOW-CEILINGED stairs into the small, empty, wood-lined reception area. He

placed the heavy room key with its leather tassel onto the desk and stepped into the cool mountain air. A bearded man in a wool cap talking on a cell phone strutted past him down the cobblestone street. Schoolchildren in uniforms ran ahead of him. The town was too sweet for his mood. It was an everything-in-its-place kind of Swiss town; if you shook it, confetti snow would flutter around it like in a snow globe. Jim felt too tall; he did not fit into its miniature dimensions.

He stopped a pedestrian, an elderly woman using a cane.

"Would you please tell me what day it is and where I am?" he asked in English.

A little translation, a few gestures, a curious glance, and an unspoken suspicion about his sanity later, and the answer was given: Sunday, September 7th. He was in the town of Lauenen, in the Swiss Alps. If he hightailed it to Geneva by—no—there was no way that he would make the international flight to JFK that afternoon. He had no passport!

He would need to get an emergency passport in Geneva. He would research the details on the Internet that day. Also, he had unfinished business: he couldn't leave Europe without knowing that Calliope had found safety and medicine.

He gazed up at the green hillside sprinkled with timber houses and, above that, at the mountains that dominated the vista from the main street. He counted eleven peaks. It was like a view into the mouth of the planet: eyeteeth at the front, molars and wisdom teeth at the back. How many hundreds or thousands of mountains rose behind these, beyond his vision?

Ambrose had described "hiker's high," the euphoria that climbers experience when they feel they are in the reach of the clouds. He'd also warned Jim that descending into a valley could bring on bouts of depression, even in the most experienced hikers. In Lauenen, closed at one end by a mountain and opening at the other end onto a large lake now filling with fog, a feeling of oppression lodged itself in the back of his throat. The perfect flowers planted in large pots, the way the people looked so confined in their clothes, the fences around the small houses and small, manicured grass plots: everything seemed contained and manmade and dull, compared to the wide-open skies and sharp peaks of the Wildhorn. No one seemed to notice that life was moving like the mountain-fed river beside the paved sidewalk— swiftly and beyond reach.

In a small Internet café, he used his credit card to pay for a seat at a desktop computer. He entered the names "Calliope and Yves Castellane" in the search engine and scrolled through a dozen photographs of the couple. He stopped at an image of Calliope on a stretcher. Her lovely face was wan; her eyes were closed. She was Juliet, carried aloft from the Capulet tombs. In the photograph, a helicopter loomed in the background.

"GRETA GARBO FRANÇAISE" was the headline. Another: "I WANT TO BE ALONE." Another: "WIFE OF PRESIDENTIAL CANDIDATE RESCUED FROM THE ALPS IN CRITICAL CONDITION." He studied the photograph of her husband, a slightly overweight but handsome man. He was gray at the temples, with brown

eyes, a strong, slender nose that oddly resembled hers, a chin that jutted out like a rock outcropping, and a broad forehead that looked higher due to his receding hairline.

No mention in any of the articles of an American named James George Olsen. According to the press, Madame Castellane had experienced an unusual "*contretemps*," a turn in the weather during her vacation in the Bernese Alps. There had also been a "*contretemps dans leur mariage*," foul weather in her marriage. Another photograph showed Yves Castellane, "the politician who had promised 'exemplary behavior' in his quest for the presidency, on a scooter departing from the local hospital in the 17th arrondissement in Paris, where he was visiting his baby daughter by his mistress, a Russian model." The writer described how the presidential candidate's shiny Ferragamo shoes in the shabby neighborhood had given away his charade.

In the leftist rag *Libération*, a journalist suggested that Madame Castellane's discovery of her husband's clandestine affair and child had sent her into the Alps. But this was France, where the populace was more tolerant of their politicians' peccadilloes. Still, the online news intimated that French women voters' opinions were changing about what was acceptable and that Castellane's support among the female electorate could erode—that is unless his wife of twenty-seven years excused his behavior as out of character and did the proverbial "stand by his side."

Castellane's party, the Union for a Popular Movement, carried 51 percent in the polls. The candidate had his anchor

on the right; immigration was his major issue: "Without border controls, there is no nation." His triumvirate platform: reduce taxes on businesses and the wealthy, reduce the number of public-sector employees, and reduce illegal immigration by 50 percent.

Jim checked his e-mail, hoping for news from one of the sisters. He and Thalia had exchanged cards. He searched "thalia" and received six results. The first was dated the day after his and Ambrose's departure.

"Jim, I know you won't receive this until you return to Gstaad, but I wanted you to know that it was a delight, the night that we met."

The second: "My sisters and I are wondering whether you are having success bringing our mother down from the mountain. By the way, I got great reviews in *Dahlia*, the play in which I'm the lead. Reviewers said I was a '*provacatrice*'!"

The third: "Where are you, Jim Olsen. We're beginning to worry. Have you come down the mountain yet with our maman? I am hoping that you are well. Call my cell as soon as you're back. By the way, I was awarded the part of Ophelia in the new *Hamlet* playing at the Athénée Théâtre starting in December."

The fourth e-mail: "We have heard that it has been snowing in the Alps, and we worry about our mother's and your safety. Where are you? I feel like I'm typing into a vortex. We hear nothing from you! Please come down!"

The fifth: "Father said that the helicopter pilots saw you

and Mother, but that you fled from them. Is this so? Please come back with our mother."

The last, from yesterday:

"You must be in Gstaad by now. Our mother is in critical condition, still in intensive care at the hospital. She was barely conscious when they landed. WHAT delayed your return? She refuses to speak. Even to me! What happened in the mountains? What happened? We are confused and dismayed, and we need answers from you."

There was a slew of messages from Ambrose, as well.

"Jim, have you fallen off a cliff? Do you know that we've had search parties out for the two of you? Your mother has been calling me, sometimes twice a day. You owe me for that, pal. Sall calls every other day. If you are still in Europe, come and stay with me in Paris, but let me know as soon as possible."

JIM MADE THE EXECUTIVE DECISION TO START WORK on Monday the 15th, a week after his official start date. He would call Jay Wolfe and apologize for the delay, which had been caused by Alpine weather conditions. On his way back to New York City, he would pass through Paris. His itinerary for the following morning: Lauenen to Geneva, where he would try to attain an emergency passport. Hopefully, that would take no more than an afternoon. He would catch a flight from Geneva to Paris and arrive Monday evening.

He e-mailed Thalia: "I plan to be in Paris tomorrow

evening. Would you be free to meet me for a drink? I will confirm arrival time."

In the quaint Swiss town, he ate a hearty breakfast. He bought new clothes and a cell phone, accoutrements necessary to conform and integrate.

From the terrace of an empty café, he called his parents. It would be cocktail time in Chicago. When his mother answered the phone, despite the static on the line he heard her take a deep breath. And then she dug in. What a relief it was to have the Atlantic Ocean between them.

"Yes, I will be back in the US soon," he said. "Yes, I know. Ambrose. Did he? Yes. I don't know when. Climbing in the Alps. Ambrose was supposed to tell you all that. Longer than expected, yes. I did not expect snow. Not sure what the temperature is here. No. I would say forty degrees, maybe warmer. Yes, early snows. I'll let you know when . . . No, no. Yes, they know. I think I still have the job. I know you worry." The energy was draining from him. "Where's Dad?"

Most probably in the basement. His mother carried the portable phone everywhere she went in the house.

"I'd like to talk to him," Jim said loudly. "You've never had a problem interrupting him before. Please put him on the line. I'm calling from Switzerland."

Jim walked to the edge of the terrace. The shadow from the tallest peak covered this part of town. He guessed it would be another hour before the sun would shine through to where he stood.

"Dad. Mom, will you please hang up. I can hear you breathing." Jim waited, closing his eyes, pacing the small terrace. An older couple, walking arm-in-arm, passed him. And then there were his parents, arm-locked in repressed rage over the decades, separated by the different floors of the house they shared. The older man in the walking couple wore a plaid hat tilted sideways in a stylish way. Jim imagined the woman pulling it down over the man's left eye before they left their home. "There," she might have said. "That's smart." The old couple rounded the corner.

The voice that had given up so many battles spoke. "Hello, son."

"Dad," Jim said. "Yes, I'm fine. Yes. Dad. Mom, I heard you pick up. Mom, will you please let me speak to Dad alone?" He wished his father would do this for him, this one time: tell his mother to put down the receiver and quit eavesdropping.

"Mom, NOW."

He waited until he heard the click.

"I know what you're going to say, Dad—yes, 'that's Mom,' but I want to talk to *you*. I want to tell you that I love you. That's all I want to say."

There was quiet on the other end, as if Jim's words were an inscrutable riddle for which the recipient had no answer. Jim continued his pacing back and forth on the terrace. He watched his breath unfurl into the cold.

Was that his mother's impatient sigh on the other end of the phone?

"Dad, are you there?"

No sound, only the static. Jim waited. "I'll call again, Dad. I'll call again, okay?"

He heard himself bark, "You will visit me in New York City when I get back."

This was the language his father understood.

"Yes, I will—yes, *we* will," his father corrected himself. No doubt his mother was back on the line.

His father would never leave his mother to visit him alone.

Jim hung up the phone. On that terrace, gazing at the mountains to the west, he vowed that he would never end up like his father. He vowed that today was the last day he would be a passive party to his mother's bullying. If his mother did not change her tone, change her tune, he would never speak to her again. *Mountains, you are my witness.*

Next call: Jay Wolfe. He decided to sidestep the hierarchy and go straight to the top.

As part of the interview process more than a month ago, Jim had played a round of golf with Jay. The way Jay had ordered golf clubs from his caddy—"Sand wedge," "9 iron"—and held out his arm without looking up or acknowledging the caddy's presence bothered Jim. It wasn't a cataclysmic character flaw, but each time Jay did it Jim found himself wincing.

It was Sunday evening, but Jay was at the office.

"I apologize for not letting you know sooner. I was in the Alps, I lost service— "

"The point is not where you were vacationing, Jim; the point is that without you here next week, you will cost us money and time. When *will* you be in the office?"

"A week from tomorrow."

Helene would have appreciated his gumption. What made him think of Helene?

Jay Wolfe hung up the phone without another word.

THE NEXT MORNING, AFTER AN ALMOST SLEEPLESS night of undefined and disturbing dreams, he hired a taxi to Gstaad and caught the 9 a.m. train to Geneva. In Geneva, three hours later, he found the passport agency and received an emergency passport, thanks to Swiss efficiency. At an Internet café, he checked his e-mails and was relieved to see a response from Thalia. After he confirmed his flight details, he wrote that he would meet her that night at 5:30 p.m. at the café Les Deux Magots.

PART THREE

CALLIOPE CAPTURED

SIXTEEN

PARIS

IT WAS THE HOUR CALLIOPE LIKED MOST: DUSK, when the day was mature and all that remained was reflection. "Sunset," she'd said—Jim remembered her flipping her palm upward—"there's mischief in a sunset, in the hush of it, when the world says *shhhhhh*." She'd paused, and with her he'd felt the resonance in the moments before the sun bowed its head—before the night animals and insects broke the stillness with their buzzing and swarming.

The buzz at Les Deux Magots was at high frequency at 5:30 that evening, not with insects but with Parisians. The waiters, tight faced, narrow eyed, and stingy with requests, zigzagged in their long white aprons from table to table. Jim was ten minutes early, thanks to the punctual Swiss trains. He'd had just enough time to drop off his things in the foyer

of Ambrose's apartment. Unfortunately neither Ambrose, Stephanie, nor the kids were home. Ambrose was away on business: a Giacometti had recently appeared on the market, the seller lived in Brussels, and Ambrose was escorting a client to view it. Stephanie was at dinner with the kids at her parent's apartment. As Jim had left to meet Thalia, he had spotted her book of poetry poking out of the pocket of the new knapsack he had bought in Lauenen. In a last-minute impulse, he took it with him. Perhaps its presence would rekindle the mood of the night with Thalia and her sisters. Perhaps she would explain why she'd translated that one stanza. Would she use the wine as her excuse? The altitude? Or had her private message been merely a device to bribe a hiker to find her mother?

It was chilly, but the sun on the café terrace tempted Jim into taking a table outside. As he waited for Thalia, he absorbed the movement and color of the Parisian boulevards, dressed as they were with dancing colored leaves from the nearby plane trees.

At first glance, Thalia was less beautiful than she had been when they'd first met. Her skin looked paler and her face smaller, her chin sharper and her eyes set too far apart on her face. But her eyes were that same light blue whose brightness had startled him at first glance in the Cabane des Audannes. He stood as she approached and he leaned over the table to kiss her on the cheek. Thalia averted her head to avoid the kiss, leaving in its wake a sweet scent that Jim did not recognize. It was different—musty, like something that

had been in the attic for too long. The fragrance lingered in the space between them. Her lips moved, but her eyes stayed watchful. With her mother's grace, she lowered herself into the chair that Jim pulled out for her.

Ah, Calliope! Where are you now, to soften the hard edges between people? Thalia twisted to catch the attention of the waiter, her wavy, shiny hair swishing along her pink silk scarf.

When their eyes finally met, Thalia quickly looked away. It was her lips that disturbed him most. They pouted oh so beautifully, with such a plump bottom lip; but the look they created was of a spoiled child.

"Mademoiselle?" said the waiter.

"Un kir, s'il vous plaît," she said. Where was the flirtatious curve of her lips as she spoke, her jaunty movements? Where were Calliope's lilting and winged melodies, silky like rose petals on their last day of bloom?

He ordered a Stella Artois.

"What happened?" Her tone was clipped; her eyes questioned him. Pigeons scattered in front of running children and flew toward them. As if Thalia and he were one person, they lifted their hands and ducked their heads in unison. If he had been with Calliope, she would have laughed at their simultaneous reaction. But Thalia was not interested in such frivolity. She placed her hands on the table; she was here to do business, to extract reasons. Tender, delicate hands, fingernails painted a light pink.

"I asked you what happened," she said.

A truck with SAINT YVES, 6 PLACE DE LA LIBERTÉ in bold black letters across the side lurched nearby, and he felt the grating grinding of the brakes somewhere deep inside him. How long would it take for him to become desensitized once again to the harsh city sounds? Where were the murmurs of the mountain winds and owls and the ever-present hum of running water? The irony of the juxtaposition of the words "Saint Yves" and "Place de la Liberté" was not lost on him.

"What happened?" she repeated. Her blue eyes searched his, then quickly moved to her slender, folded fingers. An oval sapphire surrounded by diamonds was perched on the ring finger of her left hand.

"I returned your mother," he said.

"You nearly returned her to her Maker," she said, her thick black lashes clamping shut. She touched the scarf at her neck, then clasped her hands.

"She had pneumonia," Thalia continued. "She was in critical condition and was finally released to go home this morning."

The waiter returned with their drinks and placed the torn bill in the small ashtray. Thalia sipped her kir. Her hand trembled when she returned the glass to the table. Perhaps that was why she clasped her hands together so fiercely—so he wouldn't see. The orange-pink sunset color of the kir was the hue of her lips. Her fingertips grew white as she pressed her knuckles.

"You told us that you would bring her down if you lo-

cated her . . . that you would call us from Gstaad. You were gone for a week!"

He looked down at her pink fingernails and her wrist, the delicate gold bracelet that lay around it, and followed her long, slender arms to the puckered black short sleeves of her dress. He wondered how long it had taken her to choose the dress. Had she thrown the clothes that didn't satisfy her on the closet floor, as he'd watched Sally do countless times? She'd decided on sexy. This dress dipped down in front in a shape that suggested the curve of a heart. So many small details contributed to a French woman's allure.

"We refrained from sending in the Swiss Air Ambulance for three days," she continued, "and then, with the snow, it was impossible. Did you know that for two terrifying days, the Swiss gave you both up for buried in snow? The press went berserk. We couldn't leave our homes."

"You forget—" he began. It was Helene and her wish to protect her mother's liberty, who had dissuaded her sisters from hiring the experienced rescue service at an earlier time.

Jim could have apologized, told the scowling daughter that he could have been more determined and forceful, that he shouldn't have let her mother convince him to visit the hermitess when the snow loomed. He also could have told Thalia that he had not left her mother's side during her illness, that instead of excoriation he should be receiving praise for ensuring her capture. What he was tempted to tell her was what it felt like to spend time with her mother—as if he

was drunk with life, really alive for the first time in his life.

Tilting her head, Thalia gazed at Jim from the corners of her blue-blue eyes. She'd written him off as below her noble pedigree.

"How is she?" he asked.

Thalia sipped her kir and regarded the couple at the adjacent table. They were approximately the same age as them. The woman's hair was disheveled. Lovers, perhaps, having a drink after an afternoon nap.

"How is she?" he repeated.

"You were supposed to—"

"I did."

She sighed loudly. She reached to pick up her purse beside her chair and placed it on her lap. "What took you so long?" she asked. She shook her head quickly. A strand of hair fell across her brow, splitting her face into two halves. "We misjudged you," she said. She rose from the table. He stood also.

"And I you."

"Do you know that yesterday, when she came home from the hospital she ran around the house in Paris like a madwoman, pulling oil paintings from the wall?"

"Which paintings?"

"Family heirlooms, the ones of the muses, masterpieces that belong in a museum . . ."

Calliope's small rebellion: exorcising the muses from her life. Perhaps she would change her name, ask for a divorce.

"What did she do with them?"

"Clio and I found them in a heap in the back hall to be picked up as trash the following day. She doesn't know it, but we hid them safely in the basement. When we asked her why she did it, she refused to answer. She began calling us names that weren't ours. She's still calling Helene Eleanor. She's said very little to any of us since she returned. That's why . . ."

He watched the color rise in her cheeks like a burst of flame in a fireplace. The flush settled in the lower part of her jaw. That was the face he'd remembered, Thalia of the transparent skin, the blue-blue eyes.

"I begged Clio to come with me today," she continued, "but she refused. She said she couldn't look you in the face. I don't think you understand how completely deranged with worry we've been during your absence. Clio and Helene got into a huge fight and are still not talking—"

"You haven't told me how your mother is," he persisted.

She placed a five-euro bill on the table.

He picked it up to return it to her.

"No," she said, raising her palm. "Consider it your tip. *Oui*, five euros, yes, that should cover it." She stood.

"Wait," he said, his voice rough at the edges, "I never said thank you."

"Thank you for what?" she said. Her purse swung forward and knocked over her half-drunk kir. She frowned and wiped at her dress with her napkin.

"Before you go," he said.

She sat back down in the cramped space and continued

to rub her dress with the small paper napkin. The couple next to them kissed. Thalia raised her eyes to the sky.

"I wanted to thank you for this," he said, placing on the table the tattered paperback of French poetry that had survived the snows.

She looked confused.

"That's not from me," she said.

He opened the book to the blurred handwriting in blue pen and showed it to her.

"Not my handwriting," she said, peering down at it. "It's Helene's."

"What?"

"She's the poet in the family." Thalia read the translated verse. She stood again. "This whole thing has become so, so . . ." She shook her head emphatically.

She slid awkwardly out of the tight arrangement of tables.

No backward glance. No sliver of light in the slammed door of her departure. She glided away down the street, walking as if she knew he was watching, gracefully sidestepping to avoid pedestrians, her figure growing smaller and smaller until finally she was lost in the sea of multitudes.

Helene had given him the book of poems! The verse that had told him only of Thalia's compelling emotions on a moonlit night now revealed a moon with a different luster. The world felt lighter; it reminded him of the moment when the whiteout ended and the mist began clearing, and he could see farther and farther into the distance. He called

Éditions Gallimard from his phone and asked for Helene Castellane. Out of town.

THAT NIGHT, JIM LOGGED ON TO AMBROSE'S COMputer, and the news program confirmed that the presidential candidate's wife who had been lost in the Alps had been released from the hospital and was recovering at home. Jim also discovered that Calliope was a trustee of the Musée national du Moyen Âge, the National Museum of the Middle Ages, and that her husband had recently arranged to donate to the Cloisters in New York one of the most important of the seven tapestries in *The Hunt of the Unicorn* series from late-fifteenth-century Flanders. This one tapestry had been missing from the series from the museum because the owners, the presidential candidate's family, had wished to keep it warming the hallway of their ancestral home in Limousin, where it had been hanging since before the French Revolution. (During the French Revolution, it had been hidden in the cellar as a cover for potatoes.) The tapestry would be delivered to the Cloisters after an elongated exhibition stay at the Musée national du Moyen Âge.

The image of the tapestry, *The Unicorn in Captivity* on the Internet showed a unicorn, with a placid expression on its face, chained loosely to a tree surrounded by a low, circular fence. Wasn't one of the presidential candidate's slogans "Without border controls, there is no nation"?

Unicorns, he read, were caught only by deception. Jim remembered the coffeetable book in Calliope's chalet featuring a different unicorn tapestry.

Madame was scheduled to preside over the rededication of the *Unicorn* tapestry at the museum the following week. This would be Madame Castellane's first public appearance since her husband declared candidacy.

Political campaigns aside, Jim thought, *shouldn't she be resting?*

The following morning, Jim called the Department of Development at the museum and asked the director's assistant, who spoke fairly good English, to leave a message for Madame Castellane. He left his cell phone number and e-mail address.

There was no response for the next three days. Saturday morning before his rescheduled flight, in a small stationery boutique near Ambrose's apartment on the rue de Passy, Jim bought a card stamped at the top with the silhouette of a unicorn. He would hand-deliver the note to the Castellane residence, which, to his surprise, he had been able to find online.

"Dear Calliope," he wrote. "I am relieved to know that you have recovered. I blame myself for your critical condition. I depart for NYC today, but I hope that we can continue to be friends. I can be reached at James.Olsen@wolfetaylor.com or at +1 646-535-5777.

Sincerely,

J."

• • •

He rang the bell and looked up at the lions' and horned rams' heads decorating the cornices of the mansion. A man dressed in full butler livery—complete with raised chin and open disdain for outsiders—took the envelope from Jim's hands.

"For Madame Castellane," Jim said.

White gloves! The candidate from the Union for a Popular Movement greeted the world with a butler with white gloves?

Jim was about to turn around and leave when he heard something so familiar, he wondered if he'd imagined it. It was Calliope's cough. He looked up and saw her leaning out the window, her hair falling on either side of her pale, gaunt face.

"Jim," she called. "Don't leave." Her voice was high-pitched and strained.

And then she was no longer at the window. Had she been pulled back into the room? He rang the doorbell. The butler appeared.

"Madame Castellane has asked for me," he said.

The butler motioned for Jim to wait at the door. He spoke with someone inside.

"Madame is busy now," he said, "but she says she would like to see you later, this afternoon."

"I have a flight to catch. Would you please tell her that I can only see her now?"

The butler turned back into the interior once again. This time the volley was faster. "Madame Castellane cannot see you now, but she would like to see you this afternoon."

His flight was at 2 p.m. He would communicate with her by phone, by e-mail. He could not miss a second flight. He returned to Ambrose's apartment to pick up his few things and headed to the station to catch the RER train to Charles de Gaulle Airport. "Don't leave," she'd said.

On the train, as the distance between Jim and Paris increased, so did a strange tension that made him feel as if he was being pulled in the wrong direction. He could return to Paris next week, maybe next month, within the year. Who was he kidding? At Wolfe, Taylor the chances of a free weekend were dim at best. For the next six months, his primary job would be demonstrating his loyalty by resisting life.

He caught himself wishing the RER train would derail, that his flight would be delayed or, better yet, canceled. When he arrived at the airport, Jim saw the train for Paris on the opposite track. Hadn't he felt this same sensation when he and Calliope parted ways in the Alps and he'd heard her cough? Without thinking, he ran across the platform and jumped onto the train only moments before the doors glided shut. Heart beating. Next stop: Paris.

BACK AT THE RESIDENCE, THE BUTLER EYED JIM with irritation.

"Madame is not available," he said in heavily accented English, his white glove closing the door.

"She asked to see me this afternoon."

"She is not here."

The door closed. From the street, Jim looked up at the window above the door.

"Calliope," he called. "Are you there?"

The window was closed. Jim found a pebble on the street and tossed it at the window. Calliope's aim would have been better.

SEVENTEEN

LA RÉSIDENCE

Minutes later, the begrudging butler opened the large oak door. In quick succession, a man dressed in black greeted Jim and showed him into the drawing room to the right of the entrance hall, where he was to wait for madame. A second man in black entered the room to ask whether Jim wanted a *café* or a glass of water. The two men, both handsome, between the ages of twenty-five and thirty-five, and wearing black shirts and black pants, could have been interchangeable: *très* businesslike, *très* cool, *très* streamlined. Jim was glad he'd paid a good sum in Lauenen for his dark gray suit.

The pastel-blue paneled drawing room hosted the biggest crystal chandelier he'd ever seen. In the corner, mounted on a pedestal, stood a life-size bronze statue of a falcon. He was

in the right place. From his seat on the gray velvet sofa, he had a full view of the sweeping white marble staircase with its black wrought-iron banister of whirls and arabesques.

Would she float down the staircase to greet him, or pop in from one of the three doors in the drawing room? Door number one, two, or three? As he looked above at the sparkling crystals of the chandelier and the diamond-shaped coffering in the wooden ceiling, a question popped into his mind: Had he been just a plaything for the rich and famous? An amuse-bouche before the main course?

Jim had read stories about the desires of powerful people being met at the expense of others. Was he the disposable American, a companion for a few weeks in an Alpine wilderness—only to be dropped, as a child would discard a toy?

Voices and the thud of moving furniture resounded in the next room. Jim rose from the sofa and opened one of the three closed doors. In a ballroom of huge proportions, flanked on one side by four floor-to-ceiling French windows, he counted a staff of eight, all dressed in the same black on black, setting up tables, spreading tablecloths, and unfolding chairs.

Jim guessed the ceiling height to be at least twenty feet. Ornate scrolls decorated the tops of the columns at the four corners of the room, and wavelike molding ran along the top of the interior walls. The French windows were dressed with salmon-colored curtains, drawn to the sides with similar-colored sashes and tassels. The floor was shiny parquet. The

row of three chandeliers caught the afternoon sunlight as if they were hung in such a way to capture every glistening ray. A forest-green marble fireplace occupied the length of the far wall. On the other side of the French windows Jim glimpsed a formal topiary garden, the trees shaped into triangles and balls.

A woman in black sped through the room carrying bunches of red and orange flowers in her arms. She ran so fast, it looked like she was carrying fire. Everything in the room had the effect of fullness, a lushness that overflowed.

HE HADN'T SEEN HER ENTER THROUGH THE FRENCH doors, but she was standing like a statue at the edge of the room. She wore a white satin suit. The skirt, which fell to her knees, looked as if it had been sculpted around her thin hips. Her eyes were blank, like a day without sun or rain, a day without weather.

For a moment it seemed as if she would speak, but then she closed her lips and turned her face away. Her hair was in a tight chignon; with her long neck, she was the sculpture of Queen Nefertiti that Jim had seen as a child in books about Egyptian history. A princess from a distant land. She pressed a finger against the glass pane as if she wanted to touch what was outside it. He remembered that finger on his arm as he'd carried her for miles. He had known her every breath, her every cough. After all that, would she refuse to speak to him?

"Calliope," he began, approaching her.

She continued to gaze out the window. A caged bird of paradise. He had returned her to this.

Her blue-green eyes. His eyes her target.

"I could not risk your health, your life . . ." he said.

"You did." Her voice was hollow; all the creamy richness had been extracted. "This is my life." She looked away.

The light from the windows touched her lips.

"Madame," said a slim man dressed in the black uniform, entering the drawing room from the door to the ballroom.

"Yes," she said, her voice dull. She did not turn.

"Les traiteurs sont ici."

Jim the Traitor, he thought. It occurred to him that *traiteur* was the French word for *caterer*.

"Les traiteurs sont ici," Calliope repeated, her eyes still on Jim. "S'il vous plaît, veuillez leur montrer la cuisine." Please show them to the kitchen. The man left.

"As you may have guessed," she said, "we're hosting a dinner this evening."

She took a deep breath. How different she was from the woman with loose, wild hair, laughing on the rose-petaled threshold of her Alpine chalet.

"Where are you?" He knew she would understand. "Calliope with the rose petals in her hair?"

She smiled at him, a social smile, one he knew she flashed at the hundreds who filed in to *ooh* and *ah* at the green marble fireplace, and the crystal chandeliers, and her.

"The soul which has no fixed purpose in life is lost; to be everywhere is to be nowhere," she said. "Michel de Montaigne."

Another woman in black with a blond chignon, a pale imitation of the mistress of the house, popped her head into the room from door number two with an air of urgency. Jim guessed she was the head of staff. She asked madame a question, something about *les traiteurs*.

"*Oui*," Calliope responded. "*Un moment*."

He followed her into the drawing room where he had waited for her. She took a seat on the gray velvet sofa, and he sat beside her. The woman who had dashed through the ballroom with the flowers now stood at door number three. She spoke quickly, gesturing with her hands, about the flower arrangements, he presumed.

"*J'arrive*, I'm coming," Calliope answered in a smooth voice, as if pouring out a measured batter. She was the commander in chief of decisions in this, her castle.

"I have things to take care of . . ." she said, moving to the edge of the sofa, a white egret about to take flight.

"Madame?"

The sun had gone out of the room. The Calliope impostor popped her head through door number two. Jim understood from the next exchange that more people were attending the event than had been expected. They would have to add another table or squeeze more people at the ones they had.

Calliope quickly—*clip, clip*—instructed the woman to add another table.

Jim could smell her: roses, miles of rose bushes, and bees buzzing in them.

He stood. "Leave here," he whispered. "Now. You are *free* . . ." The image of the owlet popped into his head. He hoped she would not ask about Hamlet.

She turned to look at him, and finally, once again, he was the recipient of the warm smile amid the fluttering petals under the trellis of roses at the entrance to the Chalet of Owls.

"I don't blame you, Jim," she said, sighing and spreading her arms wide. "That is why I called you in from the window the first time. Yves demanded my attention so I could not see you at that time. This is my life. Despite my bitterness about what happened at the Cabane, I chose this life once and I choose it again—to keep the family together, to help my husband reach the success he desires, to play the part of hostess with all that I have been given." The blue tint under her eyes reminded him of the hue under the surface of ice, the frigid conditions they had endured on the Wildhorn. "All I can hope is that my daughters, at least one daughter—"

Calliope and Jim saw him at the same time that he saw them. He entered from the foyer—door number three. It was as if they were onstage, but it was a breach of the script that the third actor should appear now. He strode in like a military commander; a crop would have completed the picture.

The man was the same height as Calliope and puffed

his chest out like a character in an eighteenth-century cartoon of wealthy men boasting watches that barely fit into their vest pockets. He had a chiseled chin, a wide, shiny forehead, and dark hair mixed with silver, more than the Internet photographs had shown; his sideburns were a little too long. Something about him reminded Jim of Clio, perhaps the wide forehead, the pronounced cheekbones. His intensity was like a magnet. His quick brown eyes darted at the couple, then to the doors to the right, where the three could hear the staff.

Jim stepped away from the sofa. Calliope remained as still as if she had been turned to stone.

"Calliope," said the Commander, glaring at Jim. He paused and waited. "We need to go over a few things," he continued. "The seating chart . . ."

"Fine," she said coolly, looking at him, then back at Jim. She was singing a ballad as *this* Odysseus's muse, singing to his accomplishments, to his political power and his delight.

Now would be the time for an introduction.

"I hope you'll excuse me," she said in English to Jim, her face emptied and wan.

As if as an afterthought, she added, "Yves, please meet Jim Olsen."

The flash of recognition was immediate. The words were hardly out of her mouth than her husband boomed, "*L'Américain!*" He followed the exclamation with a quick laugh.

Jim waited.

For a moment, Calliope looked disoriented.

In the tense pause that followed, Jim watched the Commander change course like a man on a ship turning the wheel abruptly starboard. The boom swung around, but Calliope did not duck.

"Women," said Yves Castellane in French-accented English, his impatience visible in his twitching eyebrows. He placed an arm around Jim's shoulder and steered him to the doorway. "We know how they can be, don't we, monsieur? They can be up in the mountains one moment and then down in the valley the next. My wife, she came running down the mountain to me, begging her way back."

Jim tried to steal a glance at Calliope, but the minister of the interior held his shoulder in a lock.

"I would like to say good-bye to her," Jim said, breaking free.

"I'm afraid my wife is very busy. We have several visiting dignitaries," he began. "Running for office, you see—it's not easy to keep it all together, the wife, the daughters, the whole world beckoning . . ."

When Jim turned back to her, she looked as if she were in a trance. A wisp of her hair had come free from the chignon and fell over her eye. She brushed past her husband to approach Jim. She kissed him on both cheeks, small, withheld pecks that barely grazed his face.

For a moment, before the butler closed the door, he caught a glimpse of Calliope facing her husband, the silhou-

ette of her curved lips smiling up at the politician to calm the furrow on his brow, to please him with the plans for the political reception, to tell him which important head of state she planned to seat next to him. So the muse could fulfill her mission: that *he* would appear the most brilliant of all.

EIGHTEEN

MIDTOWN MANHATTAN

AMBROSE WAS LATE, AS USUAL. FIVE MINUTES early was on time for Jim Olsen, the punctual Midwesterner. From the table at the far corner of the room—"Monsieur Ambrose Vincelles's table"—Jim observed the midtown New York City lunch crowd, the glossy lips moving, the stilettos prancing, the suits leaning in and the suits leaning back in chairs. He noticed the shirts straining across the bellies of middle-aged men as they unbuttoned their suit jackets. *Would someone please turn down the volume?* Jim caught flirtatious glances from the two women at the adjacent table. About his age, both wore short skirts, and their long legs were crossed, crossing, about to cross again, within his view. And this was lunchtime.

"How great it is to see you!" Ambrose's voice broke

through the drone of lunchtime voices. Jim embraced his friend heartily.

The sommelier appeared with a bottle of red wine. He bowed knowingly to Ambrose, pointed at the vintage and the vineyard, and poured a taste. Ambrose swirled the dark-red liquid in the glass, tipped it to his lips, inhaled and sipped, and then nodded.

"How is your new post, my friend?" Ambrose began.

"You make it sound as if I have a job in a sub-Saharan colony."

"Well, it certainly isn't that, is it? You're gainfully employed by one of the most established investment firms in the country. Bravo, my friend!"

"Before you continue, you should know that I quit the job before I began."

"What?"

"I was a week late to my start date," Jim said. "When I showed up and my superiors interrogated me about the reasons for my delay, I decided to tell them the truth—that I'd been stranded in the Alps, where I was trying to help a woman escape from her husband. I didn't mention that said husband was a candidate for the presidency of France. They looked at each other as if I'd lost my mind. They didn't believe me. It was at that moment that I walked."

Ambrose was incredulous. "Jim, I don't understand. This is so unlike you!"

"I told them in a very calm way that I appreciated the opportunity to work with them, but I had decided that life was too short to work with assholes."

"You didn't."

"Now that I think of it, Jay Wolfe looked at me as if I were some kind of prophet, as if by my seeing the light, he was beginning to see it, too."

"I might agree with your now ex-bosses—Jim, you *have* lost your mind! This is not the same hardworking Jim who refused all my vacation invitations these last eight years!"

The waiter brought menus.

"And the hermitess, I've been wanting to ask for the longest time—did you ever find her?"

"We did. Sadly, she'd died by the time we arrived. But now that I've had time to think about it, by watching Calliope embrace her death even as I was repulsed by it, I think somehow, in that moment, I learned how to live."

Ambrose sat back in his chair.

"You see how dangerous your invitation to the Alps has proven? If it wasn't for you, I'd be able to return to the habitual life, pay my bills, and settle quite comfortably into a ten-year oblivion at Wolfe, Taylor."

The waiter was back at their table.

"The *steak au poivre* with *frites*," said Ambrose. "You?"

Jim held up two fingers.

"Speaking of paying bills, what *will* you do with yourself?"

"I've decided to save glacial melt on mountaintops. Got any suggestions?"

"One adventure in the Wildhorn and you're a changed man! Our earth will be the better for it. Last night I dined

with a friend, Margaret Paul. She runs the Natural Re-
sources Defense Council. Their mission is right up your
alley, or, um, mountain."

Ambrose removed his phone from his inside jacket
pocket and tapped out a message. "I've just introduced you.
Now for the fun. I'm sending you a link to today's cover
story in a French tabloid about this young American and a
certain presidential candidate's wife. I'm guessing the rescue
team leaked some sensitive information along with photographs. I don't believe a word of it."

"You know me too well, Ambrose, to believe . . . Calliope
was mesmerizing, intriguing, but the relationship was pla-
tonic. The whole thing is hard to believe now as I sit among
skyscrapers that are high-rise buildings instead of Wildhorn
peaks. While I was up there in the high elevation, I had this
funny feeling that Calliope had a vision of my future from
the moment she met me." He thought of her knowing about
his arrival, the questions she asked him.

"Was she feeding you any strange-looking mushrooms?"

"Very funny!" In his head he heard the word as Calliope would pronounce it—*fonny*. "But she *was* serving me
century-old wine bottled by Benedictine monks."

"I joke, but I've felt it, too, especially in the Alps," said
Ambrose. "It's a kind of clairvoyance, a telepathy with others
and with nature. It's one of the things that makes being on
the Wildhorn or any high mountain regions so addictive.
With your newfound insight, do you think she was saving
you for the actress?"

"That's what I thought at first. But Thalia's engaged to be married. I saw her ring."

The waiter brought over an amuse-bouche of potatoes and caviar, a sprig of mint gracing the tops.

"Remember the book of poetry I thought Thalia had inscribed and left for me before our departure?"

Ambrose nodded.

"It was from Helene, actually."

"What?"Ambrose paused to sip his wine. "Now that I think about it, I remember her looking at you in a strange way. She was probably the one who urged Thalia to join our table. She seemed so shy. What a strange evening! Thalia was flirting; Helene was in love; Clio was scheming; and you and I were bewitched. I suppose all's well that ends well. Madame Castellane is back to health and to her family, and—"

"She's not back to health. She's like something out of *The Walking Dead*!"

"The press says she's out of the hospital."

"She's physically better, but emotionally she's a ghost. I remember her telling me in those days when we were lost together that the thing she feared most in the world was apathy. I remember how she spaced the syllables, pronouncing it in French: *A Pa Thy*. Et voilà, when I saw her in Paris? She had eaten Apathy for breakfast, Apathy for lunch, and Apathy for dinner, and then she served a generous portion to me. When you're living the life she's chosen, the fast-paced life, like the one I lived before my Alpine journey, there's

not enough time for the other *pathies*—empathy and sympathy. In that life, if your heartstrings pulled you to experience pathos you'd have to put it off for a time when you were less busy, but by then . . ."

The waiter appeared at the table and poured more wine. "I'm willing to postpone pathos to taste this," said Ambrose, popping the amuse-bouche into his mouth.

"The helicopter was always overhead," said Jim. "She probably had it on remote control and planned its arrivals and departures. But, Ambrose, why would she go back to such a life? When I left her in the arms of the pilot to be delivered to her husband, she told me that I had betrayed her."

"You said her husband was there, that a staff of hundreds was in your midst, including the stalwart butler. According to online gossip, the presidential candidate has forsaken his extracurricular activities and entreated his wife to forgive him. His mistress has reconciled with her own husband and they will be raising the child, and, although muddied, the wheels of life and politics roll onward."

"That doesn't—"

"Jim, he could very well be the next president of France. Not exactly what you wish to hear, I know, but he's the only one they've got who has a chance against the Socialist party candidate. After the success of the Socialists in the last election, half the wealth of France departed the country. They're hoping that Castellane will win, lower taxes, welcome investment back, and restore France's economy."

• • •

THE STEAK WAS SERVED, THE PEPPER ADMINISTERED. One of the two women of the crossing legs glanced in Jim's direction. Why would anyone wear such high heels?

"Enough of French politics. Come to dinner with me tonight with Ann and Ned Lamont. They're selling a thirteen-inch painting by the school of Giorgione, only just now authenticated, and seen by only a chosen few. They bought it many years ago for a song at an auction. It's titled *Mountain Landscape with a Hermitess by a Pool*. When I think of us searching in caves in the remote reaches of the Alps—and now the hermitess shows up in my life again! I couldn't wait to tell you about it, but I wanted to see your reaction in person."

"Hermitess?" asked Jim.

"You won't be surprised when I tell you whom I'm thinking of as the prospective buyer—"

Jim stopped his fork in midair. "No!"

"Clio Castellane has been in touch with me several times since our night in the hutte. Along with checking in to see whether I knew anything about your whereabouts—my God, you had us petrified—she told me that her mother was interested in expanding her private collection. How could I not think of the Lamonts' Giorgione, remembering madame's predilection for female hermits?"

"You'd think that in an election year, the Castellanes would not be expanding their private collection."

"You'd think . . ."

"What does the hermitess look like . . . in the painting?"

"Pale face, long gray-white hair. She's wearing a long gray frock. She's the color of the mist that drops inside the Alps. It's amazing. One moment." Ambrose dipped his fingers into his interior jacket pocket.

"Et voilà," he said, inspecting the image on his phone screen. "This doesn't do her justice. Come tonight and see for yourself."

Jim expanded the photograph with his fingers to zoom in on the face of the hermitess. She had a long nose; gray-blue, almond-shaped eyes; and long, slender arms. Was that a laugh she was suppressing? She held something in her fingers at her abdomen. It was hard to make out. It looked like the small skull of an animal.

" 'The Mona Lisa of the Alps,' " said Ambrose.

It had become loud in the restaurant. Jim returned the phone to Ambrose.

"If getting a peek at a hermitess with skull in hand is not enough," began Ambrose, "I have another diversionary proposition for you. And, Jim, you'd actually be doing me a favor if you did this. I'm on the board of the French Institute Alliance Française. Tonight there's an event that its president, Marie-Monique Steckel, has asked me to attend. Would you go as my emissary?"

"Thanks but no, thanks, Ambrose. Not in the mood." The painting of the hermitess had made Jim feel gloomy.

"It's a celebration of French poetry, something I think you've become more familiar with over the past few weeks. Say yes."

"Ambrose! You're looking at me as if my saying yes will save your, or my, life."

"Marie-Monique would appreciate the gesture. For me, stop by for a drink, nothing more."

"You're in the right business, *and* you're worse than all the Castellanes put together."

Ambrose laughed over his glass of red wine.

"That's saying a lot. Introduce yourself to Marie-Monique, one of my favorite people on earth. She'll take care of you. It's midtown, Sixtieth Street." Ambrose peered into his phone once again. "I'm forwarding you the Evite as we speak—et voilà. You need only stay for one drink."

It was a relief for Jim to finish off their lunch by listening to stories about Ambrose's family and about new clients on the brink of buying a rare collection of medieval Japanese warrior figures. By the time the bill arrived, he and Ambrose had emptied the bottle of wine.

"On me," said Ambrose, swiping the bill away from Jim's hand. "Especially for taking my place tonight at the Alliance. My flight for Paris is tomorrow midday, but call me if you want to grab a coffee in the morning."

"Will you vote for him?"

Ambrose signed his name, placed the receipt in his wallet, and stood. "Castellane?" He nodded slowly. "Probably."

NINETEEN

LE SKYROOM

J IM SIPPED CHAMPAGNE AND LOOKED AROUND the pale-blue interior of the Skyroom at the French Institute. The room was dominated by a large plate-glass window overlooking Park Avenue. There were more women than men in the room, all different ages, most in colorful dresses, not the typical New York City black. Jim towered over the men, who were slimmer and shorter than he, and, he guessed, mostly French. He walked to the window and stood, mesmerized by the view across the ravine of Park Avenue, which was shrouded by a thick mist this evening.

"Et voilà. You must be Ambrose's friend." An elderly woman wearing a light-blue dress that echoed the color of the walls approached Jim with open arms, as if he were an

old friend. Ambrose must have forwarded an image of him to the institute's president.

She rattled off a few sentences in French that Jim didn't understand and then administered the French version of a kiss on each cheek.

"Ambrose mentioned that you're more accomplished as an Alpine hiker than you are in the French language," she said in English. She winked and nodded at Jim, which made him wonder what Ambrose had really told her.

"About the hiking—Ambrose has a tendency to over-state the truth. But I suppose I learned a few things about the Alps this summer."

"We're about to start our program," she said, taking his arm and walking with him to the front of the room, to the first of six rows of white folding chairs.

"Sit here, in this chair next to mine, while I gather the crowds."

From the lectern, Marie-Monique beckoned the cock-tailers. Jim checked his phone to find many texts from Ambrose, the last "Will you PLEASE call your parents?"

He hadn't yet told them that he'd quit the job he'd never begun, and he wasn't in the mood to listen to his mother's hectoring. Since Jim hadn't responded to their calls, they'd turned to Ambrose.

"S'il vous plaît, mesdames et messieurs." Marie-Monique adjusted the microphone and waited as the small crowd settled into their seats.

"I am delighted to have the honor of introducing our

guests this evening, Charlotte Goncourt of Flammarion and Helene Castellane of Éditions Gallimard . . ."

Jim's heart skipped a beat. Helene Castellane?

Their eyes met as she walked to the lectern.

"Helene?" he said.

As Helene registered his presence, he noticed a rush of blush color her cheeks. He was reminded of Calliope's face in the warm sun, when color clung to the lower part of her cheek, near her jawline.

She stopped and leaned toward him. "How *fonny*! What are you doing here?" Her breath tickled.

"I have no idea," he whispered back and shook his head.

"Apollinaire brought you here, didn't he?" she whispered.

"All the way from the Wildhorn."

"I must . . ." She nodded to the podium.

Jim watched her compose herself as she took her place next to Marie-Monique.

"Helene Castellane will be discussing the recently published new editions of the surrealist poets, original texts complete with English translations—in particular *Alcools* by Guillaume Apollinaire. As a scholar, Helene has written several important papers on the surrealists."

Helene paused at the podium as if she had forgotten what she was going to say. She held up the book, the book that contained one verse that he knew by heart. She spoke in French.

Her voice was Calliope's, the Calliope of the Wildhorn,

a voice that sailed in the wind without a tether. The arm
that held up the book was slender and white: Calliope lifting
the heavy pot of fish stew over the fire. How strong that slender arm was. The shiny black paperback cover was different
from that of the white covered edition he'd carried down
the Alps. This one featured a starlit night, but the stars were
bees!

Jim understood only a few words. He was thinking of
the Wildhorn, of the meadows of flowers, of the lakes, of
the snowcapped mountains, of the snow, the cold, wet snow.

Was she smiling at him, and only him? She was love-
lier than she'd been at their first meeting. Perhaps because
she was alone, without the backdrop of her two sisters, she
looked more mature. He recognized Calliope's elongated
nose, the way she raised her hand to her chin, the way she
held herself still, as Calliope did, as if waiting for the right
moment to spring forth to surprise.

The audience began applauding before Jim realized that
Helene had finished. She took a seat in the empty chair on
the other side of Marie-Monique.

Jim listened patiently to the next speaker. Madame Goncourt was chicken-bone skinny; her shoulder bones poked
from the top of her red dress. She rambled on in a throaty
voice about André Breton and the surrealist movement;
again, Jim understood little of what she said.

The new editions of the surrealist French poetry were
available for sale at the back of the room. Jim made sure he
was the last in line. While he waited, he removed a book

from the pile and flipped through the pages to find the poem that Helene had marked for him back in the Cabane des Audannes.

His turn in line.

"This book of poetry . . ." he began.

She looked up at him, her hazel eyes large and luminous.

"I'll tell you one day," she said.

"How long are you in the city?"

"I'm not sure."

Jim waited.

"Possibly for a long time. I've had enough of the hubbub my father is stirring up in Paris," she said. "My mother and sisters cater to his every wish, and it makes me sick. I can't do it. I just can't do it."

Jim thought of Calliope, her hair in a tight chignon, her constricting white skirt. She had slipped into an icy crevasse, with no hope of sunlight. How long could she last?

"I don't know you very well, but somehow I would expect no less from you," Jim said.

"Also," said Helene, "I don't have a job anymore. This event is my last responsibility at Gallimard. I'll be like you when we first met. I remember you said you had spent time in the doldrums in between jobs."

Jim laughed.

"But you seemed happy with your job as an editor."

"When I refused to go to his political events, my father told me that the job he'd secured for me a year ago through connections would be in jeopardy. Naturally, I quit."

"That took courage."

"Impetuousness is often confused with courage," she said, standing.

"But your mother?"

"She has resigned herself to—" She looked down at her shoes. "You have to understand: with his veil of charm and vulnerability, my father behaves nicely some of the time, but all the while he's intravenously feeding her a regular diet of his poison. He demeans her to the point that she thinks she has nothing worthy to say, that his voice is the only one that matters."

"But her own voice is so strong," he said.

"In the Alps, it's always that way. When she's been away from him for enough time. Now that she's back in his stronghold, she's abdicated again. I refuse to watch.

"I'm sorry," she said, wiping her eyes with the back of her wrist and shaking her head. She turned away from him and raised both hands to her eyes.

Was she crying there, in front of him? If only he had the courage to take her into his arms.

"I saw her briefly in Paris," he said.

"She told me. She said it was her fault that you over-stayed your visit."

"What about your sisters? Clio?"

She turned to him, wiped her eyes again, and took a deep breath. "They say they need my father for practical reasons, for their jobs, their connections; he helps them pay for country houses, Clio's children's education . . . In return,

he and the party need his daughters to publicly support his campaign. They confuse *need* with *use*! He's using them like he uses my mother, seducing them, bribing them, and making them compromise who they are . . ."

She looked over Jim's shoulder.

"I see you've sold almost all the books!" Marie-Monique said, approaching them. When she saw Helene's face, she retreated. "I must check on the ambassador."

"How about you? Your new job?" Helene had regained her composure. The sun was out again.

"I quit before I began."

"What?" There was something giddy about her expression. "You, too?" Her wide-open eyes were not unlike those of a small child for whom everything in the world is possible, and who still believes that someone is capable of bringing it.

"I'll tell you about it over dinner," he said.

"I can't tonight," she said. "I have—" She nodded her head in the direction of Marie-Monique.

"She'll understand. I think she'll even like it."

Helene smiled, then laughed. "You're right. She *will* like it."

Hers was unlike her mother's smile, unlike her sisters'. It was quieter, more modest, the promise of a small flower bud in early spring. It knew not the trampling wind or the heavy snows. That night he would ask her about the gift of the book and the inscribed poem, and the line that had kept him walking along the endless Alpine crests: "Remember, I wait for you forever."

Hadn't that little line of six words emboldened him at the outset of the Alpine journey, strengthened him as he trod heavily through the snow, given him the patience to wait out the whiteout and the courage to quit his job and change his life? Now it inspired Jim to look into Helene's large, direct brown-green eyes and gently take her hand.

Did he really need to ask her about the book she had given him after knowing him for only a few hours as he set off on his Alpine journey?

Like Ocean Olsen on the brink of his voyage to the Great New World, he already knew the answer.

Finis

ACKNOWLEDGMENTS

I would like to thank Anthony Nahas for inspiring the Alpine hike in the Wildhorn and for embracing the idea that we might actually find the female hermit. Thank you to Emma Sweeney, my agent, for believing in me; to Jennifer Barth, for saving me from myself and for her intimate and devoted relationship with words and important fiction, and to Wendy Weil, who will always be in my heart.

ABOUT THE AUTHOR

Elizabeth Birkelund is the author of one other French-inspired novel, *The Dressmaker*. As a freelance magazine journalist, Elizabeth was the personal finance columnist for *Cosmopolitan* and wrote for more than fifteen years for *Working Woman*, *Self*, and *Glamour*, among other publications. She lives in New York City.